USE OF LANGUAGE ACROSS THE SECONDARY CURRICULUM

Educat
people
the wo
languag

Inclu
languag
commo
area of

Part
conside
literacy
successf
and sup

The f...
to review and develop policy and practice to achieve higher standards of literacy

Eve Bearne is Assistant Director in Research at Homerton College, Cambridge. She has published widely on education and the teaching of English.

USE OF LANGUAGE ACROSS THE SECONDARY CURRICULUM

Edited by Eve Bearne

London and New York

First published 1999
by Routledge
11 New Fetter Lane, London EC4P 4EE

Simultaneously published in the USA and Canada
by Routledge
29 West 35th Street, New York, NY 10001

Typeset in Goudy by Keystroke, Jacaranda Lodge, Wolverhampton
Printed and bound in Great Britain by
Page Bros (Norwich) Ltd

British Library Cataloguing in Publication Data
A catalogue record for this book is available from the British Library

Library of Congress Cataloging in Publication Data
Bearne, Eve, 1943–
Use of language across the secondary curriculum / Eve Bearne.
p. cm.
Includes bibliographical references and index.
1. Language arts (Secondary)—Great Britain. 2. Language arts—Correlation with content subjects—Great Britain. I. Title.
LB1631.B357 1999
428′.0071′241—dc21 98–21484
CIP

ISBN 0–415–16516–4

CONTENTS

FIGURES

CONTRIBUTORS

Eve Bearne has taught English, drama and language in education in schools and colleges for over thirty years. She was a project officer for the National Writing Project and editor of a number of their publications. She is co-editor of a series of books about children's literature and has written and edited several books about language and literacy, the most recent of which are *Making Progress in English* and *Use of Language in the Primary School* (both 1998). She is Assistant Director in Research at Homerton College, Cambridge.

Avril Dawson has experience of teaching students from early years to adults. She is now working in middle and upper schools with SEN and EAL pupils, as well as teaching a variety of subjects, particularly English. Previous publications include work on children's language and literacy development through storytelling and writing, and children's reading histories. She is curently researching the continuum of individual experiences of language and culture and their place in education.

Mary Earl was a secondary religious studies teacher for 15 years before joining the staff of Homerton College, Cambridge. Since then she has also worked as a freelance writer and has taught on courses in the philosophy of education and curriculum methods for secondary postgraduate students.

Peter Fifield qualified as an archaeologist before deciding to train as a teacher. He has worked in comprehensive schools and special education for some years. He now teaches history and English at a school for pupils who experience a range of medical, physical and learning difficulties. He is interested in the use of pupils' wider experience of visual texts – including media and ICT – in supporting their learning and has contributed chapters about special children's literacy and learning to *Greater Expectations* and *Differentiation and Diversity in the Primary School* (both edited by Eve Bearne).

Ian Frowe is a lecturer in education at Homerton College, Cambridge. Prior to that he worked in the Wirral. He contributed a chapter on assessment to *Differentiation and Diversity in the Primary School* (ed. E. Bearne, Routledge 1996).

Paul Goalen was a secondary history teacher for fourteen years before moving to Homerton College, Cambridge in 1988. As a teacher trainer he developed his interest in teaching history through drama with a colleague, Lesley Hendy. Together they have published a number of articles in professional and academic journals on using educational drama in teaching National Curriculum history.

Richard Hickman's teaching experience includes ten years as a classroom teacher in Leicestershire and as a lecturer in art education at the University of Reading and at Nanyang Technological University, Singapore, since 1985. He is currently head of art education at Homerton College, Cambridge. Dr. Hickman is also a specialist OFSTED inspector for art and design and for design and technology. He has presented papers at a number of international conferences and has had several articles published in professional journals on art education.

Liz Mellor is a senior lecturer in music at Homerton College, Cambridge, where she works with students who are learning to teach music at both primary and secondary levels. She came to Homerton with experience of teaching music in schools, co-ordinating music across all Key Stages 1–4 and as head of music in a tertiary college. She also works with teachers on assessing music in the National Curriculum. Her current research focus is on aesthetic development in music education, which she is undertaking with the psychology department of Leicester University for her PhD.

Helen Nicholson teaches drama and theatre at undergraduate and postgraduate level at Homerton College, Cambridge. Before that she taught drama and English in secondary schools in Bristol for eleven years. She has also worked with adult and youth groups. She has published several articles on different aspects of drama education, including a chapter in *On the Subject of Drama* by David Hornbrook (Routledge 1998) and has researched into arts education.

Tim Rowland is a senior lecturer at the University of London Institute of Education. A graduate in mathematics, Tim taught in 11–18 schools before entering teacher education. His PhD in mathematics education reflects the range of his interests – mathematics, language, epistemology and education. He is also an active mathematician in the field of number theory. Tim is a book reviewer for the *Times Educational Supplement* and his book on vagueness and mathematics is to be published by Falmer in 1999.

Nigel Spratt joined the teaching profession in 1975 after a brief spell in commerce and journalism. He is now head of English in an Essex comprehensive school and became particularly interested in exploring ways of motivating reluctant readers through his involvement in the Essex Reading Project. He has run INSET sessions on aspects of literacy and Information and Communications Technology to schools and industry.

Marie Stacey was a secondary English teacher and head of department in Hampshire before joining the National Writing Project in 1986. She became a project officer for the NWP and later General Inspector for English and drama in the Wirral in 1989. She was chair of the National Association for Advisers of English from 1994–96. She works in a fascinatingly diverse local educational authority, with all ages of pupils and has a commitment to empowering pupils through the development of language.

Ruth Sturdy is a SENCO in an 11–16 comprehensive school in Essex where she also teaches English. She studied sociology at the University of Wales and after gaining her PGCE at Avery Hill college, she entered teaching as a special needs teacher in four different schools in Essex and the London Borough of Havering. She has always been interested in how children learn and in particular how they learn to read. This prompted her to study for an MA through the Open University, an interest she was able to pursue further through the Essex Reading Project.

Ian Terrell is Head of Continuing Professional Development at Anglia Polytechnic University. He was formerly senior lecturer responsible for professional studies and the MA in educational management at De Montfort University. His work in secondary schools includes teaching, coordinating PSHE, organising TVEI and, as Senior Teacher, responsibility for INSET. His recent publications include *Development Planning and School Improvement for Middle Managers* (1997).

Gill Venn is Programme Director for Continuing Professional Development at the University of North London. She has taught in both primary and secondary schools, all in urban areas. Her research and publications include work on gender and identity. Her current research focus is on facilitating reflection on values and beliefs and the cultural experiences of teachers.

Elaine Wilson was a secondary chemistry teacher for fifteen years. She was awarded Salters' Medal for outstanding chemistry teaching in 1995 and was recently appointed to the post of lecturer in science education at Homerton College, Cambridge. She has published a range of curriculum materials to support the teaching of chemistry and has research interests in peer tutoring and learning styles in science teaching.

ACKNOWLEDGEMENTS

My very grateful thanks to all the teachers and pupils who have participated in work for this book, but particularly to Phil Jackson, Ken Johnson, Richard Landy and Marie Stacey.

INTRODUCTION

Language and literacy

> Pupils' use of language is a vital skill which influences their progress in every area of the curriculum.
>
> (SCAA 1997: 2)

It is hard to think of anyone who would disagree with that statement. Stating generally accepted truths, however, does not ensure that learners reach full and satisfying literacy. Whilst acknowledging the validity of such assertions, current educational debate speaks of literacy in terms of crisis and we have a National Literacy Strategy which aims to improve standards of literacy significantly and swiftly, such is the concern about pupils' achievements. It is worth remembering, however, that anxieties about language and education have haunted every generation of teachers – and their pupils. The Board of Education Report of 1926 *The Teaching of English in England* traces debates as far back as 1362 when English became the language of the courts of law and of parliament and schools used the vernacular as the medium of instruction (Board of Education Inspectors 1926: 27). From that time until very recently, arguments turned upon the relative merits of teaching Latin, Greek or English; it was often felt that teaching the classical languages was detrimental to English as a language. At the end of the seventeenth century John Locke ironically summarised a common view that English was being neglected in schools:

> Would it not be very unreasonable to require of a learned country school master to teach his scholar to express himself handsomely in English when it appears to be so little his business or his thought that the boy's mother . . . outdoes him in it?
>
> (Board of Education 1926: 28)

What does this suggest about current assertions that standards of English have fallen? Or that people were more articulate or literate in the past? Nearer to our own times, the comprehensive and wise Bullock Report opened with a reminder that attitudes to the teaching of English have for many years been tinged with dissatisfaction. The report warns, however, against nostalgia:

> In any anxiety over a contemporary situation there is likely to be a wistful look back to the past with a conviction, often illusory, that times were better then than now. . . . Was there a standard which we can regard, if not as ideal, at least as a criterion by which to judge other times and conditions?
>
> (Department of Education and Science 1975: 3)

This is not to suggest that, simply because these questions have been asked for centuries, they are not worth asking. On the contrary. The very fact that teaching language and literacy is the focus of recurrent debate means that issues about teaching and learning English are worth debating. Bullock points out that questions about standards are not trivial, but central to decisions about how best to provide an education for our children. As we near the end of this century, the questions are equally important. The Bullock Report commented: 'If we are to decide what kind of English is right for our pupils they are the kind of questions that need to be asked' (ibid.: 3).

This book examines some of the kind of questions which need to be addressed if pupils are to benefit from a full and relevant language curriculum. However, debates about how best to approach the teaching of language and literacy raise particular problems for secondary schools, where teachers of different subjects are not necessarily trained in the development of language. At the same time, OFSTED inspections have identified areas which need attention, particularly in the teaching of reading at Key Stage 3 and in teaching about language throughout the secondary phase. There are other areas, too: teachers' own knowledge about language; the variety of kinds of language (written and spoken) used throughout the secondary curriculum; the reading and writing demands across the range of subjects. There are questions of entitlement: the needs of pupils who have English as an Additional Language; the identified differences in attainment between boys and girls in English and how best to promote literacy with pupils who have learning difficulties. The contributors to this book have joined in the historical process of healthy argument as they consider just what kind of language and literacy teaching will be best for the citizens of the twenty-first century.

The SCAA (now QCA) document *Use of Language* sees it like this:

> Pupils should be taught to express themselves clearly in both speech and writing and to develop their reading skills. They should be taught to use grammatically correct sentences and to spell and punctuate accurately in order to communicate effectively in written English.
>
> (SCAA 1997: 2)

In this document, language is seen as 'effective communication', a matter of 'skills' and 'correctness'. Whilst not for one second disagreeing that pupils should learn how to use standard forms of English which are conventionally written, the

SCAA document offers a narrow view of language and literacy. It contrasts with an earlier view about language presented in the Cox Report, one of the most influential reports on English in education of the last decade, which offers this definition:

> Language is a system of sounds, meanings and structures with which we make sense of the world around us. It functions as a tool of thought; as a means of social organisation; as the repository and means of transmission of knowledge; as the raw material of literature, and as the creator and sustainer – or destroyer – of human relationships. It changes inevitably over time and, as change is not uniform, from place to place. Because language is a fundamental part of being human, it is an important aspect of a person's sense of self; because it is a fundamental feature of any community, it is an important aspect of a person's sense of social identity.
>
> (DES 1989: para. 6: 18)

This view captures the complexity of debates about language and offers the background to what this book is about. The contributors reflect, in different ways, a common view that:

- language is both variable and changing and because of the different kinds of change – diachronic (over time), diatypic (according to situation) and dialectal (according to speaker and background) – language has to be viewed as a product of social and cultural interaction;
- since language is systematically organised, teachers need to know something about the structures of language – spoken and written – if they are to teach pupils how to handle the range of texts they meet;
- language is central to the development of thought and that there are important links between language and a sense of self. This has implications for teaching and learning styles;
- language is the means through which learners can reflect on and evaluate what they have learned. It is also necessary to develop a critical eye about language itself in order to probe the meanings which texts carry and be able to use language to carry the force of one's own meaning.

All of these constitute knowledge about language in its fullest sense. Since pupils' use of language does indeed influence their progress through education, the way in which language is taught becomes a matter for critical consideration. One of the prerequisites for teaching language is that teachers themselves should be confident about their own knowledge about language.

On the face of it there seems very little to explain about what 'knowledge about language' means. Put simply, it means being aware of language and how it is used. However, that very simple sentence covers a wide area of information about the structure and uses of language as well as some very contentious debates about how language is – or should be – used. A familiar commonplace observation is that everyone has a great deal of knowledge about language drawn from the experience of being brought up in and living in a language community. This is referred to as implicit knowledge. Then there is the explicit knowledge which might have come about by discussion of language in the family, at school, college or university. Both implicit and explicit knowledge about language need to be considered in any definition of what the phrase might mean and imply. There are recurrent areas of difficulty, however, about how such knowledge might be applied.

Language and values

Perhaps the greatest area of difficulty lies in making a clear distinction between genuinely linguistic issues and matters of culturally based value judgements. Because language is deeply socially and personally embedded, people's emotions tend to colour views of what knowledge about language means and implies. In everyday terms, this is expressed through opinions, for example, on 'correctness', 'bad grammar' and standard English. It is important to be very clear about the difference between a judgement about correctness based on linguistic criteria and a judgement based on culturally developed criteria. Comments about 'poor grammar' are very often nothing to do with grammar at all but about the perceived value of different ways of speaking – particularly about people's accents. Whilst it is important to have a responsible view of teaching standard forms of English – particularly written English – it is equally important to separate judgements made about individuals on the basis of social or cultural opinion (perhaps prejudice) and judgements about the linguistic organisation of how people speak and write.

A very simple definition of 'grammar' is that it describes the set of patterned possibilities through which the speakers (or writers) of a language communicate meaning to other speakers, writers, listeners and readers in their own speech community. In short, it describes the syntax of a language. In English, I might say *I'm going to London today*; in German I would say *Heute soll ich nach London fahren* (Today, shall I to London travel). Those are the distinctly different grammars of the two languages. If someone says *I ain't goin'* or *She be fair mithered* they are not speaking ungrammatically since the syntax is recognisably that of English. The first is an example of colloquial speech with dialect use of 'ain't' and the second is an example of dialect use with a specifically regional way of using a personal pronoun and vocabulary. In each case the speaker may well be able to speak a more standard form of English at will. Studying grammar means looking closely at the patterned ways in which language is used to make meanings in different kinds of texts; it does not mean correcting dialect or home uses of language. There are other ways to ensure that teachers are properly developing children's knowledge about the linguistic and social differences between standard and non-standard forms of language.

Another difficulty lies in an assumption that knowledge about language consists in naming parts of speech. The idea seems to be that if you can name or define a verb or an adverb you are necessarily a more competent language user. This kind of view is based on a simplistic idea about what *knowledge* means; it assumes that knowledge is simply fact gathering. Everyday experience tells us that this is not so. For pupils to become more critically discriminating readers, writers, speakers and listeners, they need to develop a vocabulary through which to talk about language. However, it is the means by which this metalanguage is developed which is crucial to the establishment of confident and secure knowledge about language. Knowledge about the systematic nature of language has to be developed in a context where the language makes sense and where it is being used to serve particular communicative purposes.

Language as a system

Studying language means paying attention to both the large and the small shapes of text – sentence and word level as well as at the level of genres or forms of language. In the National Curriculum, the details of language study are mostly included in the English order. In contrast with most other areas of the curriculum, the emphasis is not so much on facts and concepts as texts and processes. However, since the study of language and the development of literacy are important elements in teaching throughout the curriculum they need to be seen as integrated (see Figure I.1). In this model the texts are those organised elements of language – spoken and written – through which ideas are presented to learners and which they learn to produce. The processes are the means through which these texts are approached and understood. Together these elements comprise a full language and literacy curriculum.

This model takes into account all the language modes – reading, writing, speaking and listening – and their role in learning. Traditionally, language has been seen as a proof of learning. Reading aloud has been assumed to demonstrate understanding whilst writing is often seen as the automatic end-point to any learning activity – 'do it then write about it' – giving teachers the chance to check up on what pupils are supposed to have learned. Speaking and listening have featured in the question-and-answer format of classroom work, again as a means of confirming knowledge. Such traditional practices tend to concentrate on language as an end product rather than as a means of getting to grips with learning and often concentrate largely on writing. They often fail to provide evidence of what pupils genuinely do know and understand or take into account the ways in which talk importantly contributes to learning. Employers frequently comment that they want good oral communicators in the workforce, yet forms of talk are not usually specifically taught outside English or drama lessons.

Texts	*Processes*
Study of language (includes standard English): small shapes – sentences, words, phonemes, parts of speech, grammatical organisation, spelling and handwriting	**Getting and conveying information and ideas:** reading for understanding and inference, responding to reading, writing to explain, persuade, inform, entertain, awareness of readership (audience) . . . listening and speaking for the same purpose . . .
Study of texts (includes media texts, spoken texts and aspects of standard English): structures of texts, forms and formats, different genres, poetry, plays . . .	**Developing discrimination:** becoming independent, choosing what to read and what not to read, commenting on own and other people's writing (including published authors), using different registers in speaking . . .

Figure I.1 An integrated model of the language and literacy curriculum

The uses of language

The importance of language to the development of thought is sometimes misunderstood. On the face of it, it seems obvious – we read information and write it down or answer questions as a way of showing that we know things. However, the relationship between language and thought is rather more complicated than that. It isn't just that human beings use language to clothe ideas which are already formed in the mind but that we use language to create knowledge. Language helps us to grapple with partly formed concepts and shape them; it helps us to put previously known ideas beside new information so that in forging ways of expressing those combinations of ideas we reach more developed understanding. Language helps us to *realise* – both to make real and to come to understand – knowledge and thought.

The links between language and a sense of self and the cultural relevance of language begin a move towards more difficult terrain. Knowledge about these areas is not limited to seeing language as a set of structures, but introduces the idea of language use as a social practice, and, since it is social, it carries all the weight of social judgements with it. For some people, an example of the social value attached to using language comes when their own ways of speaking are criticised, mocked or praised. This is rather mysterious; if language is a systematic set of structures, how can its use attract praise or blame? The answer lies in the understanding that language is not a neutral set of linguistic relationships, but the repository of people's ideas of what is valuable or to be valued in society. Language can conceal and reveal aspects of human relationships – of power, culture and gender.

Further to this, language is never static; it changes over time and shows variation throughout any nation sharing a common language. This does not mean, however, that there is no possibility of establishing some knowledge about language – far from it. It is *because* language is so diverse and variable that it deserves study. For teachers, knowledge about language is professionally as well as personally relevant since language is central to the process of teaching and learning. The development of a metalanguage (a language to talk about language) means being able to talk more precisely and economically about language. Greater knowledge about the uses of language informs teaching throughout the curriculum, not just in those lessons described as English lessons. For pupils, the progressive development of knowledge about language contributes towards more effective learning in all areas of the curriculum.

This book includes both the formative and performative aspects of language use – the processes and texts. It goes further than looking at language merely as a proof of learning but includes material which focuses on the three major aspects of the relationship between pupils, language and learning:

- learning to use language in specific contexts;
- using language to learn throughout the curriculum;
- learning to talk about, reflect on and evaluate language.

The parts of the book move through a series of key areas in thinking about 'Use of Language' in schools. The first issues are related to exposing the ideological elements of language. Teachers need to recognise the values inherent in particular views of language and literacy and to create classroom opportunities for pupils to explore values through texts as well as values carried within texts. Further, if schools are to promote higher standards of achievement through a more enlightened view of language and literacy, then there are management issues to be faced. Part 2 looks at how schools and local authorities have gone about making changes to improve standards of literacy and learning. Part 3 extends the focus on change by looking at the language demands of different subjects and the classroom practices which best support learning. If pupils are fully to consolidate their learning, then they need to be able to evaluate the texts they encounter and create. Part 4 considers ways in which pupils and teachers can develop a critical eye. However, there are some pupils for whom learning is not straightforward; how are they moved into more confident literacy and learning? Part 5 presents two case-study accounts which analyse some of the issues and practices to support pupils less experienced in literacy. The book ends with a practical chapter which provides formats and guide questions for any school wishing to review existing practices in the use of language in order to change practice and raise standards. This final chapter draws together all the strands of the book, emphasising that careful and structured analysis, planning and monitoring are the keys to helping learners reach full and satisfying literacy.

References

Board of Education (1926) *The Teaching of English in England*, London: His Majesty's Stationery Office.

Department of Education and Science (1975) *A Language for Life* (known as The Bullock Report), London: Her Majesty's Stationery Office.

Department of Education and Science (1989) *Report of the English Working Party 5–16 (The Cox Report)*, London: Her Majesty's Stationery Office.

School Curriculum and Assessment Authority (1997) *Use of Language: A Common Approach*, London: SCAA.

Part 1

QUESTIONS AND ISSUES

The social and cultural aspects of language

Introduction

> In 1991, Nottingham established itself as a respected national clubbing destination. For it was then that a club named Venus opened and began attracting some of the finest party heads and vinyl maestros from across the country. . . . The promoter responsible for orchestrating this genesis was a feisty wee jock and ex-miner, James Baillie. Now he's back with a new venue, The Bomb, which is already attracting a full-on party-people vibe. Musically, James is assured of its direction. 'I want to go for a new disco house sound, with the likes of Harvey and Weatherall in the main room and, say, Nuphonic and Faze Action in the back.'
>
> (*The Big Issue* 1997 No. 263: 28)

This extract comes from an article entitled 'The Bomb squad: Can Nottingham ever get cooler?' It presents no problems in terms of reading the words; most experienced readers could read this aloud fluently. Whether they would understand it is a different matter, because in order to get the meaning out of the extract a reader needs some prior knowledge – and knowledge of a particular kind. In the case of this article it is a matter of knowing some of the terminology of the modern music and night-club scene. The extract serves as a reminder that all language carries social and cultural connotations; the meaning of a text relates to the context in which it was written and in which it is to be read. The headline for this article, for example, might have been taken as something to do with urban terrorism (except for the give-away isolated capital *B* on *Bomb squad* – no capital on *squad*). If readers already know something about the club scene they will also need to interpret the references to 'Harvey and Weatherall' and 'Nuphonic and Faze Action' in order to decide whether the Bomb is a club they'd like to visit. All of the article is written in standard English, yet it is a highly encoded cultural text, fully decipherable only by those who know something about clubbing – at night spots, not with blunt instruments! Every Saturday or Sunday, articles appear in newspapers and magazines which are equally inexplicable to the uninitiated. To be fully literate in any society means having some understanding of the ways in which language is socially and culturally encoded. I may not want to delve into the argot of wine connoisseurs, but at least I need to know that's what it is so that I can decide that I don't want to know.

Effective communication

These may seem peripheral or trivial examples, but the implications are serious. Having power over literacy, measured by the extract above, means more than just being able to read the words. It signals being 'in the know' and highlights the fact that literacy can be exclusive as well as inclusive. Culturally specific texts like the extract above serve as a reminder that language and literacy are complex, not the apparently straightforward 'effective and accurate use of language' (SCAA 1997: 6) suggested by such documents as *The Use of Language*:

> Pupils should be taught to express themselves clearly in both speech and writing and to develop their reading skills. They should be taught to use grammatically correct sentences and to spell and punctuate accurately in order to communicate effectively in written English.
>
> (SCAA 1997: 2)

Looked at alongside the extract which opens this introduction, it's not quite that easy – for example, the article 'The Bomb squad' is written entirely in grammatically correct Standard English, spelt and punctuated accurately, yet it can only 'communicate effectively' if the reader knows something else besides the words. SCAA acknowledges this: 'To be successful learners, pupils need to be able to read in order to gain access to information and ideas from a range of texts and sources and to evaluate them' (SCAA 1997: 6).

The introduction of 'a range of texts' and the notion of evaluation suggest rather more complexity. However, neither this document, nor English in the National Curriculum fully embrace the fact that using language is a socially constructed phenomenon, much more complex than being able to 'use grammatically correct sentences', to 'spell and punctuate accurately' and 'gain access to information and ideas from a range of texts'.

The chapters in Part 1 of the book describe and examine some of the complexities of language and literacy, emphasising that language has to be viewed as a product of social and cultural interaction. The contributors to this part ask several questions and raise other issues; in looking at language generally, they examine the use of language in education. They echo Bruner's view that language 'can never be neutral' (Bruner 1986: 121). In commenting on the language of education, he points out that:

> Language necessarily imposes a perspective in which things are viewed and a stance toward what we view. It is not just, in the shopworn phrase, that the medium is the message. The message itself may create the reality that the message embodies and predispose those who hear it to think about it in a particular mode.
>
> (Bruner 1986: 122–3)

Bruner's words about 'the reality that the message embodies' applied to the SCAA *Use of Language* document reveal that language is to do with *accuracy*, *skills*, *effectiveness*. Nothing wrong with that; the reality, however, is made even more clear from what is *not* said. Gaps and silences can speak as loudly as words. There is nothing here about seeing language and literacy as part of a complex set of social practices, discourses which involve far more than pupils being 'taught to express themselves correctly and appropriately' (SCAA 1997: 6). Just what might be appropriate? To whom? In what circumstances?

Literacy and power

Much has been written recently about literacy and empowerment. This has become such common currency that it has been taken to embrace a whole set of – sometimes dubious – classroom practices which are supposed to assist literacy development. It is worth re-examining the relationship between literacy, power and schools or classrooms. It is more complex than a crude view that one more powerful group of people is controlling the access to literacy of another less powerful group. What is critical is that those who have power to define what counts as valuable or valid literacy hold the greatest power. Literacy can be exclusive as well as inclusive, depending on what it is taken to mean. Margaret Meek warns that: 'Differences in literacy are not only the result of social differences. Literacy helps to perpetuate them' (Meek 1992: 226). The ways in which literacy opportunities are presented in schools can themselves create divisions and exclude some pupils from ever having the chance to exercise power over their own literacy, or over the social rights which literacy confers. The texts children read and write are often linked with the values held by society about what counts as valued literacy and therefore as a valued person, as Jenny Cook Gumpertz explains:

> In early modern times literacy was regarded as a virtue, and some elements of moral virtue still seem to attach to it in that judgements about literacy skills tend to have prescriptive or normative overtones. A literate person was not only seen as a good person, but as someone capable of exercising good and reasonable judgement.
>
> (Cook Gumpertz 1986: 1)

The issue of what literacy is all about becomes more and more complex. It is not just about how pupils become successful readers and writers, but also about the kinds of texts they read and write and the value placed on those texts. Further than that, it is also about how those involved in the literacy business do their jobs. The way literacy is described by teachers, parents and others involved in education, and the kinds of texts which are given status, are part of society's theory of literacy. This theory, in turn, underpins the ways in which literacy is introduced by governments and schools. Literacy is not innocent nor can it ever be neutral; questions about literacy are bound up with questions about the diversity of cultural contexts in which texts are produced.

Active or passive?

Ian Frowe's chapter picks up on these questions, presenting the view that language is not merely a passive chronicler of events but an active determinant in many aspects of our lives. He argues that careful attention to the use of language should be a priority in all areas of the curriculum in order that the ideological and rhetorical components of texts can be recognised. By asking questions about the power of language and the ways in which it is used both within schools and in talking about schooling, Ian Frowe reminds us that 'Language influences how we understand the world and the attitudes we adopt towards it'. He questions the naive – and potentially dangerous – view that language could ever be seen as straightforwardly a matter of 'effective communication'. This chapter places debates about language firmly in the area of the social and cultural construction of meaning.

Helen Nicholson's examination of the role of spoken language in education moves questions about the power and complexity of language further – into issues of teaching and learning, looking at the school and classroom implications of seeing language as related to social and cultural values. To Helen Nicholson, 'language is part of the fabric of cultural communication and dialogue'. In line with Bruner's views about learning as a communal sharing of a culture, she argues that 'It is the ability to share language, therefore, which creates a culture and community of motivated learners'. Language not only reflects the home cultures which all members of a school or classroom represent, it acts to create new shared cultures. In Bruner's terms, schooling is a process of 'joint culture creating . . . and an appropriate step en route to becoming an adult member of society' (Bruner 1986: 127). Helen Nicholson offers a different perspective on communication, arguing that all language relies on a 'highly complex public system of communication'. Part of this complexity lies in the fact that the effects of communication are 'not determined by linguistic structures alone' but by the visual and aural dimensions of talk. Talk lies at the centre of learning, but not simply in its performative aspects or as 'oral skills' where pupils have to 'speak clearly' (SCAA 1997: 8).

Helen Nicholson's chapter raises important questions about the acceptance by the SCAA document that 'correctness' and 'accuracy' are unproblematic. Much more enlightening, as Helen Nicholson argues, is a view of language as the site for negotiation and dialogue – a language of education which takes into account the complications of culture, social life and language itself. This part of the book deals with the first category of knowledge about language as outlined in the Introduction (p. 3). Part of the knowledge teachers need to have about language is to do with understanding the relationship between language and social and cultural values. This means seeing the texts which learners encounter as produced within specific social and cultural contexts, so that the forms of language which are used by teachers and tackled by learners are looked at critically and analytically.

The third chapter in this part follows the thread of not taking forms of language for granted. Mary Earl examines the use of narrative in schools, particularly those narratives used in values education. She, too, emphasises that the narratives which enter school are not value-free but have all been constructed within particular cultural frames. Narrative is widely understood as providing, in Gordon Wells' words, 'a cultural interpretation of those aspects of human experience that are of fundamental and abiding concern' (Wells 1987: 195). He describes narrative as the process whereby:

> in every act of perception, the world 'out there' is interpreted in relation to the inner mental model in terms of which the world is represented. Making sense of an experience is thus to a very great extent being able to construct a plausible story about it.
>
> (Wells 1987: 196)

Mary Earl asks whether the stories which form a substantial part of moral education in schools are presented as complex and problematic or whether there is a tendency to suggest that story can offer 'right' answers.

Rather than narrative being seen as providing 'truths', Mary Earl argues that narratives ought also to 'enable learners to enter into a dialogue with the world', offering some practical suggestions about the ways in which this might be done. It follows, then, that young people – and their teachers – need not only to be able to look at language critically, but to use language consciously to construct their own critical stance in relation to moral values and the ways in which the language of moral value has to be interrogated. As Harold Rosen puts it:

> The very least we can do is to emancipate ourselves from the notion that there is only one good and proper way, and that that way is quite rightly prescribed by others, because they are paying the piper or because we have bowed before their assured authority without question.
>
> (Rosen 1992: 127)

The chapters in this part argue for that emancipation – for teachers to develop knowledge about forms of language which will lead to an educational theory of literacy offering a constructive critique of the cultural values attached to both the texts and processes involved in the 'use of language' in education.

References

The Big Issue: Coming up from the Streets (1997) 'The Bomb Squad: Can Nottingham ever get cooler?', *The Big Issue* No. 263 15–19 December.

Bruner, Jerome (1986) *Actual Minds, Possible Worlds*, Cambridge, Mass.: Harvard University Press.

Cook Gumpertz, J. (ed.) (1986) *The Social Construction of Literacy*, Cambridge: Cambridge University Press.

Meek, M. (1992) 'Literacy: Redescribing Reading' in K. Kimberley, M. Meek and J. Miller (eds) *New Readings: Contributions to an Understanding of Literacy*, London: A. and C. Black.

Rosen, Harold (1992) 'The Politics of Writing' in Keith Kimberley, Margaret Meek and Jane Miller (eds) *New Readings: Contributions to an Understanding of Literacy*, London: A. and C. Black.

School Curriculum Assessment Authority (1997) *The Use of Language*, London: SCAA.

Wells, Gordon (1987) *The Meaning Makers: Children Learning Language and Using Language to Learn*, London: Hodder and Stoughton.

1

'STICKS AND STONES . . . '

The power of language

Ian Frowe

Over the centuries 'Anon' has generated numerous proverbs and sayings which successfully encapsulate some truth about the human condition. In the case of *Sticks and stones may break my bones but words will never hurt me* we must assume some lapse of concentration; whilst it may be an accurate description of rhino-skinned politicians, it chimes less well with the experiences of ordinary mortals. Sticks and stones are capable of inflicting physical injury but to ignore the potential psychological damage of words is to operate with a narrow and misleading model of both language and human beings. In many cases what is said may cut and wound to a degree which is more penetrating and persistent than what is done. One of the powers which language possesses is the ability to convey strong emotions in a direct, unambiguous and forceful manner: are we really intended to believe that words such as *nigger*, *spastic*, *slut* or *queer* inflict no hurt on those to whom they are addressed? Indeed, they are usually employed precisely because of their pejorative connotations and consequent effects upon the recipient; only someone ignorant of social conventions could refer to another as a *nigger* and fail to see the entailed offensiveness of the term.

All practices such as education, medicine or science need a conceptual framework within which to operate – a set of ideas, principles, rules, values, etc. – and this conceptual framework will be linguistically formulated. In some aspects of a practice language will simply be a means of reporting 'what goes on', that is, the language functions in a passive fashion. It is simply reporting aspects of the practice in a neutral way. However, this is not the whole story.

Many practices (and the extent to which this is the case will vary with the particular practice) have elements where language does not simply report 'what goes on' but actually shapes the practice itself. In such cases the language we use is of the utmost importance because it will influence our understanding and subsequent actions. Whilst a secure knowledge of the technical aspects of language use is highly desirable, it is also important to understand the different ways in which language can function in relation to practices. During their educational lives children and students are introduced to a wide range of disciplines, all of which are language-dependent, although the functions of language across these disciplines is not always the same: the use of language in physics is not the same as the use of language in poetry. With a growing emphasis on the teaching of language in all curriculum areas, the need for a slightly more nuanced understanding of how language can work is apposite.

This chapter examines the following areas:

- the significance of being a language user
- the relationship between language and practice
- language use and education.

The significance of being a language user

There has been much debate over the extent to which human beings can lay claim to a uniqueness which separates them off from all other sentient creatures, namely, that they alone are language users. Studies of higher primates, whales and dolphins have convinced some researchers that linguistic ability is not confined to humans but also occurs in other species. This may or may not be the case, but the argument is not crucial for I do not wish to claim that the distinction between humans and all other life forms is identical with the distinction between language users and non-language users. Rather, I take as a starting point the empirical fact that the vast majority of human beings are language users and this is highly significant for understanding human practices.

We share, as physical beings, many similarities with non-human beings, for example the need for food and drink; reproductive ability; sensory awareness; mortality; a physiology. There are aspects of ourselves and the environment which exist independently of any language we may possess: the functions of the heart or the liver are not language-dependent; long before language users appeared there were beings with organs not dissimilar to our own eking out a living in a world whose own existence was also independent of language users. If someone were to lose the power of language totally, many of their physical functions could still operate efficiently. We have much in common with non-language users at the physical level but the emergence of language resulted in a leap of development which was not merely a quantitative increase in complexity (although it was that) but a qualitative change into another realm of existence.

Any social world presupposes some form of life: rocks, rivers and mountains do not have a social life, they do not engage in social interactions. The social world, unlike the physical world, is a human creation. The social world would not 'just come to be' in the manner of mountains, rocks and rivers by natural forces. So much may seem fairly obvious: it is almost platitudinous to point it out, but what exactly is it that enables a social world to exist?

The social world differs from the natural physical world in that much of it is hidden. In the natural physical world things are, in some fairly obvious way, just what they are: rocks are rocks, air is air, ice is ice. (I am ignoring questions about their physical composition.) The social world is not like this: the social world is a world composed of meanings and symbols. In the social world things are not always just what they appear to be. The social world requires interpretation. Children are socialised into this world so that they can effect this interpretation; so that they can 'read' the social world.

In the natural physical world a river may be a source of water or an obstacle to be overcome but only in a social world could a river be a boundary between two countries. In the natural physical world a shell is the discarded home of a sea creature but only in the social world could a shell be a unit of currency. The river or the shell, however, do not of themselves exhibit these properties: the river may be deep, cold and swift, the shell small, delicate and light but there is nothing about either which says that one is a boundary and the other a unit of currency. A detailed examination of the river or the shell would not reveal this function in the way that it might reveal their chemical composition. We could express the position thus: being a boundary or a unit of currency is not a physical property of being a river or a shell. Close examination of either will not reveal the territorial or monetary function.

How is it, then, that a river or a shell can fulfil these functions? It is because the social world is a symbolic world and the point of symbols is that they represent something else. Language has many functions but central is the power to represent: language is a symbolic system. The word *rock* is not itself a rock just as the symbol for a church on a map is not a church but a way of representing a church. The idea of representation is that one thing can stand for – represent – something else. There are no symbols in the natural physical world because this world is not a representation of something else; it does not stand for something else. Language enables us to operate in a world which is no longer tied to the physical and concrete, to the here and now. It provides a means by which we can represent and refer to objects, events or emotions which are not immediately present but may be remote in space and time. Language also enables us to imbue or invest physical objects, such as rivers or shells, with significance or value such that they may function in ways which exceed their physical properties. Non-language users can do neither of these things; they cannot refer to anything, for to understand something as meaning, as referring to something else, is already to have some language ability. To comprehend the idea of something meaning something else – a gesture or grunt as symbolic – is to be operating in a linguistic domain.

Consider the case of 'pointing': there is nothing about standing with one arm outstretched which, of itself, tells someone that they should focus their eyes on an object whose location is to be found by extrapolating an imaginary line from the index finger of the outstretched hand. 'Pointing' is a convention, it is a gesture which means, represents, something else, namely, *cast your eyes in this direction*. Try pointing things out for animals: they do not understand the convention and pay no attention. To understand the convention of pointing is already to understand symbolisation, to understand that one thing can represent another.

Take a mundane example such as buying something. One person gives money to another in exchange for goods or services. After the transaction each has something different from what they had before. Imagine two non-language users who are each carrying something. As they draw near, each places the object they are carrying on the ground; immediately and simultaneously each grabs what the other has put down and runs off. In terms of overt behaviour these two events may look very similar but whereas one is a financial exchange the other is what might be termed a 'double snatch'. To engage in a financial exchange there needs to be mutual understanding between the parties – a notion of trust or legitimate expectations of behaviour alongside established financial practices. Such notions are only available to language users.

The idea of 'trust', for example, requires a notion of time, of there being past, present and future; as the past no longer exists and the future has yet to come, the only way of dealing with them is symbolically. To trust someone requires a means of representing time, for the orientation of trust is towards future events and may also draw on past events. Financial transactions presuppose a network of rights, duties and obligations which are impossible without a language, for example the concept of 'ownership' – that the seller has legal entitlement to the goods, that the buyer has the 'right' to purchase through the proffering of 'legal' tender, that the buyer has legitimate cause for redress should the goods prove faulty, and so on. These features are not readily observable in the overt behaviour of those involved in the transaction; close examination of the goods will not tell us whether the seller has the right to sell them and, despite appearances, whether something is legal tender is not a physical property of those objects which are exchanged. The same objects may be legal tender at one time but not another.

The 'double snatch' performed by the two non-language users, despite a behavioural similarity with the financial exchange described above, is a completely different type of event. There is no element of mutual understanding or agreement, no network of rights, duties and obligations, no notion of trust. Searle points out that simply training a dog to catch dollar bills and return them in exchange for food is not to initiate the animal into the commercial world (Searle 1995: 70). The dog learns to respond to a signal but the dog does not consider that it has the right to purchase the food, nor could the dog take the food and feel obliged to owe the money. We could also add that it is highly unlikely that the dog will decide to keep the money and use it to engage in another monetary transaction, perhaps the purchase of a new collar, on the grounds that the possession of dollar bills entitles one to engage in exactly that type of exchange. To operate with money is to engage in a set of complex relationships whose meanings and significance are essentially hidden from view and only available and intelligible to language users.

There is much more that could be said on this topic but the central point is that to be a language user, to be capable of dealing with symbols, of understanding that something can represent something else, opens up a dimension of being and action which signals a qualitative leap from the type of existence available to non-language users. All of what we might term the complex social world and its institutions – commerce, the arts and sciences, education, leisure pursuits, the law, medicine, scholarship – are language-dependent. None of these practices could exist if we were not language users. However, to claim that these practices are dependent upon language still leaves open questions regarding the role which language may play within them and it is these issues that need to be examined.

The relationship between language and practice

Merely to argue that social practices, for example monetary exchanges, are dependent upon language leaves open the degree to which such practices are influenced by language. The fact that practices logically require the existence of language says little about the relationship which may exist between the two. The literature on this point is immense but I want to identify three possible models concerning the relationship between language and practice. The first sees language as having a passive or non-constitutive role in relation to practice and I term this the *Passive Model.* The second reverses this position and sees language as having the dominant role to play in practices: this is the *Strong Constitutive Model.* The third is somewhere between the other two and sees the relationship as one where language and practice influence each other. This is the *Intermediate Model.*

1 The Passive Model

The Passive Model sees language as having a minor role to play in social practices. Social practices need language but its role is what could be called 'secretarial'; language is a recorder or minute taker, it is a passive chronicler of events. According to this view language is a means of labelling objects or events in order that we can refer to them in writing or speech, that is, to facilitate communication. So we use words such as 'tree', *apple*, *fight* or *hate* as a means of referring to objects, events or feelings in order that we may successfully engage in communication with others and facilitate our own thinking. This perspective is often associated with empiricist philosophers such as John Locke. Locke's starting point was that there existed an external world which provided the body with sensations channelled via our sensory apparatus and from these 'impressions' the mind formed ideas. Language was the process of attaching 'labels' – words – to these ideas as a means of identification for future reference. The important point about Locke's theory was that language was at the end of the causal chain: world – sensation – impression – idea – word. The function of language was to label that which already existed in a neutral, passive manner such that it had no effect upon that which was labelled.

In this model, language has no creative force; it simply provides a means of referring to objects, events, feelings whose existence is taken to be independent of language.

2 *The Strong Constitutive Model*

This view, as the name suggests, sees language as playing a far more active role than simply a system of labelling. Here, language is constitutive of practices and strongly so. The Passive Model allows only a minor role for language whereas this theory sees language as the dominant player; social practices are language-driven. Rather than language simply providing a neutral inventory of objects, events or feelings, it actively engages with and shapes objects, events and feelings. One of the most explicit and influential statements of this position is to be found in Michel Foucault's *The Archaeology of Knowledge* (1972). Foucault's central claim in this book is that in order to understand correctly and explain human practices such as medicine or psychiatry (his most commonly used examples) it is necessary not to study the practices themselves or the practitioners but only the 'discourse' of the practice. Whilst Foucault acknowledges that practices will have what he terms 'non-discursive' elements, it is the discourse which is most significant; discourse is what unifies, shapes and gives purpose to practices.

The contrast with the Passive Model couldn't be sharper: in the Strong Constitutive Model, language, or discourse, does not simply provide a means of referring to the constituent parts of practices but is the driving force which shapes and controls practices. Foucault argues that we must resist the temptation to see language as simply 'pointing to things' (which already exist) but understand discourses as having the power to 'systematically form the objects of which they speak' (Foucault 1972: 49).

There are numerous issues raised by this account which it is not possible to pursue here but what is significant about Foucault's position in *The Archaeology of Knowledge* is that it presents a view of language (discourse) which does not view it as playing a simple secretarial role in relation to practices, as in the Passive Model, but as the active determiner of practices. Language forms, moulds, affects the nature of practices.

3 *The Intermediate Constitutive Model*

This position lies somewhere between the Passive and the Strong Constitutive Models. It sees language and practice as interconnected but argues for a more egalitarian relationship between the two. That is, it does not see practice as dominating language (Passive Model) or language as dominating practice (Strong Constitutive Model). The relationship is rather one of mutual dependence and influence: practice influences language but language also influences practice. Skinner expresses the position thus:

> It is true that our social practices help bestow meaning on our vocabulary. But it is equally true that our social vocabulary helps to constitute the character of those practices . . . if there are indeed causal linkages between language and social reality, to speak of one mirroring the other may be to envisage the arrows pointing in the wrong direction.
> (Skinner 1980: 576)

The 'mirroring [of] social reality' is a reference to the Passive Model, where language simply reflects what is already there but, as in the case of a mirror, effects no change on what is there. The vocabulary used by Skinner illustrates well the nature of the Intermediate Model: language 'helps' to constitute the character of practices; practices 'help' to bestow meaning on vocabulary. The relationship is more fluid; it is not a one-way street but a road where the traffic moves in both directions.

Skinner provides an interesting example of how language may shape practice. In Elizabethan England merchants appropriated the term *religious* as a way of commending 'punctual, strict and conscientious forms of behaviour' (Skinner 1980: 570). Their purpose was to legitimate their commercial practices by reference to the most highly approved moral and spiritual values: their undertakings were to be viewed as acts of piety and not simply as *instances of administrative convenience*. Once the merchants had decided to use the term 'religious', they could not hope to describe just any action they chose as 'religious' but only those actions which with some degree of plausibility met the accepted criteria for the application of the term. The merchant needed to 'tailor his projects in order to make them answer the pre-existing language of moral principles' (Skinner 1980: 576).

In other words, if you choose to describe your actions through a vocabulary already imbued with certain meanings, then not just any type of behaviour is possible; the actions will need to be of a certain kind. Social practices are not therefore independent of language, for language can influence the nature of the practice. Some practices fulfil the conditions of the Strong Model, that is, they are linguistically constituted. For example, the practice of promise making depends on the utterance of the words *I promise*; in their absence no promise has been made. Once uttered, a network of obligations and expectations is brought into existence. Language in this case shapes subsequent practice in a strong fashion. Similarly, saying the words *I do* in a specific situation alters the social world by establishing another set of duties and obligations. In such cases the effective power of language to shape practices is clearly seen.

There are also numerous cases where the passive role of language is evident. Many uses of language merely report or refer to events, objects, feelings, etc. without having any effect on the events, objects or feelings mentioned. If I say *I have £10 in my pocket* this simply reports a fact about my finances; it does not (unfortunately) have any effect on my monetary holdings. Or if I say *There's a cat in the garden* this has no effect on the existence or not of cats in my garden.

Because the Intermediate Model deals with the interaction of language and practice, it is slightly more complicated. Many practices may involve language use which employs all three models, and distinguishing one from the other may not be straightforward. The mistake made by several writers is to think that one or other of these models is applicable to all language use, thus either underplaying or overplaying the creative role of language. What is important is to recognise what role language is playing in a particular set of circumstances since to confuse one with the other leads to serious misconceptions. For example, the belief that language can be strongly constitutive in relation to the physical world leads to a radical scepticism regarding the nature of science, whereas attempts to reduce certain human activities such as morality or religion to, say, a genetic level go hand in hand with a view of language as essentially passive.

Language use and education

Both Foucault and Skinner, despite their differences, have a common view about the nature of language: they see it as 'interconnected'. Foucault talks about discourses as 'networks'; Skinner sees language 'holistically'. The idea is that words are connected to other words and that this is what enables them to have a meaning. Although it is possible to isolate individual words, the meaning individual words have depends upon the existence of other words. This might seem fairly obvious but, because words are interconnected, changes in one part of the language can have knock-on effects in others. Words possess what might be termed 'resonance': they form an integrated whole and changes in the meaning, use or appraisive force of one word can have implications for others. For example, consider the word *primitive* as used in the past by anthropologists. A *primitive society* was one characterised as being backward, unscientific, superstitious, perhaps immoral, that is, a society lacking the attributes of sophisticated, advanced cultures. The appraisive tenor of *primitive* was to reveal deficiencies and to judge some societies as inferior to others. The reluctance of present-day anthropologists to employ the term *primitive* signals an unwillingness to judge certain cultures as inferior to others. The knock-on effect is that the attendant vocabulary – *backward* or *unscientific* – also becomes inappropriate. The change in vocabulary influenced how the cultures were viewed and what was legitimate behaviour towards them. Compare how the perception of those traditionally termed *disabled* has been changed by a language which has moved from a (no doubt) well-intentioned paternalism which emphasised weakness and dependence to one stressing equality and civil rights. The *disabled* realised that, if they wanted attitudes towards them altered, a first, vital step was to change the vocabulary traditionally employed.

There are clearly aspects of the world which are independent of language, for example the weather or the colour of one's eyes; these are things which language cannot change or shape. However, there are also aspects of our life which language can influence, where the language we use has significant implications for how we understand and conceive what it is that we are engaged in. For example, in the development of personal relationships the role played by language is highly constitutive for the language that is used powerfully shapes how the relationship develops; *the language of love* may be a cliché but, like most clichés, it has an element of truth within.

This power of language to mould or shape perspectives, to influence thought and practice, has long been exploited by rhetoricians and ideologues to promote their own views and denigrate those of others. Because language is interconnected, because it is a resonating system, an apparently innocent or minor change in vocabulary can bring in its wake a whole set of meanings which can radically alter how a practice is to be understood. It is much easier to justify the deaths of civilians when they are described as *collateral damage*. One of the goals of education has always been to equip people with the cognitive tools necessary to examine critically the information which they receive so that they are less open to manipulation and deception. A central element of such an ability is an understanding of how language can be used to influence both thinking and action.

Let's consider a concrete example: education is a social practice; it is a language-dependent activity and the language fulfils many functions. Sometimes it merely reports what goes on: *Mrs. Jones teaches science*; *The school has 250 pupils*; *The school football team lost every game*. Although such statements need a language for their expression, their content is not 'linguistically constituted' in the sense that the number of pupils in the school or the outcome of football matches is somehow determined by language. In such cases the language is simply reporting certain facts about the (educational) world.

But education is more than simply a catalogue of facts. As a social practice it involves meanings. There is more to education than an inventory of the sites where it occurs or the personnel involved. Education is not identical with its physical manifestations. There is no one view as to what education should be; no blueprint which is acceptable to everyone; no set of practices which have universal application. Under the label *education* there are diverse and often conflicting perspectives as to how the practice should proceed. Although there is a common core of language – essential for communication to take place – each perspective also has a language which is distinctive and provides its conceptual framework. It is also the case that a 'common' language can often be less common than it appears. People may use the same terminology but understand it in very different ways. Thus the 'common' language may in fact mask a range of perspectives under a veneer of consensus. Consider how most people would concur on the need for schools to produce 'good citizens' but harbour radically different interpretations of what this should entail.

The importance of language can be seen in cases where there have been attempts to change the nature of a practice. Often the process starts with the introduction of a 'new' vocabulary which is aimed at getting the practitioners to conceptualise their activities in a different way, a sort of linguistic softening-up process. In education the move to a more commercial, business-orientated approach was heralded by the introduction of a language which couched the practice in terms such as *productivity, quality control, delivering a product, value for money*. This language was intended to influence how teachers understood what they were doing and, consequently, change their practices to fit in with a different perspective. Once established, the 'new' language ousts the 'old' and becomes the dominant means by which practitioners conceptualise their activities. As Skinner noted, once you have adopted a particular language you are limited in how you can behave, for your actions will have to be in sympathy with the vocabulary.

Language and the practice, therefore, become interwoven, each feeding off the other. When problems arise (and what counts as a 'problem' will depend on the conceptual framework being used), the action taken will be influenced by the language of the practice, thus restricting the available scope for manoeuvre. Practitioners will conceptualise using the dominant language and seek solutions which exist within that framework. If the framework is one of managerialism, then problems will be put down to 'bad' management and the solution will be 'more effective' management.

The important point here is that, far from simply being an enervated minute taker standing on the sidelines, language is in there actively shaping the nature of the practice. To see it as a passive observer is to misunderstand one of the relationships which language can have to the world; it is to fail to understand how language can work. Once we grasp the fact that language can actively shape our behaviour, then the need to pay attention to how we use it becomes apparent. Its effects are often subtle: we may unthinkingly adopt a vocabulary without realising the assumptions it contains or how it influences our behaviour. Every era has its fashionable orthodoxies but what education cannot shirk is the responsibility to hold up such taken-for-granted beliefs and expose them to critical examination. It may be a case of familiarity breeding contempt; language is such an inescapable aspect of our lives that we can become somewhat blasé about how we use it. Attention to the finer points of language use should be a feature of all aspects of education, as this is how we achieve precision and clear meaning. Its potential for affecting our thinking and actions has perhaps been unduly neglected.

Conclusion

This chapter has attempted to highlight and illustrate some issues regarding the relationships between language and practice, although it does not claim to provide any definitive answers to the questions raised. Its prime purpose is to suggest that this is an area which deserves attention and thought: language is a powerful tool which moulds and shapes various aspects of our lives. It influences how we understand the world around us and the attitudes we adopt towards that world. In schools and colleges children and students need to be made aware of how language works – what it can and can't do, how it relates to their experiences and actions. Language is organic and constantly evolves but this does not mean that all language changes are desirable or that it is not possible to adopt a critical, informed perspective on those changes.

References

Foucault, M. (1972) *The Archaeology of Knowledge*, London: Tavistock.
Searle, J. (1995) *The Construction of Social Reality*, London: Penguin.
Skinner, Q. (1980) 'Language and Social Change' in L. Michaels and C. Ricks (eds) *The State of the Language*, Berkeley: University of California Press.

2

TALKING IN CLASS

Spoken language and effective learning

Helen Nicholson

> As part of his attempt to improve his behaviour, Lee has agreed not to talk in lessons. Please initial his report form if he is successful.

I received this note on the report card of a Year 8 student whose behaviour was giving some cause for concern. It immediately placed me in something of a dilemma, as my lesson was structured around group discussion, where the pupils were preparing a presentation about the journey to Canterbury undertaken by Chaucer's pilgrims. Lee had begun reading extracts from *The Canterbury Tales* with limited enthusiasm; at that stage he found reading difficult and often irksome. However, his interest had increased when he began to participate in activities which involved talk, and he had happily agreed to take the role of the Pardoner in their own partially scripted version of the Tales. In the event, I ignored the literal message conveyed on the report card, and urged Lee to talk as much as he liked in my lesson. In fact, the more he joined in the discussions, I told him, the more he would learn. Reciprocally, I suggested, we would learn from his insights. He looked sceptical.

The incident is significant because it points to some of the misapprehensions which have surrounded classroom talk. Although the authors of Lee's report card were obviously hoping to encourage him to concentrate in lessons, the suggestion that his learning would be augmented by his silence in class implies that talk is somehow linked to bad behaviour, that it is less educationally valuable than other forms of language use. Indeed, assumptions about the relationship between language and learning would appear very different had Lee's report asked teachers to sign if he had been successful in avoiding reading and writing.

The problem for Lee, he told me, was that that he liked classroom discussion *when you can put things your own way*, but found that much of the language with which he was confronted at school *makes me feel thick* because, he said, *I don't talk like proper with my dad or my mates*. Because of his colloquial use of spoken

English, Lee clearly felt excluded from much of his education, not because he did not understand the language he encountered, but because he felt that his own spoken language was socially and culturally inferior. His response was to exaggerate his own idiom, and his stock in trade was to offer a parodic commentary on the lesson as the class joker, a process which, as his report card rightly suggested, was inhibiting his learning. Indeed, as an acute observer of human folly, Lee often sustained an emotional involvement with the lesson in his own terms, and interestingly demonstrated his attention to spoken language by picking up on the verbal and physical mannerisms of his teachers, through which he regained some control over the linguistic community of the classroom.

As Lee's story implies, the place of oracy in the curriculum is complicated by the intimate connection between talk and the ways in which social and cultural identities are constructed and valued. Because spoken English is often regarded as the most spontaneous and immediate form of communication, and is learnt in the home, playground and street as well as in school, the varied values associated with oracy are very closely allied to the unequal, asymmetrical and complex social relationships which characterise contemporary cultural life. Indeed, although linguists have usefully pointed out that Standard English is but one dialect amongst others, there continues to be a significant political currency attached to its use, of which, as a student in a large inner-city school, Lee was well aware. As Tony Edwards has pointed out, children whose home language closely resembles the 'authorised' language of school are most likely to be 'identified and sponsored' as successful learners (Edwards 1992: 68–73). I do not wish to reopen tired debates about the use of Standard English here, but to suggest that if Lee felt estranged from the 'official' language of the classroom, it was because the difficult balance between valuing the language of his home culture and the need to extend his repertoire of spoken English had not been achieved.

To address the obstacles to Lee's learning, and to enable him to learn effectively in a variety of subject areas, Lee had to be encouraged both to use the experiences of his home language in the classroom and to acknowledge that the acquisition of new vocabularies is a necessary part of understanding new ideas and concepts. As he was an expert skateboarder, it was relatively easy to explain this to Lee. He recognised that the language of skateboarding was specific and technical, and one that he used only with other participants in the sport. When I asked him why, he said that there would be no point in using skateboarding terms with me because I wouldn't understand what he was talking about. I asked if I would need to understand the words he used to describe the various turns and jumps if I wanted to learn to skateboard. Although the idea of me on a skateboard amused Lee enormously, he conceded that I would pick up the vocabulary by joining in, when I would need to know what everyone else was talking about. As Lee began to recognise explicitly that he already moved between different linguistic registers according to context and audience, he became increasingly assured in his construction of spoken texts in the classroom and, with considerable effort and struggle, eventually began to enjoy using the 'expert' languages and technical terms intrinsic to different subjects in the curriculum.

The popular perception which has surrounded the issue of classroom talk needs re-evaluation if a more rigorous theoretical understanding of the benefits of oracy are to become more firmly embedded in educational practice. This chapter aims to address two central aspects of the opportunities for learning presented by structured talk in the classroom. First, it will explore how talk enables children to experiment with ideas and, I will argue, it is through spoken language that they achieve ownership of abstract concepts and unfamiliar information. Second, effective oral communication is, in itself, a skill which can be acquired through practice, as a synthesis between the emotions, cognition and experience, a triangulation of complementary but different aspects of learning.

Shared experiences

All language, including the informal construction of dialogue and other spoken texts, relies on a shared understanding of the ways in which meanings are created and understood. If this seems obvious, it is because it has come to be accepted that language is not the private expression of personal feelings and perceptions, which are impossible to communicate to others, but it enables individuals to participate in a broader community of those who use language in similar ways. Indeed, although its meanings may be variously *interpreted* according to context and situation, all language, including both the inner language of thoughts and the more social act of speech, relies on a highly complex public system of communication. To accept this premise raises questions about how children gain access to the rather confusing range of linguistic codes which face them in the early years of their secondary education. As Jerome Bruner points out, it is through the narrative structures of language, particularly found in the act of speech, that we come to understand, construct and 'shape experience' (Bruner 1996: 109).

A theory of learning which recognises the educational importance of speech relies in large measure on the view that it is through language that thoughts, feelings and concepts are created, and not the other way round. Since Wittgenstein demolished the idea that language is an 'incorporeal process' which is private and subjective, his argument that language is a 'vehicle of thought' has been widely accepted in education. As such, the process of learning a conceptual language necessarily depends on the experience of communicating with others. Wittgenstein suggested that there is a direct relationship between understanding language and intellectual curiosity. 'Language is an instrument. Its concepts are instruments. Concepts lead us to make investigations; are the expression of our interest, direct our interest' (Wittgenstein 1963: 151). As an instrument and a symbolic system, language is part of the fabric of cultural communication and dialogue. It is the ability to share language, therefore, which creates a culture and community of motivated learners.

If language and thought are interdependent, as Wittgenstein and his successors have argued, it suggests that children's conceptual development, and their interest in their work, is dependent on how far they have *ownership* of the different forms of language used in the classroom. In this context, classroom talk has a particular significance primarily because it is both a physical act and a creative process; to speak with assurance depends on a high degree of ownership of the words pronounced, and an ability to create and construct meanings independently in ways which listeners recognise. In suggesting that speech is immediate and dynamic, Merleau-Ponty likens spoken language to a 'magic machine' which is a 'gesture of renewal and recovery which unites me with myself and with others' (Merleau-Ponty 1973: 17–19). Because speaking and listening is interactive, it encourages learners both to communicate their understanding and to explore and interrogate new insights. One of the ways, therefore, in which children might extend their linguistic repertoires is through sharing ideas and thoughts, in the public and personal act of speech. It is a dynamic process which enables individuals to become personally and emotionally involved with their learning.

Writing about the educational value of speech, Jerome Bruner suggests that dialogue enables collaborative learning, an activity which allows children, perhaps paradoxically, to develop a sense of individual agency. He argues that effective learning takes place when children are assisted by the 'give and take' of conversation, where they develop an active mind through dialogue with others. In generating and testing their hypotheses, sharing descriptions of their work, and negotiating with others, Bruner argues that children and their teachers create a classroom culture in which collaborative practices foster independent thought. As speaking and listening is an interactive and social process, children's conceptual and intellectual development is enhanced where teachers introduce new ideas with appropriately focused use of their own vocabulary. Bruner's well-known use of the concept of 'scaffolding' is apposite in this context: the teacher's role is to build on children's experiences as learners, to help them to internalise new ideas and knowledge, which may be applied *consciously* to other contexts and different situations (Maybin, Mercer and Stierer 1992: 186–95).

It is specifically through spoken language that abstract ideas are made concrete. This was demonstrated to me by a mixed ability group of Year 9 pupils who were preparing a science experiment based on electricity. Using light and sound, they were constructing a game based on the popular television show *The Crystal Maze*, which was to be used as part of a primary liaison day. The pupils had bent a piece of a wire, which would act as an electric circuit, and had attached a battery, a door bell and a light bulb to it. The game is well known, involving passing a circle of wire over the live wire which, if they touched, would ring the door bell and light up the lamp. They were discussing how to write the instructions, and how to convey the concepts of the electric circuit to Year 5 pupils.

Mark: We have to say something about this wire stuff.
Peter: Yeah . . . it's bent to make it harder . . .
Joanna: No . . . it's about circuits. We need to tell them to watch out for the buzzer . . .
Susie: We can show them . . . what to do . . .
Peter: I can do it really well . . . look . . . *(he performs the game)*
Joanna: Stop mucking about . . . if you do it right all the time they won't know about the buzzer . . .
Peter: Buzzzzz
Mark: If we show them once, then break the circuit, we can show them what the battery does . . . how it makes it . . .
Peter: . . . makes it buzz. The circuit makes it buzz.
Susie: It's not just the circuit . . . it's the electricity in the circuit. It's really important that they know that. And the way the source of electricity is conducted . . . but I think they'll know that batteries are the source of electricity . . .
Joanna: The two work together . . . they give a flow of energy and power which illuminate the light bulb. You pass the flow of charge through the wire . . .
Peter: Yeah . . . I've got it . . . it's the flow of energy . . .

This exchange is interesting because it highlights the way in which the group both consolidated their learning and built on each other's understandings. As their language became more technical, and they focused on the process of explanation, their ability to recognise the complexity of the experiment was more obvious. The task itself was multi-layered and carefully structured; their construction of the model enabled them to show their *learning* about electricity, but it was through their spoken explanations and descriptions that they understood the *concepts* which governed the experiment. Amply justifying Bruner's premiss that collaboration through dialogue leads to independent thinking, discussion enabled the experience of creating a circuit to reach cognition, a process which later enabled them to apply their knowledge and understanding to other contexts.

The raising of educational standards necessarily requires children to become increasingly independent thinkers, and to develop the capacity to use and recall the knowledge and skills they have acquired. Indeed, it is the ability to make connections between concepts, to transfer and renew ideas and knowledge, which is practised and developed collaboratively through the dialogue afforded by structured classroom talk. Because intellectual and conceptual understanding is facilitated through oral communication, talk is integral to the process of learning; the experience of using one's own language is integrated with the vocabularies which describe, create and symbolise unfamiliar concepts, as a synthesis of thoughts, feelings and ideas.

Thought and rehearsal

Implicit in the argument that language is a vehicle of thought, and that talk enables feelings and ideas to reach cognition, is the idea that different forms of talk enable different conceptual languages to become intelligible. However, the importance of talk as an integral part of learning is a highly complex process, and one which is intimately related to the inner processes of thought. Following Wittgenstein, I have suggested that spoken language, as a 'vehicle of thought', enables children to internalise external ideas and to interpret them for themselves. Indeed, the recognition that meanings are communicable only because a conceptual vocabulary is shared, points to ways in which children extend their linguistic registers and to how new conceptual horizons are opened. Nevertheless, the dynamic between learning, thought and spoken language has been further interrogated, most significantly in education by Vygotsky.

Vygotsky's distinction between different forms of speech is particularly relevant to creating a context for classroom talk. In brief, Vygotsky identified three different aspects of speech: 'inner speech' which exists silently in one's head, 'oral speech' which is vocalised and immediate, and 'written speech' which, as the most elaborate form, is planned, rehearsed and practised (Vygotsky 1962: 98–101). Although closely interconnected, Vygotsky suggested, somewhat schematically, that these three modes of speech have different educational functions. In *Thought and Language*, he argued that although all thought is conducted in language, the process of turning thoughts into speech is a dynamic process which alters, renews and recreates the thoughts themselves.

> The structure of speech does not simply mirror the structure of thought; that is why words cannot be put on by thought as a ready-made garment. Thought undergoes many changes as it turns into speech. It does not merely find expression in speech; it finds reality and form.
>
> (Vygotsky 1962: 126)

In identifying three forms of speech, Vygotsky implies that inner speech, oral speech and written speech transform thoughts in different but complementary ways. According to his argument, the varied forms of speech are related to the formation of concepts, not as a linear process of learning, but because each is integral to intellectual development.

One of the implications of Vygotsky's theories for classroom practice is the recognition that space needs to be created for children to shape and rehearse their ideas. Following Vygotsky, speech cannot simply be regarded as the articulation of pre-existing inner thoughts; learning is dependent on a rather more haphazard process of ordering, revising, renewing and recreating a web of thoughts, ideas, information, questions, experiences and feelings into increasingly coherent patterns. This is, in itself, a creative process, where inner speech is used to 'draft' ideas before they are articulated in the public context of the classroom. In explaining how she rehearsed ideas in her head before speaking, Sarah, a Year 7 student, identified a strategy she used in whole class discussion:

> If I already know the answer to the teacher's question, it's easy. I put up my hand quickly. Sometimes, I sort of half know the answer, and then sometimes I put up my hand and sometimes I don't. If I do, I think what I am going to say whilst I am waiting for Miss to decide who to ask. And then if it's me I hope it comes out all right. If I don't, I don't usually bother to think about it. Sometimes I just get a bit lost.

Sarah's response reflects the differences between 'written speech', which needs to be structured and ordered if it is to make sense to an audience, and the language of thought. She implies that she is only fully confident in speaking to the whole class when she knows that she is repeating ideas with which she is already familiar. Used in this way, talk is not integral to the processes of learning, but demonstrates only that which has already been acquired and assimilated. However, the teaching style she describes suggests that, when answering teacher-led questions, her learning is a rather hit and miss affair. As Sarah identified, without prior knowledge of the ideas or information they articulate, students may get 'lost' in their work and fail to learn effectively.

Approaches to education which have valued confident responses to teacher-led questions have often neglected more speculative and dialogic forms of talk, and have militated against those moments of learning which result from the expression of doubt, uncertainty and ambiguity. Perhaps this is the place to challenge the traditional idea that fluent and articulate speakers are necessarily intelligent and educated; such a view of oracy tends to ignore the depth of thought which is often found in those whose spoken responses are more hesitant. However, not only was Sarah able to discriminate between occasions when she was simply repeating ideas which had already formed in her mind, she also recognised that the composition of speech offers a transitional stage between thought and understanding. Indeed, there has often been either too easy an elision between 'writerly' speech and judgements of intelligence, and an accompanying lack of acknowledgement of the skills involved in creating lively dialogue, largely because written language has been traditionally more highly valued in education. Both perspectives, however, fail to take account of how ideas are shaped, redescribed and transformed by the act of speech itself.

One of the ways in which children learn is through rehearsing ideas, thoughts and feelings, as a monologue, in inner speech. In a fully differentiated curriculum, however, children will also be given space to rehearse ideas in dialogue with others. This is not a case of simply repeating information to 'make it stick', but of providing structured activities which allow students to generate their own questions, to speculate and experiment with their emergent ideas and thoughts. It is interesting in this context that Vygotsky refers to Stanislavsky, a theatre practitioner who developed a system of rehearsal which was designed to allow actors to share their motives for action. Stanislavsky's ideas depended on the view that the simple repetition of gestures, speech and movement was unlikely to encourage actors to achieve a depth of understanding of a particular role, nor would this allow an emotional engagement with ideas. His system suggests that meaningful, coherent expression is created only when actors reach a shared interpretation of the text and subtext, and when they have identified the motives for action. His advice to actors to 'always act with a purpose' might be usefully adapted to a more general educational context; children learn best when they understand the learning objectives, and are able to recognise the point of what they are doing. One of the ways of achieving this sense of purpose is through an active and enactive period of 'rehearsal', when children are able to interact with others, when the learning objectives are clarified. It is a process which allows, crucially, space for different positions and interpretations to be considered and constructed.

When children are given space to rehearse and explore ideas, they are able to make sense of their learning. The dialogue of conversation, with all its hesitancy, questions and speculations, leads children to new levels of understanding and allows them space to develop their own interpretations. I witnessed an example of this form of 'rehearsal' in a class of Key Stage 3 pupils, where Jane and Claire were looking at the changing use of buildings in their area as part of a history lesson. They had been given a selection of resources, including contemporary and old maps and photographs, taped conversations from people who remembered the district in the past, portraits of the gentry and pictures of labourers. They needed to construct a diagram in the form of a 'time-line', which showed the dates of the buildings they were studying, when and how the usage had changed, and what alterations had been made to suit their new purposes. Their teacher had stressed that it was important that they offered evidence for their ideas, and invited them to speculate about the demographic changes which had occurred in the neighbourhood:

Jane: Look at this one . . . *(she holds up a photograph)* it shows that bit near your nan's . . . it looks like there were fields down the end of her garden.

Claire: No . . . I don't think it's there . . . it's too hilly . . . What can you see on the map?

Jane: Here . . . *(she points at the contours)*. What do you think that's like when you see it?

Claire: I think that shows the hill at the back of school . . . there aren't any hills near my nan's . . . Look she lives just on this bit here.

Jane: Look at this . . . What's that woman doing with a bucket? Do you think she's . . .

Claire: She's working . . . look, there are chickens in the picture. Is that enough evidence?

Jane: Not sure. She might just be carrying a bucket for some reason. *(They giggle)* Why would you take a bucket for a walk?

Claire: Yeah . . . you wouldn't. Not unless you were really dippy. I think she's going to feed the chickens. Shall we write that down . . . *(she writes, speaking the words out loud)*. Woman feeding chickens. What can we tell about that?

As the pair worked, it became obvious that they were looking at the information from a new angle, and the urgency to make decisions and represent them in a diagram meant that their insights grew and developed. They looked at the material creatively and critically, revising and altering their views as they questioned their own and each other's opinions and observations.

This very brief example of collaborative talk suggests that the ability to rehearse ideas, to question and speculate is in itself a skill which is developed through practice. Jane and Claire, demonstrating Vygotsky's description of oral speech, were able to further their ideas and to consolidate their learning. Furthermore, and importantly, their talk clarified the learning objectives implicit in the work, and enabled them to explore new possibilities and unforeseen interpretations of the work. In many ways what is noticeable about this transcript is the number of questions it contains, and the way in which the pupils used their local knowledge to develop their insights. Working with a shared motive, their questions transformed their understanding, and the process of rehearsing their ideas through dialogue enabled them to deepen their understanding.

Composing spoken texts

So far in this chapter I have focused on the ways in which classroom talk might aid children's own understanding and interpretations, and I have suggested that dialogue with others enables children to shape ideas, in part because it is informed by both external ideas and the internal monologue which goes on in our heads as we think. But in everyday life we also use talk to affect others, to create an emotional response, for example, or to persuade an audience of a particular point of view. In this section of the chapter, I shall suggest that, although all talk is in some sense performative, there are particular crafts associated with the construction of the kind of spoken texts described by Vygotsky as 'written speech'. It is these spoken texts which children use when they consciously compose their ideas for presentation to an audience.

There are two particular, and interrelated, aspects of spoken language which may enable children to present their ideas with assurance when they are constructing spoken texts. The first is that talk has many purposes, and the various structural devices in talk can be used to influence an audience in different ways. The second is that talk has a physical dimension, and this distinguishes it from other forms of language use. As such, an explicit understanding of the crafts of performance, and the way language is structured to create particular effects, is integral to children's learning if their work and ideas are to reach a wide audience. In other words, there are specific opportunities presented both by learning through talk, and by learning about talk, where children focus explicitly on how spoken texts are constructed for different audiences and for different purposes.

In well-crafted spoken texts, the linguistic structure of spoken language varies according to whether it is intended to persuade, inform, explain, narrate, instruct, summarise, interrogate and so on. Although there can be no guarantee that an audience will be influenced in the particular way the speakers intend, knowing how to construct spoken texts enables children to use different linguistic idioms and genres and thus to become increasingly effective communicators. To achieve this aim, they are aided when they are introduced to examples of a range of spoken texts, and invited to identify the strategies used for different purposes. As Merleau-Ponty has commented, speaking and listening, action and perception are only seen as 'quite distinct operations' when we reflect upon them; the recognition of how our own reactions to speech are fostered can, in turn, lead us to create similar reactions in others (Merleau-Ponty 1973: 19). In practice, this requires an understanding of the structures of different forms of spoken language, and an awareness of how language, and the delivery of a spoken text, might influence an audience. In other words, where speakers use words and phrases which consciously anticipate audience response, and create spoken texts which are designed to fulfil specific objectives, they are often able to engage and influence their listeners. As such, the ability to explain, summarise, or present an argument, for example, is dependent not only on the knowledge that the speaker has acquired about the subject-matter, but on knowing how to present the material.

Gunther Kress, writing about the relationship between speech and writing, argues that the speaker's 'awareness of the hearer' means that the speaker takes account of the hearer's needs as 'the recipient of information' (Kress 1994: 28). As Kress points out, however, children are often in a less powerful position in their social interaction with adults. The preparation and presentation of a sustained spoken text to an audience may go some way to redress this balance, and the immediacy of audience response allows children to consider and gauge the effectiveness of their powers of communication. Children who are familiar with the great range of spoken texts available through television may have assimilated many examples of different forms of oral language in use, but are less likely to have an explicit understanding of how distinctive linguistic codes and structures influence audience reception and interpretation. It is in this context that television can provide a rich source of texts which illustrate how spoken language is used for a variety of purposes. For example, a recent television programme tested the hypothesis implicit in the folk expression *red sky at night, shepherd's delight, red sky in the morning, shepherd's warning*. Having observed the presenters' use of language, and their inventive use of white balloons (to show cloud cover), and a red light to indicate sunset, one teacher commented that Year 8 pupils were able to construct their own explanatory texts about meteorology in a similar style, and with an awareness of the different ways in which information can be conveyed and, significantly, how it might be communicated with clarity.

As this example illustrates, the effects of communication are not determined by linguistic structures alone. There is a visual and an aural dimension to 'live' talk, which means that the spoken text has its own dramaturgy and semiotics which are open to further interpretations. Some of these aspects of talk are created physically by the speaker's use of intonation, pitch and tone of voice, gesture, movement and eye contact, but the performance of a spoken text, even in an informal context, might be extended to include visual aids, sound effects, lighting and the use of props, for example. In part, as Gunther Kress comments, the emphasis placed on words by the speaker indicates the importance and significance placed on particular information, instructions or ideas, and anticipates the listeners' response (Kress 1994: 26–8). However, if the teacher aims to encourage children to construct, in Vygotsky's terms, 'written speech', their learning may need to include some explicit reference to how they use the physical languages of the body, and a self-conscious awareness of how the crafts of the speaker may be employed to reach others. Importantly, this entails the recognition of which aspects of the information the audience might find difficult to comprehend, the appropriate selection of material to emphasise the point, and a consideration of the ways in which meanings are received and interpreted.

Improving standards

The popular perception that talking in class fails to encourage students to learn, and thus to achieve high standards in education, misses the crucial role played by classroom talk in children's development as learners. On the contrary, the evidence suggests that structured classroom talk is central to effective learning, and that talk enables information and concepts to be shared and internalised, thoughts to reach cognition, and ideas to be shaped, revised, reinterpreted and communicated coherently. Seen in this light, an awareness of the different contexts and audiences for classroom talk also offers children an opportunity to gain assurance as makers of spoken texts; learning both *through* talk and *about* talk gives them control over the linguistic communities to which they are introduced at Key Stage 3.

Jean Rudduck has commented that where pupils are involved with designing their own work they are able to speak articulately about it, which she has interpreted as reflecting a 'strong sense of purpose, strategy and goal' (Rudduck 1996: 48). Indeed, if there is to be coherence in their learning within and between subjects at Key Stage 3, students are aided by the sense of ownership of the concepts, ideas and information afforded by interaction and dialogue, the composition of sustained spoken texts and the presentation of ideas in and through classroom talk.

Improving standards in education entails a recognition of the way in which spoken language is intimately connected to effective learning. Rather than invoking increasingly arid debates about the differences between traditional and progressive styles of education, teachers and policy makers have a responsibility to focus on how children learn, and to accept that the aural, oral, visual and kinaesthetic languages inherent in speaking and listening contribute to learning in a differentiated curriculum. Both as a skill in itself and as an integral part of the learning process, talking in class allows children to identify their learning objectives, and thus to recognise and build on their understanding, interpretations and achievements.

References

Bruner, J. (1996) *The Culture of Education*, Cambridge, Mass.: Harvard University Press.

Edwards, T. (1992) 'Language, Power and Cultural Identity' in K. Norman (ed.) *Thinking Voices*, London: Hodder and Stoughton, pp. 68–73.

Kress, G. (1994) *Learning to Write* (2nd edition), London: Routledge.

Maybin, J., Mercer, N. and Stierer, B. (1992) ' "Scaffolding" Learning in the Classroom' in K. Norman (ed.) *Thinking Voices*, London: Hodder and Stoughton, pp. 186–95.

Merleau-Ponty, M. (1973) *The Prose of the World* (trans. J. O'Neill), London: Heinemann.

Rudduck, J. (1996) 'Lessons, Subjects and the Curriculum: Issues of "Understanding" and "Coherence" in J. Rudduck, R. Chaplain and G. Wallace (eds.) *School Improvement: What Pupils Can Tell us?* London: David Fulton Press, pp. 48–52.

Vygotsky, L. S. (1962) *Thought and Language* (trans. E. Hanfmann and G. Vakar), Cambridge, Mass.: MIT Press.

Wittgenstein, L. (1963) *Philosophical Investigations* (trans. G.E.M. Anscombe), Oxford: Basil Blackwell.

3
NARRATIVE AND THE DEVELOPMENT OF VALUES

Mary Earl

Twenty years ago when I started teaching, the current high profile of the term 'values education' was not, to my memory, even a speck on the horizon. Now everyone seems to be worried about promoting *common values* and even *spirituality* across the curriculum. There are different versions of why this might be but, however it got there, the values education debate is high profile today and looks likely to stay that way tomorrow. Values education enters the curriculum in several areas, most notably, perhaps, in personal and social education, but also in history, science, art, music, drama, geography, religious education, English . . . and probably mathematics and design technology, too. The importance of language in these areas might seem self-evident – after all, discussion is often the basis for exchanging and articulating opinions on human values. However, there is a more precise area of language which I want to examine in this chapter – the predominant use of narrative in values education. The power of narrative to carry moral messages is widely recognised, but I want to take a good look at the educational use of narrative and particularly at its use in the area of personal and social education (or personal and social development, or personal, social and health education).

The link between narrative and the definition and structuring of values education is not new. Writers like Kohlberg and Gilligan have already used narrative to explore how adult moral thinking develops and others have investigated the use of narrative in trying to develop and promote values in schools (Duska and Whelan 1975). Their interest in narrative does not, however, specifically address how teachers can in practice use the shifts into and out of narratives, or the shifts between narrative and non-narrative, to develop a facility in young people for using the principles, concepts and technical language of the values debate. This debate surrounds them from the cradle to the grave. The ethical problems they face include everything from cloning to drugs in sport and pornography on the Internet. We are not short of narratives to show or tell them about these. But if teachers involved in values education (e.g. PSE teachers) cannot define clearly how the process, for instance, of 'having a discussion' on one of these topics is helping to 'shape children's capacities for disciplined, self-directed learning and sustained, rational thinking' about it, then it is not clear how they can justify the existence of this activity on the timetable (Wood 1988: 14).

Nor is it enough to regard the narratives that come into the classroom from various public agencies, such as the police, health authorities or faith communities as, in themselves, 'educative'. These narratives, like any other, are value-laden, not value-free. Narratives, whether sung, danced, drawn, written or spoken, encode the values they put on information and ideas, alongside the information and ideas themselves. Nowadays, and in this culture, those narratives may come as much in the form of newspaper cuttings, magazines, Internet conversations, digitised photographs or TV soap stories as much as in the form of novels, plays or other 'story books'. It is important to exploit pupils' access to this vast range of narrative in ways which effectively promote language as a key to the development of thought. Even when we take *narrative* specifically to mean a written text, we often seem to have little idea what we do with the narrative once it has arrived in the classroom. Is the assumption, perhaps, that if a narrative is any good it needs no introduction, no follow-up work and no consideration of its premisses? For some people, on some occasions and with some narratives, it may be possible, and necessary, to let a narrative speak for itself, and to let each individual take away from it what they can and will, but we can't rely on this as our sole means of promoting values education, if only because of the link between the development of that talk and the development of thought.

It seems likely that at least some of the unease PSE teachers, in particular, often feel about their role is tied into this problem. Such teachers often have a dedication to the belief that PSE (or PSD or PSHE) is an important part of the curriculum but are unsure how to justify it 'academically'. As a result, much of the rationale given tends to be a reaction to crises or initiatives of various kinds in the public domain – the need for HIV/AIDS education in the mid-1980s, the recent SCAA values forum, or the more recent demand for explicit citizenship education spring to mind. Such a reactive view can lead to confusion for teachers and pupils alike. For all our sakes, it seems important to consider carefully what underlying factors will allow PSE teachers to deal, in a more consistent way than we seem able to do at present, with the latest narrative about what being 'healthy', a 'good citizen' or 'being moral' is. Teachers need to be able, with integrity intact, to treat each narrative as what it is, one among many sorts of value-laden texts which pupils need to learn to engage with in order to make sense of their lives and the society they live in. In other words, values education is not over when you've found a good 'story' – with what you think is an important 'message' in it for young people to hear: it has only just begun.

The way narrative is used at present in PSE is often to tell a story of some kind and then to get the pupils to discuss it. Nothing wrong in that. Adults have been telling children stories in this way for as long as there have been children, and stories. Neither do children 'grow out of' this kind of learning by the age of 11;

it remains an inevitable and indispensable part of everyone's life experience and learning until the day they die. It may be that in PSE lessons in schools, the choice of which stories to tell is partly guided by public agencies. But when we consider the methodologies used in taking these narratives into classrooms, we must ask ourselves more than whether the narrative has some official sanction or other. For instance:

1 Are we telling young people that these narratives themselves all have the same value?
2 Are we teaching them to distinguish between fact and fiction, or between accurate information and propaganda?
3 Are we encouraging them to develop conceptually in their ability to evaluate critically the moral debate arising from these narratives?
4 In other words, are we ensuring that young people *learn* anything from these narratives?

The language of values education

The decisions we make in schools about what 'stories' to tell young people about human beings and the societies they live in are strongly allied to the needs societies feel, and have always felt, to pass on to their young the inherited spiritual, moral and cultural wisdom they have so far accrued. There is no shame in this. What could be more sensible? However, there are problems about how to help young people learn that:

(a) human moral debate is a rational activity requiring the application of logic to solve its problems;
(b) there is a long history of such debate and some of it is very interesting!

The term most often used to describe what PSE teachers want to do, is *values clarification*. This is 'concerned with helping students understand the values they hold and the ways in which these are reflected in their behaviour, without any judgement being passed. The focus is on greater self-awareness' (Ryder and Campbell 1988: 262).

Implicit in this and in other language attached at present to values education is the belief that values are to be 'negotiated' or at most 'guided' but never endorsed as objective and binding on all of us. I am not criticising this (though SCAA may be), just pointing out that in values education, as in all other education, our assumptions about what counts as values education are encoded in the language we use in discussing it. If we want to allow values to be clarified as part of the educational process, then presumably we should base our rationale for PSE and other values education on the sort of ground that will not shift every time there is a change of national feeling about values education. Two ideas suggest themselves to me:

1. Values education will always have a very direct interface with the public faces of society; these social implications of values education are present in school, through work experience, police and other agency links, through an emphasis on teaching pupils their age-related 'rights' (and responsibilities, one hopes) and through links throughout the school with the various socio-economic groups, faiths and ethnic groupings represented in each school. It seems to make sense, therefore, for PSE teachers (and all others involved in values education) to start to build up a language and learning theory for their 'subject' from roots which take this interface into account.
2. Values education, as the dominant cultural language about it shows, is at present believed to be about involving pupils not in passively receiving (or unquestioningly accepting) the combined wisdom or moral orthodoxy of the age about human beings and the societies they live in, but in actively enquiring into and critically understanding and evaluating such orthodoxy. If we present this 'wisdom' in the form of narrative, which we often do, the same will apply to the cultures, wisdoms and moral orthodoxies within those narratives. But to allow the narrative both to speak effectively in its own right and to be heard by the pupils in theirs is hard to do. If we are seriously going to go for values clarification we have to give young people access to narrative without pre-loading their responses with too many hidden, misplaced or extraneous agendas about what the pupils *ought* to conclude from their debates.

Vygotsky says that social interaction is inevitably part of most teaching situations and that such social interaction embodies the actions, work, play, technology, literature, art and talk of members of a society. So children learn values as much informally as formally, as much implicitly as explicitly and as much from teachers' behaviour as from anything they say or give them to read: 'A child's potential for learning is revealed and indeed is often realised in interactions with more knowledgeable others' (Vygotsky 1978: 85). This is why education itself is often defined as 'concerned with, among other things, the transmission and reinterpretation of culture' (Wood 1988: 14–36). It is only through interaction with the living representatives of those cultures which surround them as they are growing up (what Bruner terms *the vicars of culture*) that young people come to acquire, embody and further develop knowledge of its values (Wood 1988: 14–36). One defining concept behind the use of narrative in PSE/values education might therefore be that we can, should and do use narrative in values education because narrative is the form of language which is most adaptable in terms of time, space, age and ability for transmitting these values. What's more, narratives allow us to interact socially and culturally with a far greater number of human beings than we could otherwise do. Nor is the resultant learning *necessarily* a form of social indoctrination, though we must always be aware of its potential in this respect. By interacting with these narratives, young people (and adults) register, decode and draw conclusions about often very abstract concepts to do with the meaning of 'life, the universe and everything', from 'justice' and 'fairness' to 'right', 'good' and so on. In this way they can know about and respond to ideas which might otherwise be inaccessible to all but the brightest few 'philosophers' on the planet.

But how should we ask and answer questions about narratives if we want children to learn from them? Jerome Bruner suggested that if we want young people to learn (about values as about anything else) then we must pay very careful attention at all times to three things:

> 1 The language used (by the teacher about the narrative and in the narrative itself) so that it awakens or taps into already existing **curiosity** in the pupil.
> 2 The **competences** which we, as teachers, want pupils to develop through exposure to this narrative.
> 3 Our awareness of the **community** into which we are bringing the narrative and that of the narrative itself.
>
> (Bruner, in Wood 1988)

In considering these three elements of learning about values, we should be aware, as an adult is aware of the dangers an electric plug socket offers to a toddler, that interactions with narratives can produce some pretty powerful responses, both positive and negative.

The most difficult and demanding piece of values education I ever did was connected to a school production of *The Threepenny Opera*. I had been so concerned with getting the entire project up and running, finding a piece which the singers and musicians had the technical ability to deal with, of the right length and fitting into the school calendar in the right way, that I forgot, until a parent's letter arrived one day, the central problem of values education contained in the venture, which was that almost the entire female cast were required to act the part of whores! To this parent this seemed wrong, and she didn't want to have her daughter involved. I will long remember the time I spent trying to compose a letter to her which dealt with the complexities of theatre and how acting the part of a 'bad' person might or might not encourage the actor to *become* 'bad'! In this instance the narrative of the opera text began to get interwoven with our community and the expectations of the families in it and that, in turn, became part of the values education of all of us together. What would have been wrong in that situation would have been to ignore the parent's concern or to be unable to justify our choice of narrative – the educational part is the interaction between us all and between us and the aspects of our selves narrated in poetry, history, plays and music.

Developing concepts through narrative

We sometimes seem to forget that at Key Stage 3 pupils are growing in their ability to handle the language of values as they grow in their ability to handle any other information. But this means that they should not be, at the age of 14, no further forward in being able to handle values debates than they were at 9 years of age. If we want them to grow, then we have to be clear what that growth involves and what the limitations on their understanding might be at any particular age or stage of schooling. Just because 11-year-olds have grasped the *information* in a historical account of the Holocaust doesn't mean they can make value judgements about its causes and consequences at the level adults can. Nor do we expect them to. Just because we give out a sheet with fifteen good reasons for and against capital punishment doesn't mean the pupil can necessarily make sense of them; the whole point of using narratives is that they can provide a bridge between such abstract, and to a large extent theoretical, exercises and the pupils' individual, growing experience of life.

Genuine enquiry-based learning about values means interesting pupils in a narrative, or using their existing interests. It involves being aware of what competences in handling aspects of the values debate we want them to have, and keeping a weather eye on the implications for a group's sense of *community*. It also means developing a range of linguistic strategies through which discussion of values can be carried on. This could mean anything from using narratives to draw pupils into the language of ethical debate itself, or getting students to explore for themselves the values hidden in different kinds of news stories, for example. This can help young people to understand how society's dominant values are embedded in its cultures by alerting them to the dangers of propaganda, just as examining the (often hidden) agendas behind newspaper reporting of 'news' to the public can lead to an analysis of how these affect that particular kind of story telling, too. Developing the ability to use and understand the language of values involves opportunities to 'talk oneself into understanding' with one's own peers and also with more experienced (though not necessarily more morally perfect!) adults. You don't need to waken a 13–14-year-old's interest in the ethics of medicine or of the transportation of animals and their use in experiments – it is already there . . . but how carefully do we take steps to think out ways of using this interest to develop the quality and not just the quantity of their debates? In Bruner's threefold analysis, the process of arousing pupils' curiosities in order to develop competences in debating values involves consideration of the ways in which a community works. It is worth remembering that in the classroom community the strongest influence may be the teacher, and that the choice of speakers and discussion questions will need to take that into account.

It is possible, of course, to simulate a whole range of ethical viewpoints that are current in society and use them to create debate. I came across the following story from a colleague who used it annually as a starter for a course which combined PSE with religious education. She told the story to an entire year group, leaving them after hearing the story to discuss in small groups the question at the end. I have since used the story many times myself, both in this form and, with a sixth form ethics and philosophy A level group, in an extended version. The beauty of it is that, like all good narratives, it can be taken in by any group at their own age and ability level and they can all respond to it. The job of the teacher is to ensure that the quality of response grows so that, as pupils mature, their ability to handle the language of values debates grows too. Here is the story:

> Once upon a time there was a girl. She had to cross a river to meet her fiancé/beloved. But the river was in flood, and raging furiously. Nevertheless, the girl, seeing four houses beside the river, knocked at each in turn and asked if she could borrow a boat to get her across the river. At the first lived a man with his family. He opened the door, but refused to take her across. *I must put my wife and family first*, he said. *Who knows when we may need the boat?* So she went to the second house and there the door was barely opened and her request made when the door was banged shut in her face and a voice screamed, *Go away. Why should I be interested in your problems? It's every man for himself you know, in this world – get out of here!* The girl was tiring now, but she came to the third house and knocked on the door. There a man known for his holiness lived, but he, too, refused her a boat. *It is not for me*, he said, *to alter the ways things are. If it is your karma that you get across and meet your fiancé it will happen. I cannot change things in any way*. Weary and despondent, the girl knocked on the fourth door and, much to her surprise, the man inside said, *Yes, of course I will help you* – and then added – *but only if you will sleep with me*. The girl agreed and afterwards the man took her over to the other side of the raging river. There she was reunited with her fiancé/beloved. After a while, thinking that to have such a secret might later damage their love, the girl told him what had happened. Furious, the fiancé/beloved stormed off and refused to marry her.

The question is: Who of all the characters in this story, is the most moral?[1]

Values education, the sort that pervades all education at the **implicit** level, has been taking place for all children, both at school and at home, for ten years by the time they reach Key Stage 3. Culturally, this means that the values we are talking about through the characters in this story have very different meanings for them all. They are very different individuals coming from within very different communities. It is important, therefore, in such a pluralist culture, that we allow time and space for the members of a group to exchange ideas about narratives like these. This is part of our job. After all, who else will give young people the time to do this in such relative safety from any negative consequences of holding such values? The narrative, in this case, both gives them a focus for debate and sharpens their ability to hold together or deal with diverging stances on values. If we want tolerance within our pluralistic culture, then we need to expose our pupils both to differences in values and to ways of *coping* with differences in values. It also pays for us to remain humble in the face of this task. After all, we may know what we think we're saying to young people but do we know what they think they're hearing? When schools, for sound educational reasons, choose to make a values education programme **explicit** at Key Stage 3 and thereafter, they would do well, when planning their programmes, to bear Bruner's three categories in mind. The ten years of implicit values education, which each pupil has experienced before reaching the secondary stage, have shaped their curiosities, competences and sense of community. It is this kind of awareness that determines, rightly, for many teachers, not only the **methodology**, but also the **choice** of a narrative to bring into the classroom. If the group, or some individuals in it, are not ready, personally, linguistically, socially or in some other respect, for that narrative, then the story, and the lesson based on it, may die.

Narrative as dialogue

We want, we need young people to be able to enter into a dialogue with the world, not be speechless in the face of its ever-growing complexity and we need to think very hard about how to equip them with the thinking tools to do this. If people, young or old, can't make sense of the values debate going on around them because they have no facility for handling its concepts, then they can't make choices about whether it holds any meaning for them. For many of us, access to the ideas which unlock terminology about values comes indirectly, often through encounters with narrative. So which ones should we choose? Narratives which enable young people to develop conceptually are those that raise, illuminate, but do not explain away, the complexities of human life and the value placed on it by different societies. Narratives which leap right in and say *the answer is this* or *you should think about that* are rarely the ones young people learn most from, let alone remember after schooling is over. Just because a narrative is simple doesn't mean it's a 'better' one for young people to read or see – in fact, it may be the complete opposite, because it may kill the curiosity.

I recently saw a Year 8 lesson on stealing given by means of a story which I knew had been specially written to help young people see how the decisions being made by the various characters to steal, however well motivated, led inevitably to 'bad' consequences. The group lost interest when they realised who the 'goody' and the 'baddy' were set up to be, skimmed ahead to check whether they were right and then, bored, stopped listening. Paradoxically, Kohlberg's story of a man breaking into a chemist's shop to steal medicine for his desperately ill family motivated them to much more animated, and endless, debate about whether it is ever right to steal . . . or by extension, to break any of society's moral codes.[2] My point here is that young people are precisely that – young *people*. They don't necessarily have an *inferior* moral sense because they are young, but they do have less experience than adults of what is involved in making moral judgements and of assessing what the consequences of certain actions may be. That is partly why one of the characteristics of adolescent behaviour is stereotypically known to be risk taking. If we can involve them in thinking about these consequences, through narratives which touch their experience and at the same time involve them in the greater complexities of other people's wider experiences, we can draw them towards developing, in their own time and in appropriate ways, the mature sense of rational decision making society wants in all its members. However, these are complex thinking skills they are trying to develop. They are not automatically there, fully developed, in every 11-year-old. It takes discrimination and time to develop the competence to understand how in different communities a multitude of quite different ideas of 'right and wrong' may be held at any one time. But the development of such thinking skills is not magic – it takes long hard years of slog – like most other forms of learning worth their salt and it is aided by the stories we use as examples of values debates.

Children as philosophers

In concluding this chapter I would like to pass on a discussion technique I was introduced to by Karin Murris, at the Centre for Philosophy with Children. This 'community of philosophical enquiry' offers a way of both allowing young people to own debates about values as an important and natural part of life, and of sheltering them, as a good parent does, from some of the consequences of inexperience or poorly understood ideas about life. Getting young people to ask profound questions about values issues is not hard. Four-year-olds ask all the profound philosophical questions: *Where is God? What happens when I die? Why should I?* Discussion of these questions is not something unnatural, and, in Bruner's term, the curiosity about such issues, unless crushed out of us by adults afraid of where such questions lead, remains with us till we die. By developing linguistic competence and awareness of how communities through the ages have responded to these questions we do them no small service. The description below is my own version of the 'community of philosophical enquiry' method.[3]

Ideally, groups should take part in this exercise in the round. If this is impossible, it is best to arrange the class as much as possible so that they can see each other and the teacher on equal terms – a horseshoe of desks, for instance, rather than serried rows. The teacher's role is to be a *very* neutral chair in the discussion. This particular exercise is one which allow values clarification to take place, but this does not mean the teacher is doing nothing by being neutral throughout and it certainly doesn't mean that at other times and in other lessons a teacher might not choose to use the same narrative in a completely different way.

1 Select a narrative you think would be interesting and relevant to the group and either hand it out, read it out or put it on OHP for all to see. I have

recently used the short letter, quoted below, in a teacher training context and found it very effective. A picture can also be an effective narrative and stimulate just as much discussion as the written word.

> Letter from school principal to new teachers (*The London Tablet*, 10 October 1992)
>
> I am a survivor of a concentration camp.
> My eyes saw what no man should witness:
> gas chambers built by learned engineers
> Children poisoned by educated physicians
> Infants killed by trained nurses
> Women and babies shot and burned by High school and College graduates
>
> So I am suspicious of education
>
> My request is: help your students to become human.
> Your efforts must never produce learned monsters,
> skilled psychopaths,
> educated Eichmanns. Reading, writing and
> arithmetic are important only if they serve to make
> our children more humane.

2 Allow time for everyone, in silence preferably, to take the narrative in, then go round the room and ask everyone for one question that comes to mind when they read/see this narrative. In response to the letter, for instance, questions might be factual (*Who was Eichmann? What does humane mean?*) obstructional (*Why do we have to do this, Miss?*), personal (*Who was the man who wrote this – was he Jewish?*) or philosophical (*How can you be 'more human/e'?*). The teacher accepts each question, however irrelevant sounding, or even cheeky sounding, with a neutral *thank you* but does not imply by voice, subsidiary questions, body language or anything else, an emotional response to particular questions. Nor does s/he answer them. There may be a few questions which appear silly or irrelevant at this point, but the process always seems to weed them out in the next part of the activity.

3 Still neutrally, explain that you now want the group to vote on which question they're going to debate. If you get the field down to two or three questions which they're all very keen on, try to get agreement on one to start with, assuring the group that you'll come back to the other(s) when there is time. Usually, groups do find a consensus, or at least agree on a question to start with, without much fuss. You can include yourself in the vote if you want, but you don't have veto power. Go with the question the group decided on. (In my experience they are likely to choose the most interesting

anyway.) If there are factual questions which can be easily answered (like *Who was Eichmann?*) and which are relevant to the discussion, you can answer them at this stage.

4. Ask the person who contributed the chosen question to start the discussion off, keep an eye on the time and let the discussion develop. You may choose to keep the discussion alive if it really slows down or goes off course, but try to stay neutral as much as you can. Interesting things can happen, like your 'equal status' leading someone to ask you what you personally think about the issue. You need to decide how you will deal with this, but I have found that, on the whole, groups don't invade my privacy if I don't invade theirs. That in itself is a valid and valuable aspect of values education to learn – that adults and younger people can tolerate opposing views and not be swamped by each other, and that there are limits to our toleration of being questioned publicly about what each of us privately believes.
5. When the discussion on one question fades, you can go on to the next favourite, though two or three tend to be the most you ever get time for. At the end of your time, you might want to leave time to debrief the exercise (gently, perhaps) and find out how the group and individuals involved in it felt about approaching the discussion in this way. Most groups welcome this chance and will use it to build on in any subsequent return to the method.

In my limited but quite varied experience of this approach to a narrative, the level of debate reached tends to be far higher than the generalised 'let's all sit round and discuss' school of debate. The reasons for this are probably fourfold:

- the questions and the majority of the procedures come from the pupils;
- it allows for a development, within quite a short space of time, through the superficial to often quite profound levels of debate;
- everyone contributes, however bumptiously or timidly, but the group dynamics tend to allow those who do not want to speak much, or who talk too much, to be handled by the group, not by teacher intervention;
- psychologically, it is an acknowledgement that in the face of the great philosophical questions in life we're all in it together. There is a lot of space to acknowledge that people don't know the answers to all the questions that face them and that young people can contribute something useful to the sum total of the debate about these issues without either being excluded on grounds of age or put down because of inexperience.

In terms not only of self-esteem but of using a process in values education productively at both an implicit and an explicit level, I find the approach well worth trying again and again. The critical edge of language, based on narrative and using thoughtful argument, allows for genuine engagement with issues which well-chosen stories, together with careful teaching methods, can offer. It is founded on young people's curiosity about their worlds; it helps them develop competences in debating tricky issues and establishes a sense that their home communities – and the values they have learned from them – are in turn valued in the community of the classroom.

Notes

1 There are probably many versions of this story in existence, and I do not know the exact origin of this one. But my thanks go to Chris Nichol, of Chesterton Community College, in Cambridge, who introduced me to it.
2 You can find this and other stories used by Kohlberg and Piaget to assess moral development in Duska and Whelan 1975.
3 For more information about the 'community of enquiry' method, contact Dr Karin Murris at the Society of Consultant Philosophers (SCP), Old School Centre, Newport, Pembrokeshire SA42 OTS Tel.: 01239 821091, Fax: 01239 820049, e-mail: 1004452703@compuserve.com.

References

Duska, R. and Whelan, M. (1975) *Moral Development: A Guide to Piaget and Kohlberg*, Paulist Press.
Gilligan, C. (1982, 1993) *In a Different Voice*, Cambridge, Mass.: Harvard University Press.
Ryder, J. and Campbell, L. (1988) *Balancing Acts in Personal, Social and Health Education*, London: Routledge.
Van De Groot, A. O. (1965) 'Images of Childhood and their Reflection on Teaching' in D. Wood (1988) *How Children Think and Learn*, Buckingham: Open University Press.
Vygotsky, Lev (1978) *Mind in Society: The Development of Higher Psychological Processes*, London: Harvard University Press.
Wood, D. (1988) *How Children Think and Learn*, Buckingham: Open University Press.

Part 2

STARTING POINTS
Raising standards of literacy

Introduction

> The problem of brute sanity was identified by George Bernard Shaw when he observed that 'reformers have the idea that change can be achieved by brute sanity'. . . . Brute sanity is the tendency to overlook the complexity and detailed processes and procedures required, in favour of the more obvious matters of stressing goals, the importance of the problem and the grand plan. Brute sanity overpromises, overrationalises and consequently results in unfulfilled dreams and frustrations which discourage people from sustaining their efforts and from taking on future change projects.
>
> (Fullan 1988: 16)

Current brute sanity tells us that young people's language and literacy is not being fully developed; achievement is being adversely affected. Newspaper, radio and television reports detail comparative literacy levels across the European Community and worldwide, revealing that the UK is lagging behind. The origins of such statistics are rarely explained nor are relevant questions asked, but nevertheless, there is a mood in the nation that suggests a need for change. This is not new, of course, as the introduction to Part 1 detailed.

Language is not only seen as a means of learning, but as a way of demonstrating learning through 'effective communication'. This raises particular problems for secondary schools where teachers of different subjects are not necessarily trained in the development of language. At the same time, OFSTED inspections have identified areas of English teaching which need attention, particularly in the teaching of reading at Key Stage 3 and in teaching about language throughout the secondary phase. There are other areas which need attention – teachers' own knowledge about language; the range of kinds of language (written and spoken) used throughout the secondary curriculum; the reading and writing demands across the range of subjects; the needs of pupils who have English as an Additional Language; the identified differences in attainment between boys and girls in English. Schools will need to develop whole school language policies if standards of pupils' literacy are to be raised. The process of developing policy is, in itself, invaluable but presents management difficulties. It is important to remember that much of the impetus of the Bullock Report was lost because it was too often seen as the province – or even empire – of the English department. The issues go wider, reaching into the effectiveness of learning in every subject of the secondary curriculum, raising issues of whole school curriculum management and review.

There seems little doubt, however, that language lies at the centre of successful learning and attention is once more being directed towards the kinds of recommendations made by the Bullock Report in 1975:

> In the secondary school, all subject teachers need to be aware of:
> (i) the linguistic processes by which their pupils acquire information and understanding, and the implications for the teacher's own use of language;
> (ii) the reading demands of their own subjects, and ways in which the pupils can be helped to meet them.
>
> To bring about this understanding every secondary school should develop a policy for language across the curriculum. The responsibility for this policy should be embodied in the organisational structure of the school.
>
> (DES 1975: 529)

Unfortunately, the generation of secondary school teachers who made thoroughly commendable efforts to implement the recommendations of the Bullock Report during the late 1970s and early 1980s did not entirely succeed in developing a widespread view of the need for all teachers, irrespective of subject area, to accept responsibility for language teaching. There were too many constraints, often associated with brute sanity. The original effervescent impetus gradually fizzled out as organisational difficulties overwhelmed well-intentioned individuals or groups. Sadly, the wealth of wisdom in Bullock did not result in generally raised awareness of the role of language and its critical relationship to learning. As Fullan points out, it is one thing to get change on the agenda, but just agreeing that something must be done is 'not a very effective strategy for implementing change' (Fullan 1988: 16).

Creating a culture of change

Analyses of the limited success of the 'Language Across the Curriculum' initiative identify a range of factors which constrained genuine change in the perceptions and practices of secondary school teachers. Many of these were related to the very organisational factors which the Report itself highlighted. These prefigure Fullan's analysis of successful change, covering *initiation*, *implementation* and *institutionalisation*. Fullan's categories help to clarify just where earlier initiatives failed, suggesting areas where the most recent push towards higher standards of literacy and learning might be targeted. According to Fullan, successful change is related to:

> *Initiation factors* – there are four requirements:
> - educational need should be linked to an agenda of political (high profile) need;
> - a clear model should exist for the proposed change;
> - there needs to be a strong advocate for change;
> - there should be an early active initiation establishing initial commitment, as an elaborate planning stage is wasteful of energy.
>
> *Implementation* factors – some critical needs include:
> - careful orchestration. Implementation requires the clear direction of many players; a group is needed to oversee the implementation plan and carry it through;
> - the correct alchemy of pressure and support;
> - early rewards for implementers;
> - ongoing INSET to maintain commitment as behaviours often change before beliefs.
>
> *Institutionalisation* factors – an innovation will be more successful if:
> - it becomes embedded into the fabric of everyday practice;
> - it is clearly linked to classroom practice;
> - it is in widespread use across several classrooms and schools;
> - it is not contending with conflicting priorities;
> - it is subject to continuing INSET for new staff, to consolidate commitment.
>
> (Fullan 1988: 17)

Attention to these three areas contributes to the creation of a culture of change within a school or local authority. The model implied by Fullan's categories is one which aims to raise awareness first, to start small and fast, to gain some immediate and tangible benefit and build through systematic support and pressure towards practices which will be perceived by teachers genuinely to serve their classroom and professional needs. The word *ownership* has been derided as a jargon buzzword, but Fullan's model places importance on teachers feeling commitment – and being put in a position where they have to make an informal contract – to any new initiative. For curriculum development to take root, teachers need to make it their own, to take it into their everyday practice. After asking *what's in it for me?* and realising the benefits of new ways of working, teachers develop 'a new sense of meaning about change' (Fullan 1991: 43).

Previous models of change have been based on a 'medical model' of development where an 'expert' diagnoses what is wrong within an institution and prescribes a cure – often in the shape of materials which – it is assumed – will work like magic. The trouble is that this doesn't happen. If it did, none of us involved in education would need to consider these matters any more. This kind of prescriptive view of curriculum development fails because it is based on an inaccurate model of the process of learning. We don't just learn things because we are told; learning involves a complex set of processes where newly introduced ideas are set beside previous knowledge and experience and interact to transform understanding. Often this is the result of active engagement with issues, discussing, trying them out, debating and arguing their relative merits and demerits. Learning can be enhanced by working beside an already practised person who can give support and advice; by experimenting and practising in a safe environment where mistakes will not be too costly. This is why Bullock recommended continuing inservice work and Fullan identifies it as an important feature of genuine curriculum change – the shifts of belief which accompany changes in practice:

> Changes in teaching practices involve the development of new skills, behaviours, coordinated activities and the like. Changes in beliefs or understandings – in philosophy, conceptual frameworks, and pedagogical theory – lie at the heart of what education and learning are for a particular group.
>
> (Fullan 1987: 214)

Such changes in practices and beliefs come about through a combination of action and reflection – doing and thinking. In looking at the initiation factors in relation to the use of language in secondary schools it is clear that language and literacy have high political profile, expressed in the National Literacy Strategy. Many of the ingredients for initiation are already in place in national and local educational institutions. There is a political agenda and a clear model; the possibilities for advocacy and early action are there. However, if teachers are to avoid the *unfulfilled dreams and frustrations* this time round, greater attention needs to be paid to the second and third categories of Fullan's analysis – the implementation and institutionalisation factors.

Critical interventions

Implementation needs *careful orchestration.* If curriculum development is a form of learning, then, just like classroom learning, its success will depend on carefully planned interventions – the management of change. These interventions, again just like those in the classroom, should not be seen as only those face-to-face interactions between teachers and learners; some of the most effective interventions for learning happen before reaching the classroom. Critically timed interventions for learning are the plans, activities and evaluations which form part of any process of learning – with children or adults. Creating a culture for change in a school depends to a great extent on the timing and nature of the interventions – the meetings, investigations, activities, inservice provision, follow-up, reporting back, evaluation and further planning. These need to be solidly and centrally placed and taken on as the responsibility of senior management in a school. Recent research into the effectiveness of inservice in raising reading standards in some London schools revealed that:

> Crucial to the effectiveness of any inservice commitment is the element of careful and planned management of change. The role of the headteacher is central in this process and it is clear from the case studies that where the headteacher had taken a proactive role, the developments were likely to be more firmly and permanently established and staff felt more secure to extend their practice. This use of pressure in identifying areas of needed change and support in funding inservice to effect change are the markers of sound management of resources. Pressure without support leads to resistance and a lowering of staff motivation and morale; support without pressure leads to drift or waste of resources. In those schools where headteachers have found a balance, the expenditure of funding is most likely to be cost effective in terms of raised standards. This balance needs to be kept both within school and at borough level. The most effective inservice happens when pressure for change is accompanied by adequate support for innovation and development.
>
> (Bearne 1994: 76)

A (draft) report to Her Majesty's Inspectorate entitled *Secondary Literacy* confirms these factors which influence effective curriculum change. The major conclusions emphasise also that 'there is no "quick fix" solution to deficiencies in literacy' and that approaches that involve curriculum areas other than English, alongside work done by English departments, 'are more likely to be successful than initiatives that are confined to the English and/or SEN departments' (HMI 1997: para 7). Based on surveys of 49 secondary schools working to raise standards of literacy, the report also makes it clear that some of the important features of successful practice are when:

> Teachers are given the necessary training and have continuing opportunities to discuss progress. Key members of staff are knowledgeable about developments in primary schools, especially approaches to the teaching of reading and writing and the National Literacy Project framework.
>
> (para 13.xii)

and

> The headteacher and senior management team are fully committed to the literacy initiatives; have a good understanding of what is involved; and are aware of the quality of the school's existing work in this field. Their commitment extends beyond the limits of a short term project.
>
> (para 13.vii)

The chapters in this section all give descriptions of ways in which departments, schools and local authorities have begun the process of implementation and institutionalisation. The first chapter details the difficult process of starting to make changes in literacy practices in a London comprehensive school where staff morale and planned management are key factors. This account follows a group of staff who take responsibility for starting off the work and describes the difficulties and achievements. One of the interesting elements of the work was the identification by the staff of the need for changed classroom practices, for new ways of teaching language. This reflects the points made in the introduction that 'teachers need to know something about the structures of language – spoken and written – if they are to teach pupils to handle the range of texts they meet' (p. 3). As one of the teachers in Chapter 4 comments: 'People are more aware in their lesson planning structure of the four areas of language so that they can teach language through their subjects.'

Not only have teachers become more aware of their role in teaching language, but that classroom teaching and learning practices need to be carefully examined: 'Accepting that their literacy is not very high might mean using other strategies – more talking or more picture text.' However, changes in practice – in doing – are only part of the story; there is a need for reflection – thinking about it and a concomitant need for time to be made available for discussion and reflection. The value of reflection is identified by another teacher in the school who comments: *One of the most positive things is having time and space to talk with other people*. Having agreed that reflection and discussion are valuable, however, this honest account deals with the constraints which the teachers felt affected the progress of their initiative to raise standards of literacy: 'We can all sit down and come up with great ideas but actually having the time to follow these through is completely different.' This leads to the key role which school headteachers and senior managers have to play in organising for follow-through, despite the financial and organisational constraints they operate within.

Prudent management of resources has always been a feature of management concerns, but seems even more critical now. Whilst being aware that funds for inservice and curriculum development are limited, headteachers and senior managers are aware that many educational ships have been sunk because of the lack of that ha'p'orth of tar. *Cost effectiveness* may be an irritating factor when teachers are trying to raise standards of achievement, but it cannot be ignored. This means that every penny has to be fought for – as Marie Stacey outlines in her chapter on the Wirral initiatives. This chapter describes work in one local educational authority which committed itself to literacy development work with teachers from science and history departments. The work produced some sharp lessons about the need for support from educational policy makers and financial managers; the role of libraries – and librarians – as sometimes undervalued and often underused learning resources in schools; and the central role which headteachers have to play in managing budgets and school organisation to ensure successful change to raise standards of literacy. The poems which end this chapter aptly demonstrate the value of increased attention to language by teachers in subject areas other than English.

The final chapter in this part is a detailed and careful study of reading practices in an Essex comprehensive school. It is also an example of how long-term and supported inservice work, provided by a local authority, can make for considerable change in a school. Nigel Spratt and Ruth Sturdy write about their work in school as part of the Essex Reading Project. This gave them the opportunity to scrutinise their own school standards of reading, particularly in respect of the current concerns about differences in attainment between boys and girls. The research began because of OFSTED concerns about gender and reading attainment and fulfilled all of the criteria described by Millman and Shipton as necessary for successful change:

> These include the importance of changing attitudes, both by pupils and teachers, the importance of whole school approaches in which equality perspectives are central to all new initiatives, the effectiveness of a combined top-down/bottom-up approach to change, the key role played by positive role models and the importance of monitoring progress through the collection of quantitative data.
>
> (Millman and Shipton 1994: 147)

Describing the results of their research as a *sobering affair*, Nigel Spratt and Ruth Sturdy, like the teachers in Chapter 4, identify a need for teachers themselves to have a greater understanding of how to help readers tackle texts:

> There is evidence that pupils are not encouraged to delve into and interrogate the texts they are given. Texts are seen as a source of 'right answers'. We clearly need to develop a more critical approach to reading for our pupils.

The detailed statistical data in this chapter provide a very clear view of what is happening to boys' and girls' reading tastes and practices as they progress through secondary school. The chapter also highlights the need to hear the pupils' voices in any initiative aimed to raise standards of literacy. The research has led to a wider school-focused initiative which is bearing fruit. Like the schools in North London and the Wirral Project, they see the importance of acknowledging home experience of literacy, of making links with parents, of taking a good look at supporting readers who are not achieving their potential in literacy and of targeting key groups.

None of the teachers involved in the work described in this part of the book would claim to have the answers to questions about how best to raise standards of literacy. By revisiting the Bullock recommendations, they have acknowledged once more the need for increased knowledge about language, about critical readership and the development of policy. However, they go further in identifying some of the key factors which mean that, this time round, 'Language Across the Curriculum' might take firmer root. Their starting points provide pointers to ways in which schools might begin to develop a climate for change.

References

Bearne, Eve (1994) *Reading Recovery and Raising Reading Standards: A Comparative Evaluation*, Cambridge: Homerton College Occasional Papers.

Department of Education and Science (1975) *A Language for Life* (known as The Bullock Report), London: Her Majesty's Stationery Office.

Fullan, Michael (1987) 'Implementing the Implementation Plan' in Marvin F. Wideen and Ian Andrews (eds) *Staff Development for School Improvement: A Focus on the Teacher*, London: Falmer Press.

Fullan, Michael (1988) 'Managing Curriculum Change' in *The Dynamics of Curriculum Change: Curriculum at the Crossroads*, London: School Curriculum Development Committee.

Fullan, Michael (1991) *The New Meaning of Educational Change*, London: Cassell.

Her Majesty's Inspectorate (1997) *Secondary Literacy: A Survey by HMI Autumn Term 1997.*

Millman, Val and Shipton, Sandra (1994) 'Gender Issues' in Gajendra Verma and Peter Pumphrey (eds) *Cross Curricular Contexts, Themes and Dimensions in Primary Schools*, London: Falmer Press.

4

IMPROVING LITERACY

Establishing a culture of change

Eve Bearne

Encouraging colleagues to take a fresh look at their practice is never easy. The London comprehensive school in this chapter has begun looking at language across the curriculum as a starting point for raising standards of literacy. The process has been going on for just over a year, beginning with subject teachers investigating the language demands in their own areas and then participating in a half day's inservice designed to raise awareness about language issues and to kick-start a progressive development towards improved policy and practice. Getting a whole school participatory policy going is never easy – the constraints of time, resources and increased demands on teachers' energies get in the way. This chapter outlines the progress and difficulties in this school's experience as reflected by a group of colleagues who committed themselves to leading an initiative to raise standards of literacy.[1]

The school has approximately 1,000 pupils from a very wide range of cultural backgrounds. About a fifth of the pupils are bilingual or multilingual, many of them born in England, although there are constant waves of pupils new to the country whose needs, both learning and emotional, have to be catered for. The numbers of children coming in with little experience of English is increasing; there is particularly a growing number of pupils who are in the very early stages of learning English. The local authority employs a team of language support teachers to work in the school. The Language Development and Curriculum Access Team (LDCAT) work in support of developing bilingual pupils. This can include the pastoral needs of refugees to the global raising of achievement with African Caribbean learners. Part of their brief is professional development since teaching and learning styles, linked with the language activities, are key factors in promoting confident literacy with bilingual or multilingual learners. Over the past few years numbers on roll have fallen. This has an impact on the extent to which language support teams can work alongside mainstream teachers; team teaching can only develop if there is time available. Budget decreases linked to falling numbers mean that the staff generally have very little non-contact time.

One of the problems for the school has been the level of literacy of the incoming pupils. The school draws from a wide catchment with between 40 and 50 feeder schools so that it is a tricky task to get hold of children's incoming records. After a somewhat negative OFSTED inspection report, the senior management took advice from the special educational needs department and in 1996 administered a reading test across years 7–10.[2] The test results showed that 50 per cent or more of pupils in Years 7–10 had reading ages below their chronological ages. Whilst the staff recognised that reading tests do not entirely reflect the pupils' reading capabilities, these figures were a shock to them. There was a range of different problems related to reading. Some children appeared to be fluent readers when they read aloud but did not genuinely understand the texts they were tackling whilst there were others with neither fluency nor the skill of analysing and interpreting words and looking at the implications beyond the text.

A group of teachers met at the end of the summer term to begin planning for raised standards. The Improving Literacy Group was open to any staff who were interested, but each department was encouraged to send a representative. One of the first decisions the staff took that summer was to review literacy provision in each subject area. The first meeting of the Improving Literacy Group held in the new school year concentrated on setting up the departmental review of pupils' reading, writing, speaking and listening experience. The results from this survey suggested that most pupils had the opportunities to read and write a range of texts, although there was less coverage of spoken and heard texts. But if the pupils were being exposed to a range of types of text, why were they having such difficulties in making sense of what they were reading?

The main discussion centred on the fundamental question of why there needed to be a school-wide language policy at all. This was linked with issues of entitlement, as one member of the special needs department explained:

> We express ourselves through language and if children are to have access to knowledge, to any kind of relevant experience, then the vehicle through which they're going to acquire this is language. If we don't develop language to the extent that children will appreciate and value knowledge then we are shutting them off from experience. There's a relationship between thought and language – the one impinges on the other. Thought processes are directed by language. You think in certain ways because through the particular language you can handle that kind of thinking. If we don't develop that language in the pupils we're cutting them off from something.
>
> Besides focusing on reading there's also a matter of the pupils understanding what is being said, especially in subject areas. Most of the talk is casual talk. When we talk we communicate casually. The pupils find it very difficult sometimes to reframe their minds to the idea *this is*

> *not casual talk this is scientific talk, mathematical talk,* for instance – that business of register, moving from one level of understanding to another. I've got a feeling that it's something to do with the pupils not having sufficient understanding or access to the subject-specific vocabulary or the subject register. When you express something mathematically you can't say *this way and that way* you have to say *north or south* or *on an axis*; you don't go *up and down* in mathematics you go *horizontally and vertically* and if you don't know that you're lost. Subject-specific vocabulary, that's what they need.

The matter of subject-specific elements of literacy was also minuted as a key issue. The entitlement debate was widened to include writing as well as reading and members of the group agreed to report back these discussions and get response from their departments about their own priorities. At the same time, the deputy head, at the general request of the staff, had asked the English adviser to come in and lead a half-day staff training day on literacy. A meeting in December began to draft some of the material for a policy. By the end of the first term, the work done by the Improving Literacy Group had begun – slowly – to develop some shared perspectives on the major issues to be tackled and to begin to consider some ways forward.

Identifying priorities

By January the group's agenda had firmed up. In moving towards a draft policy they needed to identify the key tasks to be addressed, the proposed time scale for action and the level of involvement of the staff generally. This last point was considered essential because some of the staff could remember the last time schools attempted to get issues of 'language across the curriculum' going. The Bullock initiative had not fully succeeded in this school. Whilst in the early 1980s the school had established some shared approaches to writing and teachers' responses to writing, only a small number of departments had fully embraced the idea that language teaching is everybody's responsibility. The Improving Literacy Group felt that a key to getting greater success this time round lay in helping staff identify something in the initiative which would serve their own purposes – *what's in it for me?* – and which would contribute towards more effective teaching and learning.

After some discussion in this meeting, it seemed that tackling reading first might be a useful starting point. The group also returned to the language demands of particular subjects as an important factor in pupils learning different reading strategies. Each subject uses learning commands or instructions which may have specific meaning within that subject, for example *analyse* or *examine*. They looked at a list of key terms used in examination questions (Figure 4.1) and agreed to consider subject-specific terminology with their own departments.

Account for	Explain, examine the points that make up the subject you are being asked about.
Analyse	Explore the main ideas of the subject, show why they are important and how they are related.
Calculate	Find out by using mathematics.
Comment on	Discuss the subject, explain it and give an opinion on it.
Compare	Show the similarities (but you could also point out the differences).
Complete	Finish off.
Conclude	Decide after reasoning something out.
Contrast	Show the differences ('compare and contrast' questions are very common in exams).
Criticise	Analyse and then make a judgement or an opinion. You could show both its good and its bad points. (You could refer to an expert's opinion within this question.)
Define	Give the meaning. This should be short.
Describe	Give a detailed account.
Differentiate	Explore and explain the difference.
Discuss	Explore the subject by looking at its advantages and disadvantages (i.e. pros and cons, for and against). Attempt to come to some sort of judgement.
Distinguish	Explain the difference.
Enumerate	Make a list of the points under discussion.
Estimate	Guess the amount or value of.
Examine	Look at something closely.
Explain	Describe, giving reasons and causes.
Explore	Look at something closely; investigate.
Express	Put the ideas into words.
Evaluate	Give an opinion by exploring the good and bad points (pros and cons). Attempt to support your argument with expert opinion.
Give reasons for	Explain why something is the way it is.
Identify	Recognise, prove something as being certain.
Illustrate	Show by explaining, giving examples.
Indicate	Point out, make something known.
Interpret	Explain the meaning by using examples and opinions.
Justify	Give good reasons for offering an opinion or reaching a conclusion.

Figure 4.1 Some key terms used in examination questions

It was also decided to review how different subject areas help pupils learn to read the types of material relevant to the subject. Some staff explicitly teach this, but the group felt it could be a useful area for more general discussion. Examples might be teaching pupils to read diagrams in science; to sift through historical information to sort out fact from opinion; to identify the difference between the structure of a newspaper and a fictional narrative. The discussion raised some important points generally about improving the profile of reading in the school and making reading strategies more explicit.

With reading identified as a school priority, plans went ahead for the half-day of staff training. Part of the preparation for that was a staff meeting where the head of English explained what the Improving Literacy Development Group had been doing and charted progress up to that particular point. This highlighted some of the key issues that had come out of the discussions so that the whole staff could then consider them. At that meeting the staff were given a preparatory task to select a lesson or unit of work and think about the language demands it required so that on the inservice day there was informed discussion. The input from the adviser, the preparation, the workshops and discussion heightened awareness of the key issues. One of the outcomes was a series of statements identifying important issues raised. What emerged quite strongly was that the priorities for each separate group went across all departments. The two most frequently mentioned were: developing the use of writing frames[3] and the importance of teaching pupils the terminology and specific language of subject areas.

The work of the Improving Literacy Group was now permeating whole staff discussion and there was a growing feeling that there were issues which could be tackled effectively which would not be too daunting to staff and which could make a significant difference to the pupils' reading and writing. Departments were beginning to develop their own plans. After the session on the training day, they were asked to outline areas of focus and to identify how they would work on these, who would be responsible within the department for the work, deadlines and success criteria (see Figures 4.2 and 4.3 – examples from maths and science). Another suggestion which had been taken up by departments was to allocate one lesson each half term with each class to reading for enjoyment within the subject area. Staff would find information books, biographies, magazines and other material which was related to the subject but which was not text designed deliberately to teach. They planned to read extracts in order to excite interest and generally widen the pupils' reading experiences then to encourage pupils to browse and enjoy the material.

Looking at special educational needs

Whilst the general work throughout the school was taking shape, one of the members of the special needs department had been analysing the language demands made on the pupils who need extra support. She describes the work so far:

Whole School Approach to Literacy

Department MATHEMATICS

Areas of Focus

1 Use "framework" method from Year 7 to facilitate the writing up of Mathematical Investigations.

2 Excite Mathematical discussion within the classroom to enable written work to be more meaningful.

Action / Task	Person Responsible	Deadline	Success Criteria
① Produce a generalised framework which can be adapted for each investigation	Department in faculty meetings	Half-term	Whether pupils' written work matches up criteria for Ma 1
② Introduce practical work but followed up by formal written work connecting facts established by the practical work. Extrapolating tests the theory ensuring vocabulary is understood and pupils use confidently	Whole dept.	On-going	Comparison of pupils' ability to remember – increasing achievement levels.

Figure 4.2 Whole school approach to literacy (mathematics)

Whole School Approach to Literacy

Department SCIENCE

Areas of Focus

1 Resources to support literacy

2 Improve classroom practice to include simple strategies to aid pupils with literacy difficulties.

Action / Task	Person Responsible	Deadline	Success Criteria
1. Gather all support materials (existing). into a central location available to all staff.	H.A.	25/5/97	Resource available for use.
2. Place materials support into relevant S.O.W/s (K.S.3 first)	All Each person responsible for different units	7/97	
3. Incorporate list of 'useful' exam terms with 'easy' definitions into KS4 teaching laminated on walls – translated into major languages.	J.O/H.A	before 9/5/97	
4. Use different strategies in lessons e.g. several different explanations of each thing to be done or more definitions. Break up language and groups of similar words to give confidence. Perhaps focus on prefixes (cross-curricular use of as well)	J.O/E.D + All	Immediately	Judged by effectiveness of delivery of lessons – shared by observation + 'good practice.'

Figure 4.3 Whole school approach to literacy (science)

> I've designed a progress booklet for the learning supported children. When they come in to school they write two things that they wish to achieve and they fill in the date that they do it. When they read a book independently at home then they write down the title, author and when they read the book. When they do their spelling tests they have to write down which spelling pattern they've learned, what the result was and they're supposed to write down their homework. This book goes into lessons and in each lesson when they learn a new word associated with their subject, they should write it down. So they build up a list of subject specific language and we reinforce them and talk about them. At the end of a term they have to review the things that they have learned: *I can now successfully* . . . whatever it is and how they did it. Then I write a little comment there and it goes home to the parent; at the back there are some handy hints for reading, writing and spelling.

She feels, however, that these supportive booklets should be used in every subject: 'every child should have a glossary of terminology, concepts, whatever, like a little reference book which they can refer back to.'

These aspects of terminology were being taken on by the staff more generally, but she felt that there was a need for more explicit teaching of how to structure writing for different subjects:

> One of the things that I also feel strongly about is the level of note-making skills, note-taking skills, researching skills. Some of the pupils can't use their notes for revision purposes. Because I work with Year 10s and 11s who have to finish coursework, I've designed some guidelines to do with completing coursework. It might not work for every subject, but these are general pointers. I say *When you complete your coursework you have to go through these stages*: And this also matches up with an action plan with dates and completion times: these are things which have to be done and you tick it as it's done.
>
> But as I was doing this, I sat down and I said to myself *Am I expecting the kids to be able do all of that? How do they know what to do?* I noted the skills they need to be able to do to complete an assignment. I linked up the skills with the processes. If they can't do that adequately, the question is, *why?* Is it because they haven't been taught? Is it because their lessons haven't given them access to the kinds of skills they need to be able to do that? Is it the kids? If they're failing because they're not putting into practice what they've been taught that's another issue. But if they're failing because they haven't been taught at all, then that's our problem and I think this is where we've got to ensure that we've given them access to certain research skills, reference skills, reading skills. These are the things they should be able to do.

These guidelines (Figure 4.4) were later made the focus of a meeting between staff in the school whose role was specifically to support learners with different needs – SEN staff, the bilingual team, the head of Year 9 and Year 10 and the deputy head who has responsibility for the curriculum. One of the practical initiatives taken on during the year was to use the schema outlined by one of the special needs staff about the processes pupils need to go through to do project work (Figure 4.5). The group spent two days planning and discussing. Their aim was to create a structured programme that would support the pupils across their KS4 curriculum. Using the reading test results and other assessment data they identified twenty pupils who needed special support at this level. There were some who had learning difficulties, some bilingual pupils at the early stages of learning English and some whose performance was below their potential because their behaviour was having an impact on their education. They will be taught as a group but there will be differentiated approaches within it. Two teachers will work together, some from learning support and some from the bilingual team at different times. There is now a planned programme based on supporting the pupils in all aspects of their learning and trying to help them develop the skills that they are going to need to be able to cope with the Key Stage 4 curriculum.

Reviewing the first year

As the Improving Literacy Group analysed and evaluated their first year, there were different perceptions. Most of them felt that the group had been able to make a significant contribution:

> There's been a real heightening of awareness across the whole staff and within the working group as well. Although it's been hard work I think we've achieved quite a lot. We've got to a point where it's an issue for everybody; we've made them aware and people can see the importance of it and have agreed to do something about it.

However, the head of LDCAT felt that many of the suggestions were matters that should have been attended to already:

> I think that the training day revisited a lot of the areas about language skills and the need to work further on those. People are more aware in their lesson planning structure of the four areas of language so that they can teach language through their subject. With differentiation or heightening awareness about language, some departments are further ahead than others. In those classes where we've been able to work in partnership with certain teachers, it's perhaps been more effective and those teachers have got further forward.

COMPLETING COURSEWORK

There are four essential steps in completing coursework. Successful completion of coursework and meeting deadlines depend on your ability to progress smoothly from stage to stage using the skills crucial to each.

STAGE 1

Here are the stages you need to follow to complete your coursework.

Go through each stage diligently.

Planning and Preparation

Define the problem/task, i.e. ensure that you understand exactly what you are required to do.

What are the essential aspects, areas, issues, problems that you need to address?

Write down the vital ideas associated with the task – brainstorm.

Alternatively, present the main ideas graphically, i. e. as a diagram, flowchart.

Perhaps a design or a sketch is more appropriate.

Where are you going to locate the information that will assist you?

What materials/resources will you need to complete the task?

Which people will you invite and involve to help you?

What is the best method that will help you to complete the task?

You should now have a plan to guide you through the next stage.

GO ON TO STAGE 2

STAGE 2

Information Gathering
Locating Resources

Use your plan as a guide to help you to gather whatever information, materials, resources you will need to complete the task.

Will a questionnaire help you to amass some of the information?

How about collecting ideas by interviewing different people? Perhaps you will have to use notes, textbooks, reference books, magazines, encyclopaedia to gather in information.

Do you need to produce a sketch or design based on the information you have gathered together?

You may want to make an investigation.

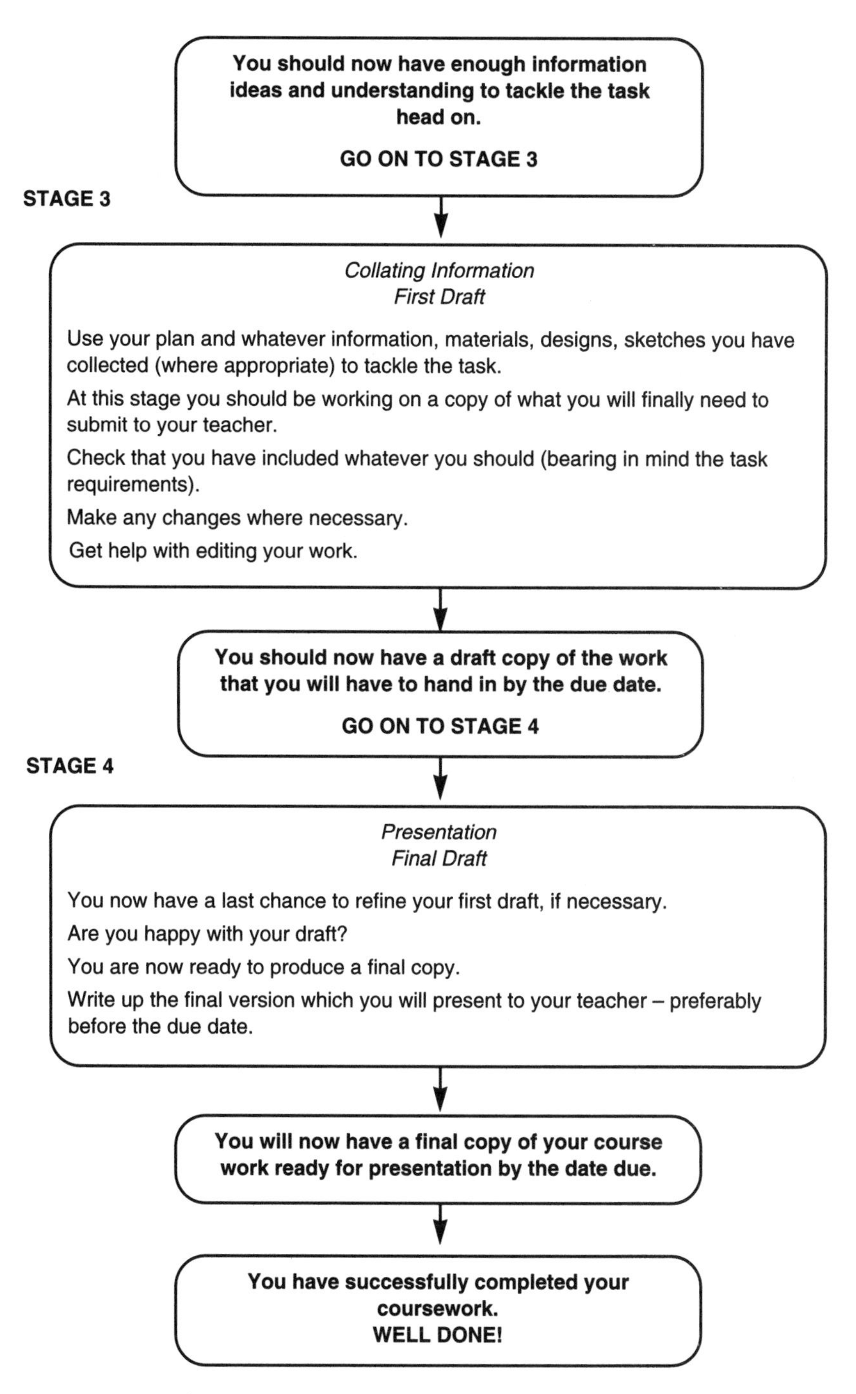

Figure 4.4 Completing coursework

Processes and skills needed for coursework completion

Process	Skills	
STAGE 1	*Planning and Preparation* Defining the problem/task. Asking relevant questions. Brainstorming ideas. Presenting ideas graphically: Diagrams Flowcharts Designs Sketches Identifying sources: Information Materials Resources Identifying best-fit methods. **Producing a blueprint/plan.**	Interpreting Generating questions Recording Presenting ideas Graphical presentation of ideas Locational Making choices Devising plans
STAGE 2	*Information Gathering* *Locating Resources* Researching: Questionnaires Interviews Investigating. Making notes from references. Gathering materials and shaping. Producing sketches. Making designs. **Producing notes/plans.**	Research/library Reference Reading Note-taking Presentational Creative design method Organisational
STAGE 3	*Collating Information* *and Materials* Arranging and manipulating: information materials Selecting information. Creating documents. Producing: models designs **Producing a draft/preliminary design/model.**	Application Organisational Decision making Writing Presentation Editing
STAGE 4	*Presentation* *Final Draft* Presenting final: document design model Evaluating **Producing final effort.**	Redrafting Presentation Evaluating

Figure 4.5 Processes and skills needed for coursework completion

Whilst there was understandable frustration that more could have been done, other members of the group felt that there had been positive outcomes in terms of time to discuss ideas and develop enhanced understanding between colleagues:

> One of the most positive things is having time and space to talk with other people instead of getting snatched conversations in the staff room that start and then you have to finish because the bell's ringing.

> It's made me far more aware. It's also built links between different subjects and with the Language Development and Curriculum Access Team. We've been making things more cross curricular.

Dealing with constraints

In reflecting on the year's work, however, members of the Improving Literacy Group identified blocks to progress when they were trying to develop a culture of change across a whole school. Some comments echoed what previous teachers had felt over the Bullock initiative to raise awareness and standards of language across the curriculum. However, there are other factors which act against staff commitment and energy being directed into new initiatives:

> There are still some people who think *That's the English department's problem; it's got nothing to do with me* but not too many.

> I still think that there's a sort of idea of *Well, that's to do with English and arty subjects and it's not got much to offer . . .*

There were other problems related to finding a focus for action:

> I think the problem for us first of all was not knowing what to do and not quite knowing how to go about things so a lot of the talk was quite exploratory. In some ways the talk was valuable and enabled us gradually to work out what our priorities were.

One of the constraints mentioned by all members of the group was lack of time and this raised issues of management within the school as a whole. In this school teachers have little non-contact time so development work is necessarily constrained by that:

> There's a real issue about time; it's as though Improving Literacy is another task. I think that the school really has to take stock of what its priorities are going to be. When you look at the reading test results that's the priority – literacy. There has to be some coherent plan and strategy that will have some impact on moving reading scores up. That means

> making reading a really important priority across the whole school and being prepared to accept that other things may have to wait.

This means that time has to be found on the school development plan not just to get initiatives going but to implement, review and evaluate them: 'We can all sit down and come up with great ideas but actually having the time to follow these through is completely different.'

But there are wider problems associated with teaching and learning more generally which raise matters of differentiation and resourcing:

> Teaching and learning styles are an issue. Talk is very important in terms of promoting literacy but it's marginalised because there are issues to do with control. It's much more difficult to manage groups for teaching and learning. People who feel they can't take the risk withdraw into a much more traditional and didactic type of style – not so much emphasis on speaking and listening but providing work that's going to occupy the pupils.
>
> Differentiation is another problem area. Some departments cope with that much better than others in terms of looking at their resources and adapting them. There is a genuine lack of understanding or knowledge of how you adapt resources to cope for varying abilities.

There were other problems related to resources. The group felt generally that resources had become depleted and damaged. There was not only a need for a big injection of money, but they needed to improve ways of looking after resources.

The next steps

Priorities varied within departments, ranging from consolidating existing practice to developing new approaches and attitudes to teaching and learning. The English department had already focused on reading, designating one lesson a week as a reading lesson in order to give reading a much higher profile amongst the pupils as a worthwhile and enjoyable activity in itself, not just as a means towards getting something written down. The mathematics department has invested money and effort in the Success Maker computer program as well as developing lists of vocabulary for each module in each year. Science has made similar key words sheets for individual use and as a classroom prompt, displayed in each science teaching room.

The LDCAT team wanted to:

> pursue partnerships to promote language support work in mathematics, science and English. We've made a bilingual support booklet with key words, particularly English and Turkish, which seems to be the main language needed as far as newly arrived pupils are concerned.

The deputy head felt that the process was going to be a long-term matter, beginning with the establishment of a draft policy:

> The next move is to get a bit more clarity about a draft policy statement, getting it agreed and accepted by governors. It'll then be an ongoing process to run it through for, say, twelve months with observation and monitoring processes at different stages and some kind of detailed evaluation then at the end of the academic year. When you're embarking on this you're talking about years – a continuing development. That's the initial way forward then revisit the identified priorities so that there's an agreed procedure and a commitment from everybody. There should be some critical points during the year designated for a review of progress involving the whole staff. There's a need for the language group to continue to meet and work; they might not meet as regularly as they have this year but there'll still be a need for that group to continue to drive it and people can feed back from the departments in terms of aspects covered. It needs to be an agenda item on departments' meetings.

What factors contribute to raising achievement in literacy in a school?

The year's work has established some important practices, but it has also revealed some key issues about the organisational principles which need to be in place if a school is to promote change. To the members of the group interviewed, these fell into four main categories:

- responsiveness to the pupils' needs;
- attention to teaching and learning practices;
- support from the school management;
- closer links with parents.

Responsiveness to pupils' needs

This was expressed in a variety of ways, but generally reflected a desire to take the pupils alongside any initiatives to raise standards and recognise their strengths. The teachers wanted to convince the pupils of what was in it for them – to build on:

> the attitude kids have to learning and their enthusiasm. They come in with particular enthusiasms and maybe we don't feed them. I think we've got to be very quick off the ground to capture the enthusiasm and channel it.

As far as literacy is concerned this means trying to *get their get reading ages to a point where they can become independent readers and learners*, which raises, for these teachers, some important points about teaching and learning styles and strategies.

Attention to teaching and learning practices

A prerequisite for closer attention to ways of presenting learning needs:

> First of all a real commitment from all staff or a significant number of staff. And then establishing some shared principles about what good practice is. The major whole school issues need to be tackled by everyone.

However, it was recognised that this was not easy. One of the reasons why a generation before this the Bullock initiative had not taken root more firmly was related to the experience that: 'Whole school issues across the curriculum are difficult to manage because sometimes people in knowledge-based subjects don't feel that it's important; they're more interested in the content of the curriculum, not the processes of literacy.' Nevertheless, there was a sense that, as well as raising awareness, attention to classroom teaching was one of the keys: 'I think it's really careful, planned, focused teaching and accepting that (improved standards) just don't happen.' The close attention to literacy throughout the year had made some teachers much more aware of assumptions about teaching and learning:

> One of the main things we've realised is that we're asking children to do things which we haven't necessarily taught them. We've suddenly realised that if they're all doing badly it's because they haven't been taught how to do it.

In terms of language and literacy, the teachers' reflections were specific, taking account of the role of talk – teacher talk and pupil talk – as an important element in communicating ideas:

> Accepting that if their literacy is not very high it might mean using other strategies – mean more talking or more picture text.

> I've come to see the importance of asking positive questions or open questions. I've also been more aware of things like not relying so much on books; having a lot more talk about things, doing less written work and using more talk and diagrams, which seems to have worked.

> In the very early stages children should be encouraged to actually say what's happening in sequences and things like that – *adding four, each*

> *one is a multiple*, and all these sorts of things. They get to learn to like these words and there's a rhythm about some of the words. Even the spelling children can come to enjoy – there's a lovely rhythm to *parallelogram*.

This realisation that talk can demonstrate learning has an impact on teachers' attitudes to writing as the usual proof of learning: 'And then, in myself, just to be more willing to let things go away from the writing; that's part of it as well, being willing to spend a lesson not writing.'

Being explicit about teaching strategies highlights the centrality of language and the links between areas of the curriculum through language:

> It's like the numeracy initiative. In many respects the same things come up – raising awareness, getting kids to use maths in so many different ways, including story. I've got lots of histories of mathematicians that would give lovely fifteen-minute story-times to Years 7, 8, 9 and 10 which we're thinking of putting into the numeracy slot, but they're also about literacy. There are lots of parallels – rhyming, etc. – across the two. They are so interrelated it's difficult to pigeonhole them.

One ingredient of raising standards of literacy was seen as beginning to work in a more coherent way to *try to do more cross-curricular things*. Whilst this is not always easy, there are informal opportunities: 'I think it's a matter of knowing which ones to work with, working with your friends. Half the time, discussions take place in the pub and that's the way things get going.'

Support from school management

There was a strong sense that the school management should offer structures to help teachers make changes to practice in accordance with newly developing principles. This requires 'time to facilitate planning, training and classroom observation'. Structured support from the school management is essential:

> There also has to be some monitoring of the quality of teaching and learning. I think that's a key issue. We've been trying to get some peer observation because I think it's an important tool for raising achievement; if you can get people involved in discussing aspects of teaching and learning then things might move on in terms of people's practice.

Some procedures are already in place. The school is working through a programme now where all heads of department will have a period of observation alongside an LEA subject inspector who can offer useful advice about classroom observation and the management of monitoring teaching and learning within a department. Another plan for structured support is a procedure where heads of department are attached to a designated member of the senior management team. Regular meetings are held which provide the heads of departments with the opportunity of frequent dialogue. They are notified before any meeting what the focus will be so that if there is any particular information needed, they can provide it as the basis for a productive meeting. The attached senior management team member may also attend some departmental meetings.

However, simply setting up structures does not necessarily ensure that they offer the support needed for genuine change: 'There are lots of good structures in place but it needs that push to hold it together with follow-through to keep the emphasis on teaching and learning.'

Closer links with parents

There was a general sense that there needs to be greater liaison between home and school to support literacy. This is an area which all the staff interviewed saw as a significant gap:

> We need to work with children and their families and so far that's not been really tackled. It's the sort of thing we need to look towards. I know how hard infant schools work to involve parents in the teaching of reading. Parents are made to feel quite confident and powerful by infant schools; regardless of your own reading ability you are seen as a model for your child. I think in secondary school that has disappeared and parents feel quite intimidated and powerless in the face of teachers. I feel that needs to change and we need to tell them that they've still got a real role to play.

Some shifts had already begun to happen which demonstrated the value of closer links with homes over literacy:

> There are a lot more parents, regardless of economic background, who are very committed to education and are studying themselves or have studied. And that's beginning to change the culture of the school in a very positive way.
>
> We've got to work much more closely with the parents particularly of pupils who are experiencing difficulties or who have low literacy levels. We've had a number of parents' evenings recently which have had an educational focus; some of them have been related to aspects of school improvement and I think we've got to the point now where the parents are responding very positively to some of those evenings; it's a relatively small number of parents but the numbers are increasing. The last one we had about 30–40 per cent of parents. We have workshop sessions, perhaps on aspects of school improvement, and try to tell them the sorts of things we've been doing and get their ideas and perceptions of things

that we need to do to improve the school – find out what are the priorities for them.

However, there are difficulties for any school in promoting closer links with parents over literacy – or any other aspect of the curriculum – since not all parents are able to attend meetings. There need to be some ways of reaching out to homes where it is not easy for parents to visit school:

> I've got a pack of (maths) activities which I would like every first year parent to have to do with the children; it's a practice pack, it's fun to do and even if you've got parents who don't speak English it's accessible. Presumably with literacy there could be something like that sent out.
>
> A lot of the kids come in here having experienced some experience of PACT reading practices and I think there's a need for that to continue but that's got resource implications.[4]

This returns to a factor in promoting raised standards which was identified earlier as a resource and for which there are no ready-made solutions – the need for:

> Resources – money and human and material resources.

Conclusion

After just over a year some important work has been done. One of the critical factors in curriculum development is to establish a culture of change – a shared understanding that development is not only desirable but possible, that change can happen in small ways – providing glossaries of subject specific terminology, for example – as well as in whole school structural changes to support departments in developing new approaches to teaching and learning. The problems of time, resources and energy are still there, but in this school at least, the commitment of the Improving Literacy Group has resulted in changes in attitude, principles and practice. In time, this investment of effort should pay off in improved standards of literacy for the pupils who are the main concern of these teachers.

Notes

1 I visited the school during the year, sitting in on meetings and interviewing some of the staff involved in the Improving Literacy initiative. This chapter is a compilation of my observations and their reflections after the first year.

2 They used the Spooncer test, which is a test of reading for understanding. It involves two 10-minute tests. In one, the pupils read a passage and cross out the incorrectly spelt words and decide on the correct ones; the second sheet has a passage where the pupils fill in missing words.

3 These are the writing frames described by David Wray and Maureen Lewis.
4 PACT – Parents and Children Together. A scheme for supporting home-based reading used widely in London (and other) schools.

Reference

Wray, David and Lewis, Maureen (1997) *Extending Literacy: Children Reading and Writing Non-Fiction*, London: Routledge.

5

LEARNING THROUGH LANGUAGE

Wirral takes action

Marie Stacey

The Wirral Key Skills Project was established as a result of national concerns over an apparent decline in numeracy and literacy standards in 1995. Within Wirral, there was an alarming rise in the number of youngsters transferring to local secondary schools with a reading age more than two years below their chronological age. The Key Skills Project is a cross-phase, umbrella project, containing a number of mini-projects, all meeting clearly defined criteria, with the purpose of improving the strategies for quality teaching and learning in key skills. A fundamental principle underpinning the project is the desire to avoid the cascade model of training, where one person from a school is trained, and returns to school to train other staff. Similarly, it was important to train class teachers, not subject co-ordinators. Political support from Wirral Education Committee funded the establishment of a team, co-ordinated by a seconded primary headteacher. The literacy team adopted a long-term training model, where input sessions were followed by opportunities for teachers to try out new techniques in the classroom, reflect on their practice, and share ideas and experiences, before the next input for the trainers. Support networks and regular meetings have been established for when the initial training period has finished.

The literacy adviser and I (general inspector for English) worked together closely in order to ensure a cohesive policy for language and literacy which is informed by the same principles at all key stages. The work of Marie Clay and Reading Recovery provided a solid foundation.[1] A large central library of resources for loan to schools is an important feature of the project, particularly for primary schools.

The structure of the secondary project, Learning Through Language, is more easily shown in diagrammatic form (see Figure 5.1). In Wirral, the decision was made to work with two important and distinctly different subject areas, science and the humanities. There were lessons to be learned from the problems related to the attempted implementation of the Bullock Report in the 1970s. The Key

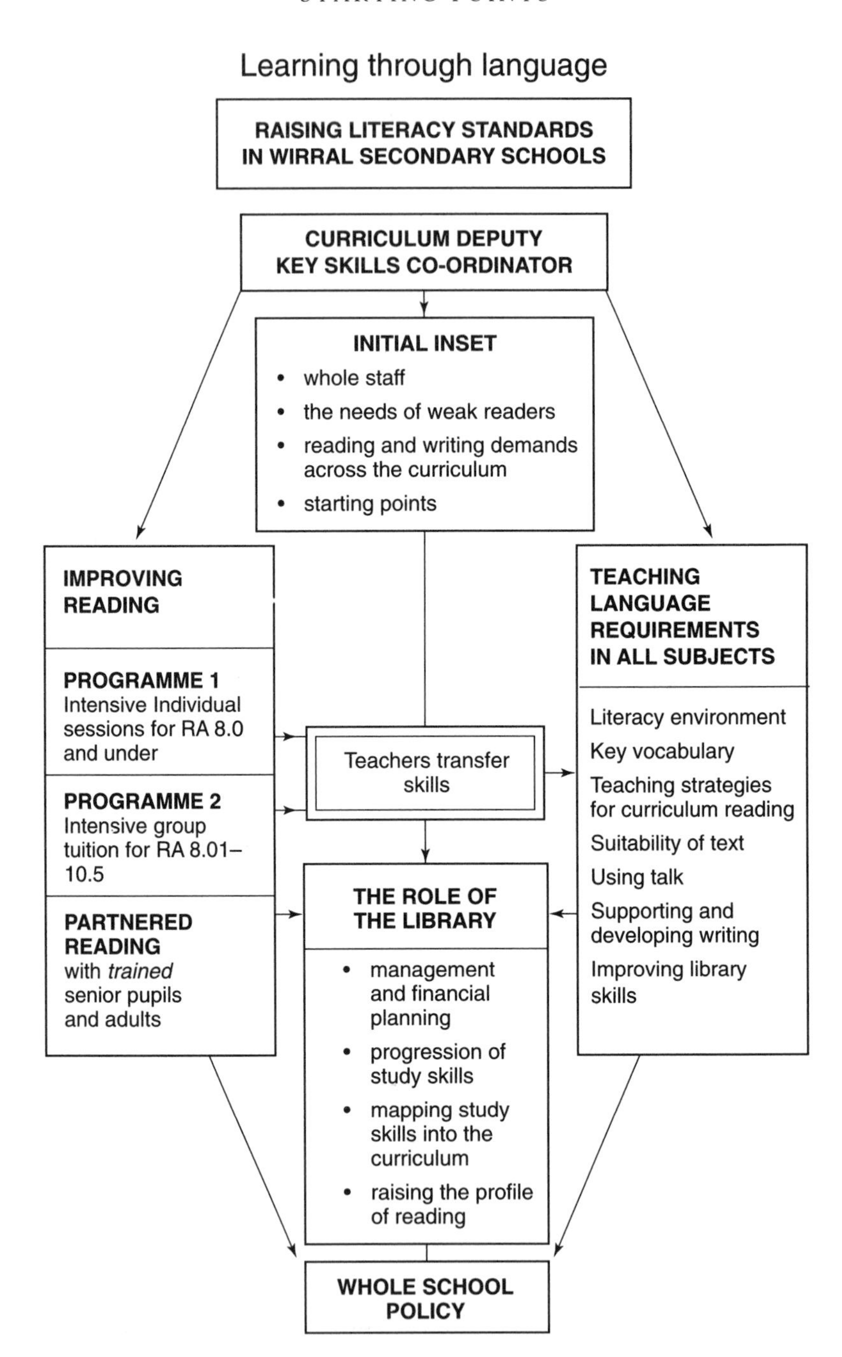

Figure 5.1 Learning through language

Skills Project left English departments to sort out their own huge commitments, of much increased programmes of study post-Dearing review, new GCSE syllabuses, and all the problems of the KS3 tests and the never-ending concerns about grammar teaching and testing. As English inspector, I had the full support of both science and humanities inspectors, but managed the work for secondary schools myself, using the expertise of advisory teachers in science, humanities and English, and the Schools Library Service. Most of the training was provided centrally. The amount of advisory support to individual schools is finite; more schools asked for support than could be accommodated, but a limited amount of training and awareness raising for whole staffs has been available.

The fragmented nature of the secondary curriculum means that development of a whole-school approach to language is problematic when a range of initiatives is undertaken simultaneously. They are complex issues, and require skilful management and monitoring. It is essential that the senior management also develop a fair degree of specialist knowledge in the field if they are going to be able to carry out their monitoring and support role well. The development of whole school language policies is a lengthy process. Short-term successes must be celebrated, while the long-term objectives are not allowed to drift. It isn't easy. The knowledge and commitment of senior managers is crucial to success. INSET was provided for headteachers and deputies on the language requirements of all subjects of the curriculum, the needs of struggling readers and writers, and their role in leading and managing developments within school.

In order to support senior managers, a small consultation group of curriculum deputies was formed, with the brief to discuss the considerable management issues involved, including working with heads of department, monitoring standards in literacy across departments, the use of data, and outside funding. The group helped to develop guidance, and to provide a step-by-step framework for developing management strategies. A key function was to ensure two-way communication between the Key Skills (Literacy) Project and senior managers of all secondary schools. In addition, schools were asked to nominate a Key Skills Co-ordinator, whose chief function was to co-ordinate the project within the school, and to disseminate the information about training. The sheer amount of training provided made it quite a mammoth task for the Key Skills Team Co-ordinator to organise centrally.

An important strand within the project was training secondary teachers to teach reading, when few had any previous training in this area. The pupils who had difficulties with reading had frequently developed passive learning styles, and some were disaffected. One programme was aimed at the individual tuition of pupils with reading ages of around 7.5, for a minimum of three periods of 20 minutes a week, for about a term and a half. Most of the teachers we trained (although not all) were either special needs teachers or English teachers. The other programme was aimed at pairs of form tutors from a range of curriculum areas, and provided for small group teaching (of those with reading ages of 8.6–9.6) throughout the year, with three sessions of 20 minutes a week. Both programmes are underpinned by the same philosophy as Reading Recovery, and follow similar content and training model. There is a focus on instruction and the fostering of independent problem-solving on text.

When we started, it was with some trepidation; however, the response from secondary teachers was enormously positive. Coming to the training without previous experience, nor weighed down by years of contrary practice, they took to the model with ease. Some of the best teaching of reading seen in the authority has resulted from these two programmes, and schools are building teams of trained teachers of reading. Aspects of the training programme have also been used to train hundreds of older pupils in partnered reading. For example, this was a successful part of the recent summer literacy school at Ridgeway High School, where local sixth form pupils provided excellent support to the trained teachers. The Wirral Successful Reading Partnership[2] also trains adult volunteers to work in schools. The initial training, for about eighty people, focused largely on classroom assistants employed by both primary and secondary schools; there were also some governors, and parents. There has been a massive demand for the courses which take one full day's training, followed by three half-days. All participants are matched with partners in school; each child has at least three 15-minute sessions of help a week (over a 10-week period). The training has now been accredited with Merseyside Open College. The local business community, the Wirral Investment Network, has approached us to provide training and appropriate accreditation for them as part of their contribution to the National Year of Reading (1998–9).

Work in science and humanities departments

The work to develop language and learning within science and humanities departments was based on the principle that all teachers have a responsibility to teach the specific language and literacy skills required in their subject areas. The draft materials developed by subject associations for SCAA (background materials for the papers on the Use of Language requirements) were extremely useful starting points (SCAA 1997). The work done by Richard Bain for NATE was also helpful.[3] Training was provided on:

- the experience of struggling readers, based on four days shadowing exercise undertaken by the advisory teacher for English;
- readability of text, and the needs of less confident readers when reading textbooks;
- active approaches to understanding and retention (Directed Activities Related to Texts);[4]
- use of the classroom environment to support literacy, particularly to promote independence and confidence in writing;
- teaching specialist vocabulary;
- whole school policies for teaching spelling;

- use of writing frames and other appropriate formats;
- the use and organisation of talk to develop learning and active listening in the classroom.

None of this was particularly new, but during the training sessions there was a lot of cross-subject sharing of expertise which was undoubtedly beneficial. The three subject advisory teachers involved were particularly gifted practitioners. Working collaboratively across subject boundaries was, for them, a novel and exhilarating experience where their areas of subject expertise complemented each other to great effect.

The library

If pupils are to become independent learners, they must be confident users of libraries, and able to access the wealth of information available in books and via technology. A key area for development was the organisation and management of the school library. All too often, this resource is underused and undervalued in secondary schools and because of other priorities often escapes serious attention. We were anxious to tackle the following thorny issues :

- the role of senior managers in the management and financial planning for the development of the library;
- a definition of the role and status of the school librarian;
- a definition of the roles and responsibilities of others involved in the development of the library (governors, senior management, cross-curricular library management team, teacher/librarian, clerical assistants).

The Key Skills team also needed an agreed progression in the teaching of study skills, and a system for mapping the teaching of study skills across the curriculum. The pack of materials developed as a result of this training is now widely used in Wirral schools; a primary pack is in the process of development. Many librarians who lack professional qualifications undertake a City and Guilds course in librarianship run by the local FE College, but there is nothing related to school libraries within that course. We therefore devised a training package on National Curriculum issues to improve the skills of non-teacher library assistants, which is equivalent to one module of City and Guilds.[5]

We worked with librarians, teacher-librarians, heads of science and humanities and deputy headteachers. The most contentious areas are connected to financial provision and strategies to identify an appropriately high level of funding to renew and develop resources. Teachers also sometimes find it difficult to acknowledge qualified librarians as equal professionals, and this has caused a considerable degree of tension and unhappiness in the past. On the other hand, many teachers are given responsibility, with or without extra payment, for the library, but no allocated time in which to perform this massive task. The level of pay offered to qualified librarians is sometimes insulting, and this is an area where governors need to be fully informed of the responsibilities involved. As a result of the difficulties we have identified, and the heated debate which often arises about proper payment for library staff, we are now suggesting throughout the authority that there is a 'library' governor in secondary schools, performing perhaps a role similar to that of the named literacy governor in primary schools (required by the National Literacy Strategy). The provision of separate clerical assistance can be enormously helpful. After much debate, discussion and discovery, the Key Skills team now recommends that all schools identify the roles and responsibilities of staff and governors in some detail, since the library is a key learning resource which cannot be undervalued if a school is genuinely to commit itself to raised standards of literacy and learning.

Teaching Key Skills at school level – the experience of two schools

There was a complex programme of central LEA INSET for the first two years of the Key Skills Project. All Wirral secondary schools were involved, to varying degrees. Some have been particularly successful. Wallasey School, for example, was the only secondary school in Merseyside to be awarded the Basic Skills Agency Quality Mark, and generously acknowledged the leadership provided by the Key Skills team. An HMI monitoring team, undertaking work for the National Literacy Strategy in secondary schools, commented on the consistency of practice within the three schools visited as examples of good practice. However, the key factors for success lie within schools, and the overwhelming evidence from within Wirral is that the leadership from the head and senior managers is the most vital factor of all.

John Hassall was appointed as headteacher to Rock Ferry High School in Tranmere, an area of urban deprivation, in 1992. Some local estates have 50 per cent male unemployment, and generations of unemployment generally. Measured by the NFER reading test, about 15 per cent of pupils arrived at the school with severe reading difficulties in 1991. There was a good special needs department, which had devised 'Readalong', a successful system of providing less confident readers with tapes to listen to as they read books at home. In 1995, the number of struggling readers arriving in Year 7 doubled. The head recognised the urgency of the problem, and took the leading role in devising strategies, supporting particular individuals to promote the literacy initiatives, and building teams. An experienced headteacher, one of John's first priorities on appointment had been to develop the library, through improving the environment, redecoration and recarpeting (at the pupils' request, as they had helped the school set its priorities), relocating the careers library and reprographics, and most importantly, employing a qualified librarian, on decent pay. Another key task had been to develop the senior management as a team, and to improve inter-departmental communication. The head of science (who was seconded to the

LEA as advisory teacher, and became an important member of the Key Skills team) started some very useful work on readability of texts across the school, and fed in ideas from other schools he worked with as advisory teacher. The head of Year 7 and the head of special needs worked closely to identify those individuals in need of support through careful use of primary liaison information and baseline data. High-quality whole-school INSET converted even the cynics to the importance of language development across the curriculum.

When the LEA offered training in the teaching of reading, John joined it himself, with two colleagues. This one strategy gave the project enormous status, both within the school and with parents. Family attitudes to school and learning are of course very significant. A number of the Rock Ferry parents have had unsuccessful experiences themselves in schools, and the head felt it was extremely important to create the right welcoming and friendly atmosphere within the school. The school nurse has a responsibility to make links with the families of primary age pupils, and to develop social networks. The headteacher makes a point of dropping in casually to greet parents when they come to the meetings about the expansion of the Readalong scheme, and invites the parents of the pupils he is teaching to read to come and observe him teaching. He keeps in touch by phone about individuals' progress, and reading homework. John Hassall feels strongly that the variations within pupils' achievements are determined largely by family attitudes, which he sees as much more important than peer pressure. Homes which are in poverty may provide rich language environments, where books and language are valued highly. However, poverty is an important contributory factor to the lack of development of many pupils' literacy. Some families living in poverty have developed what has been referred to as a 'culture of idleness'; others are determined their children will succeed. It seems that one dominant family figure, often a grandmother in his experience, can make all the difference to a child's self-belief and subsequent success. Fortunately, the job prospects on Wirral are looking brighter now than for many years, and a new spirit of optimism is percolating through the area. We hope that pupils' raised expectations of getting jobs will reduce that apathy about education which has been a blight in certain parts of the borough.

At Wallasey School, the headteacher, Peter Johnson, was one of the leading figures in the secondary heads' group who asked the LEA to take action over the problem of low literacy standards in 1995. His commitment and leadership, and the proactive way in which he has sought outside funding, have been crucial factors in Wallasey School's achievement. Like John Hassall, Peter also recognised the importance of a whole school approach led by key figures across subjects who take responsibility for development in a Basic Skills Steering Group which has been set up to guide the schools' work on literacy. The group reports to the senior management team and to the governors' Curriculum Committee through the deputy head who has responsibility for the curriculum. One of the key factors there has been that the school has set targets for continuous improvement. These are focused and precise, identified by staff observation, formal assessments and discussion. The school has targeted four groups of pupils for specific support – those with reading ages below 7.5 years; those whose reading ages are between 8 and 9 years; those with reading ages around 9 years and all Year 7 pupils. These pupils are given a combination of specialist help, in-class support and support within subject teaching. Pupils whose reading ages are below 9 are withdrawn from French lessons for one hour a week and follow a programme of reading enrichment. The improvement in literacy more than compensates for the temporary loss of experience of a modern foreign language. Furthermore, the greater awareness about language, fostered by close attention to the structures of language, means that, on return to a full French curriculum, the pupils are more adept at handling language generally and find their grasp of a new language enhanced by their increased fluency and confidence in English.

Through the provision of whole school inservice sessions, the Basic Skills Steering Group has worked on policy and practice in the school. The development of a whole school policy is translated into practice through a consistent approach to spelling and reading, which has been extremely beneficial to all pupils. Staff have identified talk as the next priority in their development initiative on language and learning and have received INSET in preparation for further work. The school made a successful bid to the Basic Skills Agency in 1996 for a Local Initiative Grant which helped to subsidise the considerable cost of extra staffing and resources. The Basic Skills Agency had previously funded a successful Family Literacy project which had been piloted in Wallasey School in 1994.

Reflections

The key determinant for success in raising standards of literacy and learning is the leadership provided by the headteacher and the senior managers within the school. They must combine successful management of staff and complex webs of changed practice with rigorous monitoring procedures. It is important that they have sufficient detailed knowledge to be able to recognise and analyse both strengths and weaknesses in language development. In particular, the senior managers must not only promote good practice, they must also recognise mediocrity, and critically, they must be prepared to take action themselves to remedy it. Identifying the right heads of department and others within the staff who are going to lead the various initiatives, and providing appropriate support and encouragement, are also important. Within departments, all teachers (perhaps working in pairs) have a role to play in both the creative and monitoring aspects of the initiative. Newly qualified teachers are just as capable of monitoring aspects of pupils' achievement as their more experienced colleagues, given the support. Indeed, the head of department has a role similar to that of senior management in energising the support and commitment of the departmental team, and managing the learning of pupils. It is what happens in classrooms which counts, not the quality of the paperwork.

One excellent example of this in practice the history department in Wallasey School, provides a rich language and learning environment for pupils which is evident as they walk down the corridor towards the suite. Teachers have made word walls, with key historical concepts defined and colour coded according to year group topics. Pupils have also been involved, representing some of these concepts in highly imaginative and often witty graphics. Mark Bailey and his colleagues place great importance on the use of talk in the development of intellectual skills of analysis, justification and proof, and one of the rooms is set out as a 'senate' for a range of oral and discussion activities, with study carrels set at angles around the walls. These provide a place for quiet reflection and individual work, but are also easily shifted when group work is appropriate. History is made exciting, and significant to pupils' lives. Teachers use a great variety of source material and facsimiles in their crafted display, which is used as part of the teaching repertoire. Pupils demonstrate their historical understanding and empathetic response in a range of ways. In summary, ample proof of what can be achieved when close attention is paid to language and learning is evident in the poems which close this chapter. They were written by Year 9 pupils after studying aspects of the First World War in a history lesson. This is what learning through language should be about.

Death Haunts the Trenches

Death haunts the trenches.
Screaming men in agony.
Do they die for their country?
Dignified and proud?
Ask their friends and family,
You may find opinions vary.
Dug out hide outs,
Like graves waiting to be filled.
Shells that pound from trench to trench,
Wipe out anyone who takes the risk.
A dead death trap,
Labelled No Man's Land,
Separates the enemies,
That fight like there's no tomorrow.
But tomorrow comes too soon,
And here it is again.
Death haunts the trenches.

by Joan Travis

Figure 5.2 Death Haunts the Trenches

Attention!

Attention!
Did the radio cry out.
The deep dark ditch,
Full of brave soldiers,
Full of death marsh.

Attention!
Did the bombs cry out.
The loud lost land'
Full of strong men,
Full of blinding gas.

Attention!
Did the injured cry out.
The screams, smells and sickness,
Full of mighty destruction,
Full of powerful strength.

Attention! Attention!
Did we all cry out.
The raids, running and rushing,
Full of darkness,
Full of the dead.

Attention! Attention!

by Rachel Graham

Figure 5.3 Attention!

Trench Life

I hear machine guns rattle in the distance,
As I lie, dying slowly and painfully.
My blood helps form the giant,
Pitiful lake of hero's blood.

I have nothing left to live for,
Our Generals are the real enemy.
Forced us to be hacked to bits,
For no reason at all.

Death is ever present,
The infamous king of war.
It is a haven for the devil,
A mini hell.

Millions of us go over the top,
To fight in a place worse than hell.
Fighting for who? Fighting for what?
Never to return again.....

by: Richard Citrine

Figure 5.4 Trench Life

Acknowledgements

Gill Jordan, literary adviser; Mo Miller, advisory teacher for English; Phil Weston, advisory teacher for science; Bill Birney, advisory teacher for humanities; Mary Bryning, Schools' Library Service; Mike Ashton, Key Skills Co-ordinator; John Hassall, headteacher, Rock Ferry High School; Peter Johnson, headteacher, Wallasey School.

Notes

1 Reading Recovery is an early intervention programme where pupils are taught to focus on text and on print. Letter recognition, phonological awareness, spelling conventions, punctuation and grammar are taught as part of a meaning-driven approach to reading and writing.
2 Wirral LEA acknowledges with gratitude the help and advice offered by Kevan Collins and the Bradford Better Reading Partnership in setting up our own programme.
3 Richard Bain and the Curriculum Committees of the National Association for the Teaching of English produced a guidance document in 1995 edited by Terry Furlong.
4 Directed Activities Related to Texts (DARTS) are activities designed by Lunzer and Gardner to increase the effectiveness of reading.
5 This training package can be obtained from Wirral LEA, Professional Development Centre, Acre Lane, Bromborough, Wirral.

References

Furlong, Terry (ed.) (1995) *Use of Language in the National Curriculum: Guidance for Developing a Whole School Policy in Secondary Schools*, Sheffield: NATE.
Lunzer, A. and Gardner, K. (1979) *The Effective Use of Readings*, London: Heinemann Educational.
SCAA (1997) *The Use of Language*, London: SCAA.

6

READING AND GENDER

Nigel Spratt and Ruth Sturdy

The Cornelius Vermuyden School is a mixed sex grant maintained comprehensive school situated on Canvey Island. It caters for the 11 to 16 year age range and has approximately 800 pupils on roll. There are two other comprehensives on the Island and the competition to gain available pupils is healthy as very few pupils live off the Island. The catchment areas of the three schools are quite wide and flexible but we receive the majority of our pupils from three local feeder schools. Our catchment area is predominantly from a large housing estate that experiences some social and economic difficulties although the parents are generally supportive of the school.

Our English department had been concerned with the poor achievement of boys at GCSE for the last few years, although this concern had not been restricted to the English department. Only 38.6 per cent of our boys gained GCSE English language at grade C and above in 1995 compared to 54.3 per cent of girls; the difference was even greater in English literature.

OFSTED identified the differences of achievement between boys and girls in English as a national problem. The report *Boys and English* based on research between 1988 and 1991, sparked our interest in looking more closely at the reading attitudes of our own pupils.

> APU research suggests that there is little difference in performance in tests of spoken English. Research has also shown that there are contrasts in boys' and girls' attitudes towards writing and reading – girls are more likely than boys to be enthusiastic about these aspects of their work in English.
>
> (OFSTED 1993: 27)

A further exploration of statistics showed that boys' levels of attainment in English were lower than those of girls in the lower school, where we prided ourselves in the way we motivated our younger pupils. As a department we felt that some of the problems could be the result of a higher percentage of boys than the girls being reluctant readers. To test this hypothesis we needed to assess our reading programme and analyse the problem. Using the time available through the Essex Reading Project we were able to work out a research strategy. We had been aware for some time that a high percentage of our Year 7 pupils arrive at the school with reading ages below their chronological ages. According to the 1995 results of the reading test which is used by the learning support department, 70 per cent of our pupils arrive with a reading age below 11 years and 42 per cent arrive with a reading age below 9 years of age.

These statistics were recognised by our OFSTED inspection in October 1995. The inspection report noted:

> The department is determined to improve reading skills which are often low on entry. There is a structured programme to develop reading in class, supported by an effective library skills programme. Standardised test results show a substantial improvement during Key Stage 3.
>
> (Inspection report, October 1995)

With the co-operation of the combined studies department, the learning support department has monitored the reading ages of its new entrants for the past three years and has followed these up at the end of each academic year with a repeat test as one way of measuring progress. The limitations of such methods are well documented and we would not like to try to defend the notion of reading tests. For the purpose of this project, however, they were a crude but nevertheless useful indicator of the fact that we *do* seem to make a difference to the reading competencies of our students and in that regard they were worth a closer look.

The test administered is the Suffolk Reading Test. Our choice was influenced by the need to find a test which was group administered and which was quick to mark. This test makes some attempt to use context and understanding in its method of testing and so is nearer to the way that experienced and successful readers read than a simple word recognition test would be. In this regard it seemed a reasonable compromise for our needs. We considered the reading ages in relation to the whole population of a particular intake. For the purposes of this study we focused specifically on the current Year 8, separating them into gender groupings. While we have kept statistics for several years, the project focus made us think more specifically in gender terms and as a result this is the first time we specifically looked at the gender split. We noted the following results for the current Year 8 when they entered as Year 7 in 1994–5 (figures are percentages):

Students with reading ages below their chronological age on entry	73
Students with reading ages below their chronological age at the end of Year 7	45
Boys with reading ages below their chronological age on entry	40
Boys with reading ages below their chronological age at the end of Year 7	28

Girls with reading ages below their chronological ages on entry	**33**
Girls with reading ages below their chronological age at the end of Year 7	**17**
Pupils with low reading ages at the end of Year 7 by gender:	**88 boys** **12 girls**

In crude terms we found that, in line with national statistics, the boys did less well on the standardised tests, making less progress than the girls during Year 7. This is also borne out by the referral process, in line with the Code of Practice for Special Needs, where we find that the boys in the school are referred to the learning support department at a rate almost double that for girls. While the remit of the Code of Practice is clearly wider than simply reading problems, there would seem to be a correlation between poor reading, failure at school and low motivation found amongst boys both at this school and at a national level.

Clearly we needed to find out what it was that stopped these pupils from making progress. Our next step was less easily quantifiable but perhaps gave us a better insight into what was going on in reading for these boys. Before describing this we should explain our present methods for improving reading skills.

The English department's present reading policy

The school curriculum is organised along traditional lines except in the lower school. In Years 7 and 8 pupils spend 50 per cent of their timetable in an integrated course known as combined studies. They are taught English, mathematics, geography, history, art and drama by one teacher, who may not be a specialist in English.[1] This cross-curricular structure has allowed the department to adopt a pupil-centred approach to teaching reading. Traditionally, reading for enjoyment has held a very high place in the department's philosophy and the library has always been seen as the heart of the school; consequently, the library plays an important part in our reading scheme. We are fortunate that our library is computerised, very well resourced and has a full-time librarian.

As the lower school curriculum is loosely based on a primary school structure in the sense that there is a main classroom teacher, we have adopted a primary-based approach to reading. All pupils choose a fiction book from the library with help from their combined studies teacher or a member of the learning support staff. Time is allocated for private reading where the class teacher listens to individual pupils read and monitors their progress. The reading time is structured so that there is a member of the learning support staff helping especially with pupils who have difficulty with reading. Our philosophy is not to extract pupils with special needs but to give support in the classroom.

To encourage pupils to read as much as possible, a reward system has been designed which includes certificates and badges. In Years 7 and 8 certificates are issued after a specified number of books have been read and a school badge is presented by the headteacher once a target has been reached. We have found this method of motivation very successful and reading ages had improved, sometimes quite impressively, as seen in Figure 6.2. At least two periods a week (40 minutes each) are given over to reading skills. In Year 8 the average increase in reading age during one year is approximately two years, so we felt confident we were doing a good job with our pupil-centred approach.

Although we realised we were improving overall reading ages we knew from our statistical analysis that there was still a marked difference in improvement between boys and girls. We decided to investigate the following questions:

- Are boys in fact more reluctant readers than girls or is it just the perception of teachers that they are?
- Are we really better at getting girls interested in reading or are they more conforming so that it looks as if they are interested?
- What are the differences between boys' preferred reading material and girls' preferences?
- Can we develop the reading habit in boys by gaining a greater understanding of their likes and dislikes in reading material?

We felt that the best way of obtaining this information was through a survey and by talking to pupils. We also felt it was essential a large survey group be used if the statistics were to represent the whole school. We decided to adopt the following routes of investigation:

- a reading survey questionnaire given to Years 7 to 10;
- limited shadowing of pupils over a school day;
- talking to pupils and staff to gain an insight into their perceptions on the importance and relevance of reading.

The survey

The questionnaire had to be kept relatively simple yet the questions had to concentrate on relevant areas of research (see Figure 6.1). We needed to know:

- which pupils enjoyed reading and whether there was a difference between levels of enjoyment between girls and boys;
- whether there are differences between years;
- how pupils perceived their reading abilities;
- favourite genres and whether preferences differ between boys and girls.

The survey was returned by a large and diverse sample of 519 pupils. Fortunately, there were equal numbers of responses from boys and girls, which made comparisons easier. We found the results very relevant, informative and, in some cases, surprising.

Reading Survey

To all pupils:

We are trying to find out what types of books you like to read in order to help us with some research we are doing.

Please can you help us by filling in the following questionnaire:

It helps to know if you are a boy or a girl so please tick the correct box: ☐ Boy ☐ Girl

Do you like reading? ☐ YES ☐ NO

If not why not? Not enough time ☐ It's boring ☐

I find it difficult ☐ Other ______________________

What type of material do you like to read? You can tick more than one box

Adventure books ☐ Science Fiction ☐ Horror ☐ Romance ☐

Humorous books ☐ Non-fiction books ☐ Magazines (Type?) ____________

Comics ☐

Do you think you are a good reader? ☐ YES ☐ NO

How do you know? ______________________

Do you prefer to read quietly to yourself or to read aloud to someone?

ALOUD ☐ QUIETLY ☐

Does anyone read with you / to you at home? ☐ YES ☐ NO

Who? __________

Does any of your family read a lot? ☐ YES ☐ NO

What type of books do they read? ______________________

What year are you in? __________

Figure 6.1 Reading survey

The first question we asked the pupils was *Do you like reading?* The answers were fairly predictable, with more girls than boys saying that they enjoyed reading. Almost twice as many boys as girls disliked reading so the next step was to try and find out whether this difference in the enjoyment of reading was consistent across all years. Figures 6.2, 6.3 and 6.4 demonstrate the differences.

Although there are some differences between the level of enjoyment in Years 7 and 8, with more girls preferring to read than boys, the differences are marginal. It was in Year 9 that we began to notice a difference. There was an almost equal response of *yes* and *no* from the boys, yet the girls continued to enjoy reading,

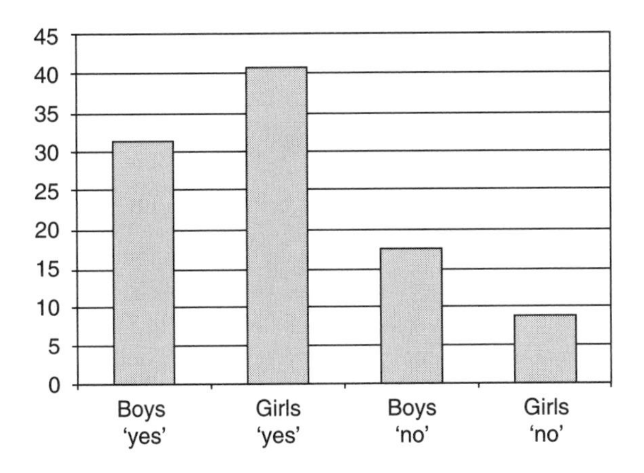

Figure 6.2 Year 7 percentage responses to the question *Do you like reading?*

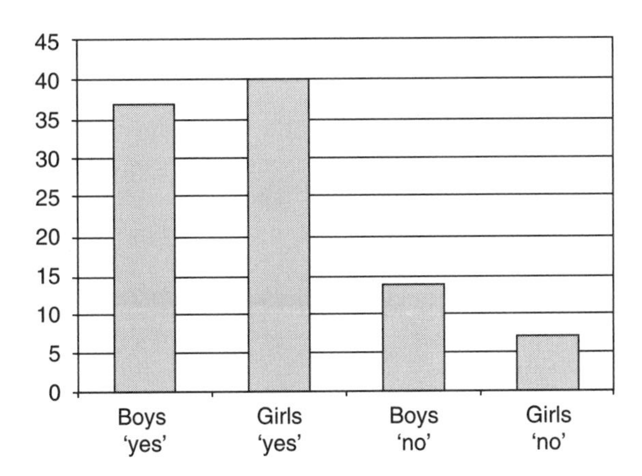

Figure 6.3 Year 8 percentage responses to the question *Do you like reading?*

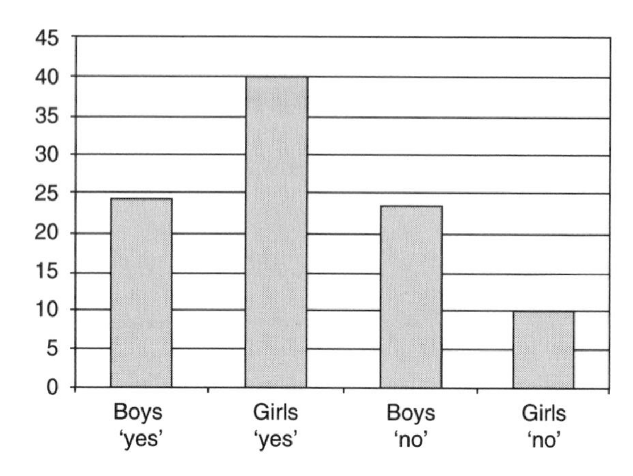

Figure 6.4 Year 9 percentage responses to the question *Do you like reading?*

recording many more *yes* responses throughout. This decline in the boys' level of enjoyment of reading raised a number of questions:

1 Is the decline due to the more restricted curriculum in Year 9 in both time and content? The Year 9 English time is reduced to four periods from six. This means that the individual reading programme could not be maintained in Year 9 except for those pupils who have reading difficulties. It is also the year of the SATs, which means that there is a greater concentration on Shakespeare and a more critical approach to poetry as the latter is written into our schemes of work. Could this result in a 'turn-off' for the boys?
2 Is it because, as Myra Barrs points out, boys begin to see reading as a way of extending knowledge rather than purely for enjoyment (Barrs and Pidgeon 1993: 10)?
3 Could it be because, as research has indicated (see Barrs and Pidgeon) 13 is about the age when boys seem more interested in computers and prefer more visual stimulation?

Clearly, we needed to look closely at the type of material boys and girls preferred to read. However, another factor became apparent at this stage. We had not yet looked at Year 10 as we didn't expect much difference from Year 9 . When we decided to look at the results as a matter of course, they came as a shock (see Figure 6.5).

The figures startled us. The boys' response to the question on enjoyment of reading barely changes but the girls' response is clearly worrying. Although there are slightly more boys than girls in the sample, there is a clear indication that the girls are losing their enjoyment from reading. This struck us as a serious matter for further investigation. The next stage was to look at what genres pupils preferred reading and to find out whether there were any difference in preferences between boys and girls.

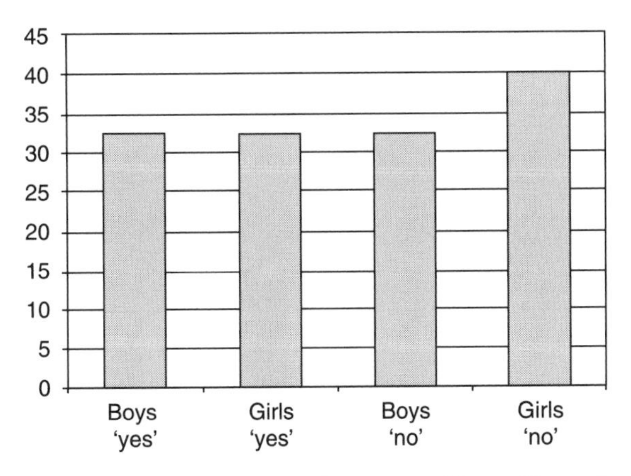

Figure 6.5 Year 10 percentage responses to the question *Do you like reading?*

Reading preferences

The survey had asked pupils to indicate which genres of reading material they preferred. We could not make the choice as detailed as we would have liked because it would have been too time-consuming and maybe confusing for some pupils, so we restricted our research to the following categories:

- adventure
- science fiction
- horror
- romance
- humour
- non-fiction
- magazines
- comics

We have looked at individual year groups, comparing the responses of boys and girls.

We first analysed the Year 7 returns (see Figure 6.6). Surprisingly, perhaps, the preferences are very similar between the boys and girls, with horror taking the predictable lead, bearing out Charles Sarland's research (Sarland 1991). There is also a predictable result as far as the preference for science fiction is concerned, with boys enjoying this genre far more than girls.

The boys do not seem to prefer reading any more non-fiction than the girls, which starts to answer the previously posed question concerning boys' preference for reading non-fiction in order to extend their knowledge. However, we have to consider the fact that all Year 7 pupils are asked to take out a *fiction* book for their individual reading programme, which could influence their choice of genre. The

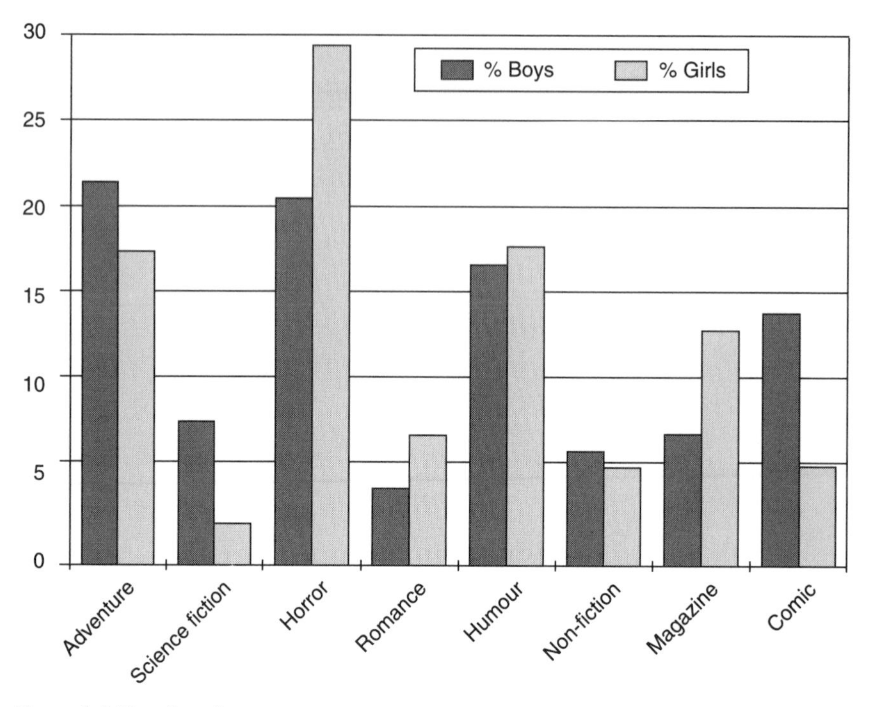

Figure 6.6 Year 7 preferences in genre

other marked difference is the boys' greater choice of comics. The girls lean more towards magazines – which could be attributed to the girls' greater maturity at this age. One factor which needs to be taken into account is that girls' comics are often more magazine-like than the boys' comics, which makes the term 'comic' difficult to define. It is useful to compare the above statistics with those of Year 9 (Figure 6.7).

Horror is still the most popular genre, increasing in popularity with girls. Perhaps unsurprisingly, the reading of romance shows a considerable increase among the girls; this could also account for the increase in magazine reading by girls. The questionnaire shows that teen magazines are the most popular type of magazines for girls (31 per cent) while the boys prefer football or computer magazines, although in lower numbers (7 per cent and 5 per cent respectively). A small number of girls (1 per cent) mentioned horse magazines and 3 per cent of boys recorded music magazines in their preferred reading. It is interesting to note that comics still remain a popular read for boys even in Year 9 but we must take into consideration that comics progress from the *Beano* and *Dandy* format to the more graphic and adult style of the Japanese manga comics, which appeal to boys of this age. Figure 6.8 shows that, in Year 10, magazines become a far more important source of reading; this follows the trend noticed in Year 9, eventually overtaking other genres including the ever popular horror.

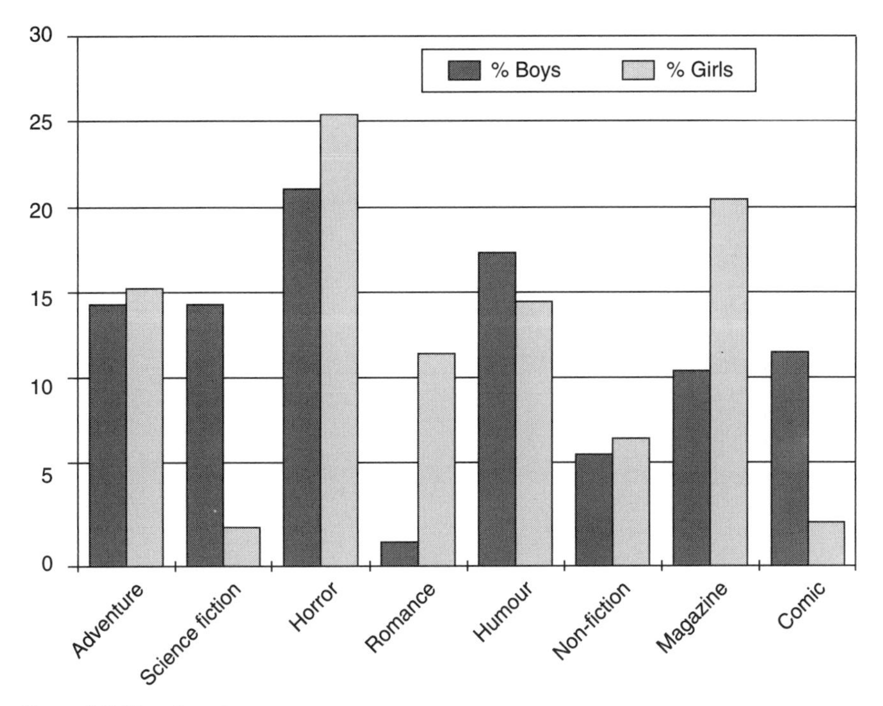

Figure 6.7 Year 9 preferences in genre

These results give a broad impression of the reading habits of 519 pupils (266 boys and 253 girls) and allowed us to look closely at our future plans for reading. It was quite surprising that non-fiction gained a low response from both sexes in all years. This clearly needs further research when the whole school implications are being considered.

The survey also gave us the following information:

- a comparison between pupils who enjoy reading but feel they are not good readers and those who don't like reading but feel they are good readers;
- the main reasons why pupils do not like reading. With hindsight we wish that we had included a question that asked why pupils enjoy reading;
- how pupils know whether they are readers or not.

It is interesting to note that the majority of the pupils in the lower school perceived themselves as good readers because they had been told so by their class teacher. The responses from Year 9 and 10 pupils indicated that they were not sure how they perceived themselves as good readers and often gave the response *because I just know*.

We feel that this is another indication that older pupils become disengaged from the reading environment that we have created in the lower school. One

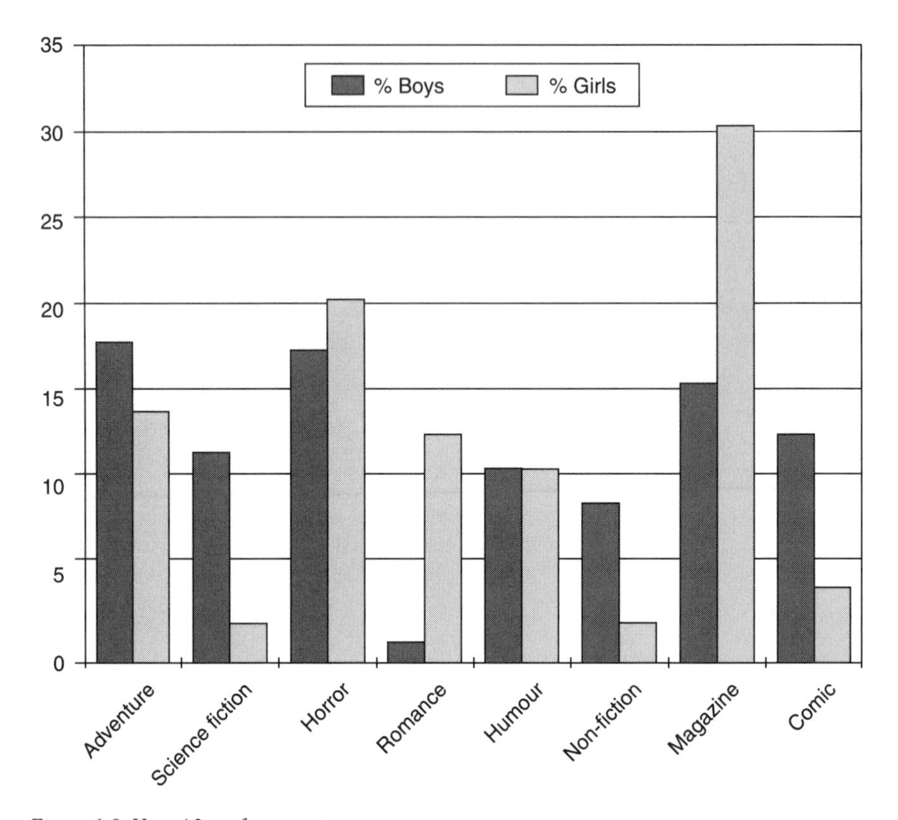

Figure 6.8 Year 10 preferences in genre

of our strategies must be to extend the provision of a stimulating reading environment into the upper school – and not just for the boys. This may well need to be accompanied by more talk about books, as indicated by the next stage of our project.

Reading conferencing: *Well, it's all right sometimes*

The worst thing about reading is really thick books.

One way in which we began to look at individual reading was by introducing a form of reading conferencing which allowed us to ask those pupils we had identified as the weakest what they felt about reading. We later extended this to look at readers who identified themselves as 'good' or 'bad'. They were given an interview in which they were asked the following questions:

- Do you like reading?
- What is the last book you enjoyed reading?

- When do you like reading?
- What is the best thing you have read?
- What do you think can be done to make reading better for you?

The answers were noted and followed up halfway through the year. The exercise proved such a good way of gaining an insight into the difficult and sensitive issue of attitudes and feelings about reading that we intend to incorporate it into the assessment of reading that we carry out in the future. In that sense, almost from the start, the project had an effect on practice for the better. Our aim in developing a structured way of discussing how pupils feel about reading was to widen our method of assessment. We had done enough talking about reading and had gained enough knowledge of theories surrounding reading to know that simple word recognition or even being able to read a passage and answer some questions did not necessarily make a good reader. We began to search for other ways of :

(a) giving readers a chance to say what they feel about their reading, having noted informally that those who make the most progress in reading seem to be those with positive attitudes to it;
(b) finding out for ourselves whether it was possible to measure progress, in an informal way, by detecting changes for the better in the way reading is regarded by those who, in a sense, have been most let down by the process.

To achieve this we selected a group of pupils whom we knew to be 'weak readers'. We did this by first of all using the initial screening information from the Year 7 Suffolk Reading Test, which confirmed information received from primary school liaison. We then interviewed the pupils and asked them for their views on themselves as readers. Results seemed to indicate a great feeling that reading was without doubt important but little idea seemed to exist as to why it might be so. Among those who appeared the most reluctant and least confident readers there seemed to be an almost mystical aura surrounding reading. Comments like *My Nan's got a big TV but she just reads* were spoken with such awe, as if the key to the mystery of why she should do such a thing was one this particular boy could never hope to hold.

There was evidence that reading was seen as a chore and the only reading that was considered legitimate was that done to a teacher in a classroom. When pushed on what reading they did outside school, it was only with reluctance that reading for information, sports results and television guides, etc., was mentioned. There was a definite expectation that this was not what the teacher wanted to know about and that competency in this sort of reading was not valuable in a school context.

In her book *On Being Literate*, Margaret Meek points out:

> The great divide in literacy is not between those who can read and write and those who have not learned how to. It is between those who have discovered what kinds of literacy society values and how to demonstrate their competencies in ways that earn recognition.
>
> (Meek 1991: 9)

The idea that being a good reader would help get a good job was another common view. And yet pupils were invariably unable to say why that was the case. For these failing readers, reading for pleasure was not an option. Reading needed to have a clear purpose.

Yet the same pupils would, in a follow-up group discussion, talk about how they would like to read books that they had seen the film or television version of. They often drew conversations back to films: My *favourite film* . . . became a frequent response to the question *What is your favourite book?* These pupils were desperate for narrative in an accessible form and turned to television to provide it. As one girl said, *I get bored with a big thick book. When you watch it on the tele' you don't have to work so hard. It's just sort of there for you.* For the more able reader, however, the fact that they can engage with a text and 'use their imagination' makes reading appealing. As another girl said: *The worst thing about reading is when I pick up a book and can't stop. Especially when it is a good story such as one that keeps you on the edge of your seat.*

For another boy, the best thing about reading is *You never know what will happen next.* In conferences with these young readers it appeared that reading is a quest for narrative and success is seen at least partly in terms of whether one can break the code well enough to get the story. For those who feel that they fail at this, the alternative is to find different ways of achieving access to stories – usually in the form of television or film. This is not perceived by the pupils as a legitimate way of joining the narrative club and comments relating to television watching are punctuated by much giggling and self-deprecation. These pupils feel that their entry to story is at best through the back door and at worst is gatecrashing. For those like Jenny, who think that the best thing about reading is *When you get right into the story and you feel like you are there*, the decoding aspect of reading has been solved. For those boys who are still unable to grasp that reading is about making sense of the text rather than simply decoding it, notions of choosing to read when you can avoid it are incomprehensible. As one such boy succinctly put it *You're mental, it's on the tele'!*

For these pupils we need to ask whether 'literacy is better understood not as an isolated social skill as something one can do on demand, but as a social process on the daily landscape' (Meek 1991: 11) and whether we are doing anything to engage these pupils in reading. Similarly, are we doing enough to tap into their experience of gaining the information they need from alternative sources, in particular the audio-visual route of television?

Teaching reading

In an attempt to look at how reading is taught throughout the school, we set aside some time to track a lower and upper school pupils across the curriculum. We drew on the experiences of the learning support team in an attempt to look at the way reading for information was dealt with in the school and to discover whether there was any evidence of much use of alternative information sources in classrooms.

It is clear from frequent discussions between colleagues that reading is a major concern to teachers of pupils in the lower school. This is particularly evident in the combined studies department where considerable attention is given to reading. To this end the learning support department is often requested to make the written word more accessible to the weakest readers by rewriting texts, adding other visual information or sometimes simply reading information to the pupils. However, as the pupils go further up the school and GCSE examinations loom, less account is taken of reading difficulties in many subject areas, not through lack of awareness necessarily, but through a feeling that there is simply not the time to spend accessing texts for the few who still have problems. This feeling is first noticed by the pupils in Year 9, where in a discussion about reading one pupil said that *You [teachers] stop teaching us. There isn't the time to do reading any more.* He went on to say that he felt that the school made a difference to his reading in the first two years because *You made us do it* but that he doubted he would make any more progress now that we had stopped insisting. When asked to expand, on this he admitted that he would not read without pressure and although he was aware that he was not as good as he might be he was unlikely to seek help because of peer attitudes: *You get the mick taken out of you if you go to the reading clubs. They all know we are thick anyway, being in the bottom set, without going to extra help.* This was an articulate boy who was anything but 'thick' but who did have a significant problem with literacy and who desperately wanted help of some kind. The question is *What help?*

We accept Frank Smith's assertion that we should 'make reading a meaningful, enjoyable and frequent experience for pupils' (Smith 1984:12) but we must begin to ask ourselves whether our practice, as a school, reflects this. We might argue that our investigation shows that we have met one of our aims – that of making reading an important issue for pupils. But we must also consider that we need to follow this right through the school by making time for reading at all stages.

The need for a broader approach to reading throughout the school was borne out on our shadowing day when we found that the written word was used almost exclusively as a way for pupils to gain information. This clearly posed problems for those pupils who lacked confidence in their ability to read. The types of reading pupils were asked to do tended to fall into four categories:

- knowledge and understanding (comprehension)
- application

- analysis
- synthesis

Books were used as a source of information in technology, with the teacher encouraging the pupils to use ideas from books for a project and to *take them a stage further*. In other lessons the emphasis was on a more passive use of the written word to achieve the 'right answers', with the impression being given that the process of information retrieval is straightforward and unproblematic. The implication is that the answers from the book must be right and they will be easily found just by looking. There was little use of original sources and the 'sanitised' textbook was the source of information. This tends to make reading passive and tedious for pupils.

There was no evidence of evaluation of the text or that texts could have more or less value. This causes problems in the upper school where, in English lessons, pupils are asked to look at texts in this way – something they find very difficult. There is evidence that pupils are not encouraged to delve into and interrogate the texts they are given. Texts are seen as a source of 'right answers'. We clearly need to develop a more critical approach to reading for our pupils.

It is likely that as a school we encourage a narrow concept of what reading is and one of our main tasks must be to develop a wider responsibility amongst the staff for teaching reading in the widest sense. For this to happen we need to establish a better understanding of what reading involves and ways in which this can be incorporated into the curriculum. Over and over again pupils made comments like *I watch TV for fiction* and while no one would want to advocate that this should mean we do not encourage reading of fiction we do need to expand our concept of reading so that we can teach pupils to be critical readers of all sorts of text – fiction, fact and the communications media.

Looking to the future

In conclusion, our research was a sobering affair. We know how to teach reading and how to encourage a critical response in our readers. We believe in Frank Smith's maxim that in order to read well we have to encourage more and more reading in our pupils and that 'it is only through reading that children learn to read and that a teacher's role must therefore be to make reading easy for every child' (Smith 1984: 34). In the lower school we achieve this but, as our upper school research shows, we fail to motivate readers. To blame the narrowing of the curriculum on National Curriculum tests and GCSE syllabuses is only part of the answer to this problem. We need to look again at our teaching methods at this level. Do we give our pupils the message that from now on we are the gatekeepers of 'good knowledge' and culturally acceptable responses? If so, are we empowering them to become critical readers? Or are we encouraging them to believe, as Margaret Meek says, 'what counts as literacy' (Meek 1991) is not what *they* value but what we and the examination boards value, therefore denying older pupils their say.

In order to address these issues, our plans for the future include:

- INSET to raise awareness for all staff of ways into reading and as a consequence encourage a move away from the 'find the answer' style of using textbooks to a more critical look at information;
- sampling of books in English where teachers read extracts in order to tempt readers into exploring unfamiliar texts;
- regular reading sessions throughout the age range (extended to other subjects);
- parents' information sessions;
- achieving the Quality Mark from the Basic Skills Agency;
- working closely with the feeder schools.

We started with questions about gender and these are still on our minds. However, this project has shown that questions about gender and reading are related to much wider issues about the ways in which we introduce young readers to texts in school, the extent to which we value and listen to their opinions and the need to develop a whole school coherent approach to reading in its widest sense.

Note

1 This curriculum structure will be changed by the time this chapter goes to print. Year 8 will no longer have an integrated curriculum, for reasons not related to this research.

References

Barrs, Myra and Pidgeon, Sue (eds) (1993) *Reading the Difference: Gender and Reading in the Primary School*, London: Centre for Language in Primary Education.

Meek, Margaret (1991) *On Being Literate*, London: Bodley Head.

Office for Standards in Education (1993) *Boys and English: A Report from Her Majesty's Chief Inspector of Schools*, London: Department for Education Publications Centre.

Sarland, Charles (1991) *Young People Reading: Culture and Response*, Buckingham: Open University Press.

Smith, Frank (1984) *Joining the Literacy Club*, London: Heinemann.

Part 3

LANGUAGE AND LEARNING

The three Rs – rights, responsibilities and resources

> It is a confusion of everyday thought that we tend to regard 'knowledge' as something that exists independently of someone who knows. 'What is known' must in fact be brought to life afresh within every 'knower' by his [*sic*] own efforts. To bring knowledge into being is a formulating process, and language is its ordinary means, whether in speaking or writing or the inner monologue of thought. Once it is understood that talking and writing are means to learning, those more obvious truths that we learn also from other people by listening and reading will take on fuller meaning and fall into a proper perspective.
>
> (DES 1975: 50)

This extract from the Bullock Report places language centrally in the process of taking on knowledge. In Language and Learning, Part 3 of the report, emphasis is placed on exploratory talk as essential to the construction of meaning and knowledge. Accompanying this was some useful advice about the style and context for talk, pointing to the importance of classroom organisation:

> There is no need to repeat here the points we have made earlier in this section about the role of exploratory talk in the classroom. For such talk to flourish, the context must be as informal and relaxed as possible, and this is most likely to occur in small groups and in a well organised and controlled classroom.
>
> (DES 1975: 189)

Despite the still very relevant advice about teacher–pupil talk, the main force of the comments about language and literacy development in secondary schools failed to take root and the implicit messages about teaching methods went almost unnoticed. For example, it took another twenty-five years before the National Oracy Project was set up to reinforce and extend Bullock's messages about the relationship between talk and learning.

Pupils' language and learning rights

In considering the use of language which is the focus of this book, one important aspect of *Language Across the Curriculum* is worth a second look. This is the idea that every teacher is a teacher of English. This is very true, and all the contributors to this book bear out the same message, but the notion needs to go a little further in outlining what kinds of responsibility for language teachers should take. The findings of national projects indicate that one aspect of a teacher's responsibilities is to provide a classroom environment which allows for the learner to be rather more than just a passive receiver of facts and messages. Before considering the second R – **responsibilities** – however, it is important to be clear about what is implied by pupils' language **rights** in relation to a teacher's responsibility for language and learning.

The first right is the pupils' right to be involved in learning. This means revisiting just what 'learning' in school looks like and where language comes in to it. The most obvious language mode when the representation of learning through language is being considered is writing. Writing pervades all aspects of school life. An immense amount of time is spent in writing in secondary classrooms, yet the paradox is that teachers are still concerned about pupils' standards of literacy. If there is so much of it, why can't young learners achieve more highly? As contributors to this book have already emphasised, language and literacy are the bedrock of successful and satisfying learning, so what can be done to raise levels of literacy and learning? How can language be used to help pupils make the most of their abilities? A substantial part of the answer lies in theories of what 'knowledge' is and how language helps to create that knowledge – back to Bullock's comments of 1975. But the analysis needs to be taken further to include teaching practices and learning possibilities.

The relationship between language and learning needs to be unpicked because the emphasis in the past has been on assessing learning by using language as a form of evidence. Studies carried out as part of the National Writing Project during 1987–90 provided some startling results. This project worked with twenty-four different local authorities in England and Wales to investigate the writing practices and achievements of pupils aged from 4 to 18.[1] In the worst cases writing was a proof of physical, if not conceptual and emotional, attendance at lessons and an indication of a general level of technical competence. Painting the most gloomy picture: writing in school bears very little resemblance to any writing which goes on in most people's home and work lives. The variety of ways in which people give and receive messages, explain, amuse, convince real readers who are reading for the meanings carried by writing, are very rarely seen as relevant to classroom writing. Similarly, the ways in which talk is used to explore ideas, to wonder and hypothesise, find little space in a classroom where the talk is largely teacher-dominated. In this worst case classroom, reading is merely decoding the surface messages of selected fragments of text, and this can be done without genuinely understanding a word. It is small wonder that, in this kind of setting, young learners fail to become the enthusiastic, fluent, versatile people that employers want.

Evidence came from teachers and pupils keeping diaries of the kinds of writing done during the course of the week in hundreds of secondary schools involved in the project. Richard Landy, a local project co-ordinator wrote:

> Aware of the dangers of generalisation, we agreed to begin our investigation by trying to obtain some sort of snapshot of our pupils' writing diet, first by looking at some samples of written work that pupils had recently done, and second, by persuading two classes of pupils to keep writing diaries in which they recorded: what they wrote, the nature of the task, the amount of writing done, the time available, the audience and any further comments they wished to add.
>
> (Landy 1990: 23)

Richard Landy found that the message which many school pupils get from classroom practices in relation to writing are clear – that writing is done for teachers to mark and then tell the pupils where they have gone wrong, either in grasping the facts and concepts which were on offer or in the technical and secretarial aspects of literacy:

> The diaries, rough and ready blunt instruments that they were, turned out to be a good place to start, particularly in a secondary school where, of course, there is a real danger that nobody is taking an overall view of the writing that pupils are asked to undertake during the course of a day, a week or a year. Those dividing walls of the secondary curriculum can be very high and rigid at times. When we peered over we were all genuinely surprised by the sheer quantity of end-product writing that pupils were expected to produce, the limited opportunities available for redrafting or editing, the lack of choice of task or format and the 'teacher-centredness' of an activity for which the teacher was, invariably, the only reader. It was a picture which didn't seem to vary much from subject to subject.
>
> (Landy 1990: 23)

Although this work was carried out almost ten years ago, the findings ring some uncomfortable bells now. Very similar experiences were recorded during the

National Oracy Project, where teacher talk was perceived as instructional and the pupils' role was to listen and take it in. Even the most committed teachers were surprised by their own investigations (see Norman 1992). They discovered that, very often, classroom collaborative talk was perceived by teachers and pupils alike as *not working* and the most common form of classroom utterance was the answer to a teacher's question, to which the teacher already knew the answer anyway – the whole process being a kind of ritualised mind-reading game.

The traditional model of learning outlined above takes a narrow view of the relationship between language and learning. A more developmental view looks not just at the end points of learning as evidenced by language in some form or another, but at the ways in which language can also be seen as a tool for learning – a means as well as a proof. The psychologist Vygotsky distinguished between two kinds of learning: the first is the kind that we absorb as part of our everyday experience, from being in a social group or a community. An example of this might be knowledge of how toys float or sink in water (*spontaneous* concepts). The second is a type of learning which comes when children are deliberately taught something. In Vygotsky's terms, for these *scientific* concepts to be fully understood they need to be reflected on and talked about. If learning means adding new concepts and experiences to existing ones to reach wider and deeper understanding, then the process of deliberate teaching, or drawing explicit attention to learning, is essential. This is where teachers' responsibilities enter the domain of pupils' language and learning rights. Spontaneous learning is just not enough. Rote learning is not enough. Copying is not enough. There needs to be a planned deliberate set of interventions, if *information* is to become *understanding*. Pupils have a right to these carefully staged interventions.

The psychologists Bruner and Vygotsky place great emphasis on the role played by culture and its systems of symbols (languages, science, books, diagrams, pictures, etc.) informing the child's concept formation. Such systems have a dynamic, structuring effect on learning and development. Another important aspect of learning theory is that learning is not just about cognitive development, but also involves the affective and experiential ways in which we learn – not just using the brain, but the emotions and the experiences of learning. This introduces the second language right: the right to one's own community uses of language. While it is essential that teachers help pupils to develop standard forms of writing and speech, as Part 1 explains, this should never be achieved at the expense of pupils' cultural or personal pride. Tim Rowland explores this in some detail in Chapter 7. Traditional models of teaching and learning do not capture the dynamic, interrelated, recursive nature of the development both of language and of thought. Neither do they adequately take into account the social and cultural elements of learning and their implications for the contexts in which people may best learn.

Teachers' responsibilities for learning

Language can be seen not just as proof of learning, but entering all stages of the process. We use language – speech and writing – in:

- preparation, getting ideas going, framing questions;
- gathering, organising and categorising information;
- exploring ideas, hypothesising, predicting, explaining, describing, persuading, arguing, etc.
- giving information to others, communicating ideas;
- reflecting on learning, evaluating and reviewing progress;
- demonstrating that something has been learned.

Bruner describes the process of good teaching as *scaffolding* learning, seeing teaching-and-learning as a series of deliberate, planned and careful interventions to help pupils get better at it – whatever 'it' is – maths, history, drama, science, art, language itself (Bruner 1986). Some of the most effective interventions often happen before teachers even reach the classroom – in the plans and strategies to scaffold learning – and effective planning will be linked to what teachers want the pupils to learn and how they are going to evaluate that learning. And this, of course, leads to the responsibilities teachers have for language and learning.

Many of the formative uses of language – devices to help get ideas going such as brainstorming activities or flow charts of ideas, or the use of pupil questions to guide investigations – depend on the pupils themselves becoming much more central to the process of learning. Tentative uses of language, as Tim Rowland explains in his chapter on the language of interaction, depend on small group talk and this can sometimes worry teachers who 'can't be everywhere at once'. He explains his view that 'pupils have a right to some personal stake in and commitment to the things they are expected to come to "know" '. Rowland links pupils' language rights to the teacher's responsibility by considering the idea of *fallibilism* – an experimental approach to constructing knowledge. To Rowland, this is firmly interrelated with the value of indirectness in inviting pupils to investigate and explain their developing concepts: 'The teacher who is aware of such linguistic devices may achieve more comprehensive understanding of what it is that pupils are trying to communicate through speech.' Having a more 'fallible' approach to the learning in the classroom does not mean an abdication of responsibility or loss of control; it means careful planning and observation. It allows the teacher to find out what pupils already know in order to plan future teaching more effectively and ensure that time is not wasted in teaching pupils what they already know – a more productive type of responsibility than just making sure that the syllabus has been covered. It also ensures that the learning sticks. As Rowland remarks, 'when pupils have been encouraged to take an active part in their own learning, to reflect on action' then they can 'articulate how they have made sense of it'.

Another area of responsibility which Elaine Wilson discusses in Chapter 8 is to introduce pupils to subject-specific discourse. Different subject areas have their own specific vocabulary, forms of writing and types of reading which need to be made explicit to learners. We do not emerge on this earth with a ready-made ability to make notes, for example; we have to be taught – and that is one of the elements of planned intervention for learning – making explicit the particular demands of using reading, writing, speaking and listening in each subject. To Wilson, the ability to operate within the subject-specific discourse is directly linked to language as a means of communicating ideas, not just proving that concepts have been covered. She points out that: 'Good communication in the scientific community is more than the simple transmission of information from one person to another; it is also about the formulation and sharing of ideas.' Her research into science teaching in twenty comprehensive schools revealed that whilst genuine communication is part of scientific exchanges, 'communication in the school science laboratory is almost always about the teacher providing answers to questions posed by the teacher'. She gives a range of examples of language in science to develop and communicate ideas – from role-play to writing poetry in chemistry lessons. In this way, Wilson summarises the responsibility of the teacher to create an environment for learning which transforms some of the more traditional practices. She argues that 'telling needs to become interpretation' and she demonstrates convincingly the benefits for learning when teachers create the conditions for more genuine communicative purposes in talk and writing.

Resources for learning

Teachers often point out that *you can't do anything without the appropriate resources*. Absolutely true, and in considering the three Rs, this part of the book largely concentrates on the human resources of the classroom. Tim Rowland and Elaine Wilson focus on teacher language as important in structuring learning, but Paul Goalen extends this to include pupils' own language as a resource for teaching and learning. He links this with teachers' responsibilities for creating a successful learning environment through looking at learning objectives and the assessment of how far they have been achieved. Goalen makes a convincing case for using the collaborative techniques of drama to enhance learning. He points out that the success of drama in developing children's historical thinking and writing 'must in part be due to the transactional nature of drama, to the fact that control over the content and direction of lessons is shared between pupils and teachers in different ways'. This suggests a shift in thinking about the language resources which pupils bring to the classroom. He urges that teachers should not be *frightened into abandoning active learning*. On the contrary, echoing Elaine Wilson's findings: 'The adoption of a more restricted diet of formal teaching strategies could quickly result in sterile responses lacking both in historical imagination and analytical skill as pupils opt out intellectually from the learning process.'

That is the danger. The responsibilities are wide – teachers need to see the use of language as a means or tool of learning as well as in the various forms which a developed language user can draw on. This involves conceiving the texts pupils produce – spoken and written texts – as part of a process of getting to grips with ideas as well as a product of learning. Success in learning needs to be judged by both the formative and the performative uses of language evident in classrooms and schools. Acknowledging the relationship between language and learning – the acceptance that talk is a valuable tool for learning and that collaboration is important, for example – does not mean that if you put pupils together in groups they will automatically learn. Deliberate planned interventions are necessary and this means that the progressive development of language, literacy and learning is related to pupils' language rights, teachers' responsibilities in scaffolding learning and the resources teachers can draw on. This part of the book gives some examples of the three Rs in action.

Note

1 See National Writing Project publications, particularly Nelson/National Writing Project 1989 and 1990.

References

Bruner, Jerome (1986) *Actual Minds; Possible Worlds*, London: Harvard Educational Press.

Department of Education and Science (1975) *A Language for Life* (known as The Bullock Report), London: Her Majesty's Stationery Office.

Landy, Richard (1990) 'Rewriting the Syllabus' in Nelson/National Writing Project, *Ways of Looking*, Walton-on-Thames: Nelson.

Nelson/National Writing Project (1989) *Writing and Learning*, Walton-on-Thames: Nelson.

Nelson/Natonal Writing Project (1990) *Ways of Looking*, Walton-on-Thames: Nelson.

Norman, Kate (ed.) (1992) *Thinking Voices: The Work of the National Oracy Project*, London: Hodder and Stoughton.

Vygotsky, Lev (1978) *Mind in Society: The Development of Higher Psychological Processes*, London: Harvard University Press.

7

WILL IT WORK?

The language of interaction in mathematics

Tim Rowland

> Knowledge is not a transferable commodity, and communication is not a conveyance.
>
> (Ernst von Glaserfeld 1983: 66)

My purpose in this chapter is to draw attention to some of the subtle ways in which teachers and pupils use language to achieve their personal and interpersonal purposes in the classroom. The teacher who is aware of such linguistic devices may achieve more comprehensive understanding of what it is that pupils are trying to communicate through speech. Since my business is mathematics education, my discussion is set in mathematical contexts. A brief classroom episode will serve to set the scene: Judith is a newly qualified mathematics teacher in an 11–16 secondary school. She has introduced her class of Year 9 pupils to a mathematical investigation. They have various rectangular arrays of points on 'dotty' paper, and have to connect them by drawing line segments between pairs of points. What is the least number of segments necessary so that they form a continuous line connecting all of the points? Encountering a 4-by-4 grid some way into the activity, she asks Allan, one of the pupils:

Judith: Right. Can you make any predictions before you start?

Allan considers the question, and answers:

Allan: The maximum will probably be, er, the least'll probably be 'bout 15.

A first reading may suggest that there is nothing unusual about this interchange. Our familiarity with the possible forms of language dulls our capacity to be surprised by the forms that we choose, and our curiosity about the reasons for making those choices. But look again. If, as it seems, Judith's intention is to request information, why does her question address Allan's ability to supply it? And why is his answer, ostensibly a mathematical utterance, so notably devoid of precision? What might we infer about Allan's attitude to his prediction from the manner in which he formulates it?

Knowing and talking

The acquisition of mathematical knowledge entails the construction of an elaborate edifice of facts, concepts and strategies. For each individual, the process of construction is the outcome of reflection on action (including actions of a mental kind). This 'constructivist' view of learning asserts the active sense-making role of the individual learner in assigning meaning to mathematical experiences, including the experience of being 'taught' or 'told':

> Constructivism is a theory of knowledge with roots in philosophy, psychology and cybernetics. It asserts two main principles . . . (a) knowledge is not passively received but actively built up by the cognizing subject; (b) the function of cognition is adaptive and serves the organisation of the experiential world, not the discovery of ontological reality.
>
> (von Glasersfeld 1989: 162)

The constructivist-oriented mathematics teacher must endeavour to access and describe the mathematical frameworks and private constructions locked away in each child's mind; to uncover what they know and how they structure that knowledge. Language offers one important means of access to thought, and the role of language in teacher–pupil discussion is crucial for this purpose. Talk with children can offer insight into the structure of fragments of their mathematical understanding. For the teacher, the primary purpose of such talk is to gain insight into the nature of children's knowledge and misconceptions, adopting a transactional approach to language which presupposes that a speaker's primary intent is to transmit (or elicit) information.

In the exchange between Judith and her pupil, Allan, it is certainly possible to detect some transactional elements in each of their utterances. Yet the indirect and vague forms in which they clothe their intentions suggest some subtlety in the way they trade question and answer. I shall argue that the transactional purpose of their language is overlaid with pragmatic personal and interpersonal goals of an interactional kind. Judith and Allan's interactional purposes are coded in the form of the language that they use. I shall show how that linguistic coding works in teacher–pupil conversations about mathematics, and hope to demonstrate the pedagogic value of some knowledge of that code.

Inductive inference

Discussion of motives and purposes in the mathematics classroom needs to be set in the context of mathematics ideologies and classroom practices. What are we trying to do in mathematics education? To pass on the discoveries of the past, certainly, but also to share the experience of mathematical discovery, of coming-to-know as the outcome of mathematical activity. Therefore we need to motivate some actions for pupils, to provide some tasks to them to engage with.

By way of example, here is one rich classroom mathematics task. The specification of the task proposes some activity – things to do – and poses a question – things to think about – in consequence of the activity.

> *Partitions* The number 3 can be 'partitioned' into an ordered sum of (one or more) positive numbers in the following four ways: 3, 2+1, 1+2, 1+1+1. Find all such ordered partitions of 4. In how many ways can other positive numbers be partitioned?

Suppose the mathematics teacher introduces this task to the whole class, and organises further activity and discussion in pairs. Two girls, Cathy and Emma, work on this activity. They soon produce some data: as well as the 4 given partitions of 3, they find that there are 2 partitions of 2, and 8 possible partitions of 4 (try it for yourself!). Emma notices that, as the number to be partitioned increases from 2 to 3 to 4, so the number of partitions doubles from 2 to 4 to 8. Cathy assents, and predicts that there will be 16 partitions of 5. Such a prediction is amenable to empirical confirmation. In this case, to achieve confirmation, the two girls undertake identification and listing of the partitions of 5. There are 16 of them: very neat, very satisfying.

Cathy goes on make the conjecture that *this always happens*. The teacher draws their attention to the fact that 2, 4, 8 and 16 can be written as 2^1, 2^2, 2^3, 2^4, and discusses choice of notation with them. Cathy eventually formulates her conjecture as: the number of partitions $r(n)$ of every number n is 2^{n-1}. Emma checks that this fits with their data, and consents to the conjecture.

Such a conjecture is a mathematical generalisation, arrived at by process of inductive inference; a statement (of belief) about properties of an entire class (of natural numbers), a statement made despite the fact that the whole class has not been directly inspected and tested – indeed, could not be – for the property or properties in question. The information-in-hand is limited, and in any case is bound to be insufficient in itself for Cathy and Emma to know the values of $r(n)$ for values of n beyond those for which they have data. It is, however, sufficient to cause them to form some tentative beliefs about those unknown $r(n)$ values, and to be prepared to articulate beliefs in terms of predictions and the generalised conjectures. We should expect such statements to convey not only propositional information but propositional attitude – not just to tell what they know but to explain the extent of their convictions. The language used will be chosen to fulfil both transactional and interactional purposes. I shall return to this later.

Half an hour into the lesson, the teacher calls the class together for reporting back. Cathy and Emma are invited to share their findings, and how they arrived at their conjecture. They explain the notation in which their generalisation is formulated. Other pairs report different strategies in their approach and different forms of representation. Not all are comfortable with the powers of 2, but there is a consensus about the universal validity of the doubling pattern.

The teacher goes on to pose a homework question, for later discussion: *Why is it that the number of partitions doubles at each stage?* In the next lesson, the class develops an explanation of the doubling – a deductive argument outside the scope of this chapter – which demonstrates that their shared belief, the inductive generalisation, is indeed valid. The girls who articulated the generalisation have made a significant contribution to a mathematical common-wealth, to shared knowledge of process and product, and to their own self-esteem as working mathematicians.

In some influential writing on the logic of mathematical discovery, Imre Lakatos (1976) coined the term 'fallibilism' to denote such an experimental approach to the generation and confirmation of mathematical knowledge. Sandy Dawson (1991) characterises fallibilism in terms of a social process in which a conjecture is created, shared, and then critically examined. As a result, pupils' conjectures are tested and proved, or refuted and modified. The purpose is to determine whether the conjecture is true or false, but this is invariably associated with the judgement that the pupil who articulated it is right or wrong. Laurie Buxton identifies a related difficulty for the pupil – and hence, for the teacher also:

> Most classroom maths sets tasks, often with very clearly defined goals; whether they have been reached or not is seldom in doubt. . . . This clarity tends to enhance the sharpness of emotional response. There is a nakedness about the success or failure in reaching a goal that evokes clearly defined emotions whose nature one cannot disguise to oneself.
>
> (Buxton 1981: 59)

Anne Watson recognises how, in time, this can generate inhibitions in pupils, who 'are worried about being wrong and nervous about asking for help if "being wrong" and "needing help" have, in the past, been causes of low self-esteem by leading to ridicule, labelling or punishment' (Watson 1994: 6).

This tendency is illustrated in the words of two 16-year-old girls (C and S), reported by a teacher, Susan Hogan (at a research seminar at the Open University, November 11th 1995). The two girls had decided not to continue mathematics studies at school. Here, Susan asks about their experience of 'speaking out' in mathematics classrooms:

SH: And do you need to be confident in order to speak . . . ?
C: Yeah, because there were people in the class that were so good that you kind of . . .
S: . . . thought well, they're gonna laugh at me if I get it wrong.

Students' self-constructed mathematical beliefs may be fragile; in particular, any inductive conjecture would be expected to be tentative. The burden of the affective baggage associated with mathematics in school then necessitates that the pupil articulate the belief whilst distancing her/himself from full commitment to it. That is to say, they must convey their propositional attitude to the substance of their assertion. The teacher's subtle task at such moments is to promote, first the utterance, then the trial – including possibly the rejection or modification – of such assertions as regards their truth, whilst minimising the personal sense of threat to the students who utter them.

I now want to shift attention from these interactional requirements of the mathematics classroom, to consider how they can be achieved with particular kinds of language.

Indirect speech acts

Not long ago, I organised some research into counting and estimation. This involved a large number of pupils tackling three short tasks involving a number of coloured sweets in various containers. The first task, for instance, involved 19 sweets on a white plate. We planned to enquire of each pupil about the number of sweets shown to them. Given that there were two interviewers and over 200 pupils, we decided to standardise the presentation of the task to the extent that we would pose the question identically to every pupil. We had, therefore, to decide on the precise form of words that we would use. The most direct form of question would be something like:

How many sweets are there on this plate?

Whilst we did consider this direct formulation, we never seriously entertained it; we rejected it without trial on the grounds that it came over as too direct, somewhat aggressive and 'testing'. In fact, we came down to a choice between two possible, preferred formulations:

1 *Can you tell me how many sweets there are on the plate?*
2 *How many sweets do you think there are on the plate?*

We piloted both, and eventually settled for the first (*Can you tell me . . . ?*). Only much later did we rationalise the guidance of our intuition in preference of the indirect presentation of the question, in the following terms: statements normally declare things that are either true or false. Such propositions have traditionally occupied the attention of logicians and philosophers of language. In the 1950s, John Austin highlighted the importance of utterances such as *Wait for me!* and *Good luck!* which cannot be evaluated as true or false. Austin (1962) called non-propositional requests, wishes, warnings and the like *speech acts*, whose essential property is that they bring about a change in some state of affairs.

Knighthoods, marriages and prison sentences are all made effective by the utterance of such words by an authorised person.

Now, there is often a mismatch between the form of a speech act and its function. Three broad categories of language function are normally identified – statement, question and command – having typical realisations in declarative, interrogative and imperative verb forms. These conventional agreements between language function and form break down in *indirect speech acts*, in which the form of an utterance does not correspond with the intended force of the action which it performs. For example:

Teacher: I'd like to take in your exercise books.
Diner: Can you bring me the wine list?

The teacher achieves a command by declaring that s/he wishes to receive the books; the diner by questioning the ability of the waiter to provide the list. These are both instances of a fascinating, everyday linguistic phenomenon – how speakers frequently accomplish a speech act indirectly, by stating or questioning one of the so-called *felicity* conditions which would legitimate the request, command or whatever (Gordon and Lakoff 1971). Common forms of this are to state a preference or use of an interrogative form in order to convey a request.

It is now possible to recognise the formulation of the research question *Can you tell me how many sweets there are on the plate?*, intuitively determined in preference to possible alternatives, as an indirect speech act, a request achieved by questioning the ability of the child to do what could be expressed directly by the imperative sentence *Tell me how many sweets there are on the plate*. Indirect speech acts are commonplace in the classroom. Judith's question at the beginning of the chapter is a case in point:

Judith: Right. Can you make any predictions before you start?

The indirect form of Judith's request for a prediction (questioning the boy's ability to provide it) is very characteristic of many of the teachers whom I have studied through transcripts – for example Hazel, a mathematics specialist in her third year of teaching. In a discussion with two girls, Faye and Donna, in her class, Hazel explores their findings to do with certain relationships between consecutive numbers. Hazel's instructions and requests to the two girls are invariably presented as indirect speech acts, for example (there are many):

Hazel: Can you tell me what the difference in the answers of the two sums that . . . the two multiplications you're doing . . . would be when you have a difference of 4 between each number?

The form of this question *Can you tell me . . . ?* is precisely that which I chose for the research study. It emerges that Hazel is the doyenne of the indirect speech act. I return to a fuller analysis of this episode at the end of the chapter.

Politeness

So why should speakers in general, and teachers in particular, be indirect in this way? A particular quality of insight into such indirectness in classroom mathematics talk is provided by a sociolinguistic theory – of *politeness* – developed by Penelope Brown and Stephen Levinson in the late 1970s. In essence, the theory is constructed to account for some indirect features of conversation; it claims that speakers avoid threats to the 'face' of those they address by various forms of indirectness, vagueness, and so on, and thereby 'implicate' (hint at) their meanings rather than assert them directly. Politeness theory (Brown and Levinson 1987) is based on the notion that participants are rational beings, but with two kinds of *face wants* connected with their public self-image:

- positive face – a desire to be appreciated and valued by others; desire for approval;
- negative face – concern for certain personal rights and freedoms, such as autonomy to choose actions, claims on territory, and so on; desire to be unimpeded.

The *model person* described by the theory not only has these wants but recognises that others have them too; moreover, s/he recognises that the satisfaction of her/his own face wants is, in part, achieved by the acknowledgement of those of others. Indeed, the nature of positive face wants is such that they can only be satisfied by the attitudes of others.

Some acts intrinsically threaten face. These are described by Brown and Levinson as *face threatening acts*. Orders and requests, for example, threaten negative face, whereas criticism and disagreement threaten positive face. The model person therefore must avoid such acts altogether (which may be impossible for a host of reasons, including concern for her/his own face) or find ways of performing them whilst making them less of a threat.

Imagine, for example, that someone says something that the model person believes to be factually incorrect and would like to correct. Such an act would threaten the first speaker's positive face – the esteem in which s/he is held as a purveyor of knowledge. Or suppose that the model person would like someone to open the window, but is aware of the threat to the other's negative face. Brown and Levinson identify a taxonomy of strategies available in such circumstances.

1 Don't do the face threatening act – simply agree or keep quiet.
2 Do the face threatening act: in which case there is a further choice of strategy:

    2.1 Go off record – don't do the face threatening act directly, but imply it by an indirect request, e.g. *Don't you think it's hot in here?*
    2.2 Go on record: either

2.2.1 'baldly' – essentially making no attempt to respect face;
or
2.2.2 with redressive action: having regard either for the other's
 2.2.2.1 positive face (*You're the expert in these matters, but I thought that . . .*); or
 2.2.2.2 negative face (*I'm sorry to trouble you, but would you mind . . .*)

Redressive action is a way of indicating that no face threat is intended.

Indirectness

Brown and Levinson identify and catalogue a number of linguistic strategies associated with the face-respecting options which redress the threat to a person's autonomy, respecting their right to refuse. Recall Judith's request to Allan:

Judith: Right. Can you make any predictions before you start?

The indirectness softens the force of the face threatening act. However, there may be mutual recognition that refusal is not a real option. The following example is from one of a number of interviews which I conducted with 11-year-old pupils:

Tim: OK, now let's think about two numbers that add up to 20. Would you like to start off, Caroline?

Both Caroline and I know that this is an offer which she is bound to accept! – that the indirectness (marked here by the avoidance of the imperative) is conventional. Caroline knows that she has no option but to 'start off'. I am nevertheless sincere in my wish to be seen by these young students to be gentle, considerate and non-threatening.

Hedges

Indirectness is one strategy used to avoid face threatening acts. Another is the use of vague language of various kinds. Here, a teacher (Hazel) is asking pupils whether they perceive a mathematical generalisation:

Hazel: What's the pattern then? Can you sort of explain the pattern for me?

In addition to cushioning the request by her indirectness (*Can you . . .*), Hazel is vague about what she is asking for – a *sort of* explanation. This exemplifies an aspect of vague language which is of particular interest to me – the use of 'hedges'

(Lakoff 1973), which are essentially one of two types (Prince *et al.* 1982; Rowland 1995):

- Approximators: which blur measures (e.g. *around, about*) or categories (*sort of, basically*);
- Shields: (e.g. *maybe, I think, allegedly*) which withhold the commitment of the speaker to the propositional content of what s/he says.

Consider the response of the boy, Allan, to Judith's, request (above). Allan did in fact make a prediction, but the vagueness of his answer suggests that it was far from secure:

Allan: The maximum will probably be, er, the least'll probably be 'bout 15.

Allan hedges his prediction in two ways: the Shield *probably* is reinforced with the Approximator *(a)bout*. The very act of complying with Judith's request for a prediction is a threat to Allan's positive face, since he could be thought foolish if his prediction were subsequently found to be in error. The Shield 'probably' is a let-out for him, for it makes his lack of commitment explicit; use of the Approximator 'about' is a more subtle protective strategy, for it renders Allan's answer almost unfalsifiable (Sadock 1977: 437)!

Using the language of conjecture

To demonstrate the relevance and the application of the analytical framework introduced so far, I want to return to Hazel's classroom, to examine fragments of transcript of teacher–pupil mathematics talk. Hazel describes Faye and Donna as able mathematicians who often work together. Her discussion with them is essentially an exploration of the following problem.

> Take three equally spaced numbers, such as 10, 13, 16. The equal steps of 3 (in this case) are called the common difference. Compare the product of the outer pair [$10 \times 16 = 160$] with the square of the middle term [$13 \times 13 = 169$]. In this example, the difference is 9. What will happen if you take other similar number-triples? What if you take a common difference other than 3?

Hazel's conversation with the two girls falls into four episodes, although most of the examples which follow are taken from the beginning of the conversation:

- investigation of the case when the common difference is 1;
- investigation of the case when the common difference is 2;
- investigation of the case when the common difference is 3;
- search for a higher-level generalisation which includes the three generalisations arrived at inductively in the previous episodes as special cases.

In every case Hazel's instructions and requests to the two girls are presented as indirect speech acts, for example (there are many):

Hazel: Shall we try it out and see what happens? Do you want to each choose your own set of consecutive numbers?

Hazel: Right, would you like to try out with 10, 12 and 14 one of you and the other one can try another jump.

Hazel: Can you tell me what the difference in the answers of the two sums that . . . the two multiplications you're doing . . . would be when you have a difference of 4 between each number?

The first two are face threatening acts, 'orders' presented as questions out of respect for the children's negative face, as Hazel imposes on their personal autonomy of action. These are conventionally polite, indirect speech acts (like *Can you pass the salt, please?*). She believes that the investigation will be a worthwhile, educative experience for them with a potentially stimulating outcome. Nonetheless, she recognises the risk taking which is inherent in her quasi-empirical approach, and that she requires their co-operation as active participants in the project as they generate confirming instances of generalisations-to-come. In *Shall we try it out?*, she uses the plural form, including and identifying herself as a partner in the enterprise. In the third, she probes for a prediction, and realises the threat to the girls' positive face – what if they fail to make a correct prediction, will their reputation as 'good mathematicians' be dented?

Fallibilistic teaching, inviting conjectures and the associated intellectual risks, is unimaginable if the teacher is not aware of the face threatening acts that are likely to be be woven into her/his questions and 'invitations' to active participation. Redressive action dulls the sharp edge of the interactive demands that this style places on the learner. For Hazel, notwithstanding her authority in her own classroom, the indirect speech act has become a pedagogic habit.

Early in the conversation Faye observes a difference of 1 between 10×12 and 11^2. Somewhat precipitately, perhaps, Hazel asks:

Hazel: One number difference . . . do you think that will always happen when we do this . . . ?

Faye readily agrees, but Hazel, perhaps realising that she has not probed but has 'led the witness', seems to want to give them more of an option to disagree.

Hazel: What makes you think that? Just 'cos I asked it . . . or . . . ?

Donna gives hedged agreement and Hazel invites her to account for her provisional belief:

Donna: I think so.
Hazel: Why?

Arguably this is a tough question – to account for a belief that one is not really committed to anyway. Donna's justification is phenomenological rather than structural.

Donna: Well if um . . . if it's after each other like 10, 11, 12 . . . um . . . it will be one more because it's 1 more going up.

It is the basis of a subsequent higher-level generalisation earlier in the exchange:

Hazel: Okay. Right, what would happen if you had numbers that jumped up in 2 instead of 1, so you had 10, 12 and 14?
Faye: I think the answer is a two number difference. So 2.
Donna: Yeah, yeah. So do I.

The substantive proposition that Faye gives – that there is a 2-number difference – is, in fact, false. By prefacing it with a Shield, she marks her utterance as a conjecture and withholds commitment to it.

Earlier in the exchange Hazel encourages the pupils to try out two more examples with three consecutive integers. They obtain a difference of 1 in each case and Faye affirms her belief (unhedged) that, as Hazel puts it, *that will always happen*.

Hazel: Do you think that will always happen then?
Faye: Yes.
Hazel: How can you say for certain 'cos you've only tried out three examples?

Donna offers a brief diversion:

Donna: I don't think it will happen if you do like 11, 14, 22.
Hazel: But you're talking about the one that . . . if you always have a set of three consecutive numbers will it work?

Her *like 11, 14, 22* is a delightful example of a vague generality; what like-ness does she intend to point to with this single example? It is difficult to judge how Hazel interprets it, except that she takes it to *exclude three consecutive numbers* – and perhaps this is precisely what Donna intended to convey through her example. Evidently *consecutive* is a useful but neglected item in the mathematical lexicon.

Faye brings the discussion back on course with a request for what philosophers of science might call a 'crucial experiment' – testing the conjecture with an example well outside the range so far considered, to discover the extent of its validity.

Faye: I'd like to try it out in the hundreds

Donna's choice for the experiment seems to be guided by Hazel:

Hazel: [*to Donna*] You want one difference between each of those. If you're going to start with 100 you could have 101, 101 and 102. Would you like a calculator . . . ?

Faye makes an independent independent choice of 110, 111, 112:

Faye: I still get one number different.
Hazel: So that . . . so do you . . . will it always work d'you think?
Faye: Yeah . . . I think.
Hazel: How can you be sure?
Donna: Umm . . .
Faye: [*laughing*] Well . . .
Hazel: Are you sure?
Faye: Well not really, but . . .
Donna: Quite yeah.
Faye: I think so. Yeah quite sure. Because it has worked because we've done ten, eleven . . . Well I've done 10, 11, 12, 9, 10, 11 which are quite similar and then I've jumped to, um, um . . . 110, 111, and 112. It's quite a big difference. So yeah?
Donna: Yeah so do I.

By this stage Hazel seems reluctant to influence their commitment to the generalisation (the *it* that *always works*). Faye's intellectual honesty is very evident here. Her crucial experiment provides another (presumably weighty) confirming instance of the generalisation yet her assent to it is still hedged, partial. One senses that Hazel has created, or nurtured, what I have called a Zone of Conjectural Neutrality (Rowland 1997) in which Faye understands that it is the conjecture (*it always works*) which is on trial, not herself. She is free to believe or to doubt. Nevertheless, her *wells* indicate that she senses, perhaps, that it would be easier if she agreed – that agreement would better respect Hazel's positive face wants – for Hazel would gain satisfaction from Faye's coming-to-know. At the end of this part of the discussion she goes some way towards agreement, reviewing and reflecting on the variety of evidence which she has assembled, to account for her willingness to make the inductive leap into the unknown.

Not only are the two pupils' generalisations tested empirically, but they are subjected to deductive scrutiny. On a number of occasions, Hazel asks *why?* and requests and elicits explanations with regard to generalities. The transcript is pure delight, a fine example of fallibilistic teaching and learning of mathematics, supported by a skilful and sensitive teacher.

Implications for classroom practice

In this chapter, I have examined a number of ways in which indirect and vague language are used by pupils and teachers in the mathematics classroom to serve their interactional purposes. An inductive, fallibilist approach to pupils' learning that I have described, and that Hazel proclaims in her practice, holds that pupils have a right to some personal stake in and commitment to the things they are expected to come to 'know'. Such a claim is perhaps one that teachers of English would find unremarkable in relation to the pedagogy of their own subject.

Fallibilism in practice necessitates classroom interaction. I am not arguing that mathematical knowledge is arbitrary, or that one self-constructed conjecture is as good as any other – any more than one would wish to argue such a case for a poem or a painting. Whilst pupils must and do construct their own mathematical meanings and beliefs, these must be tested for social and conventional validity, and sometimes be modified or even refuted. The best forms of testing are discursive, open and rational, and the role of the teacher in the testing discourse is both crucial and subtle.

It is insufficient and ineffective for her simply to sit in judgement on the correctness of pupils' conjectures. Mathematics teachers' professionalism can extend to awareness of the role of language in facilitating and interpreting the interchange of mathematical ideas, having regard for a wide range of human sensibilities and pragmatic goals.

First, pupils' conjectures must be elicited so that they can be considered. Austin raises our awareness that questions – requests for information – are not neutral; they are actions performed by words, whose effects are sometimes only loosely related to our intentions. The theoretical notions of speech act and politeness suggest that indirect request forms show respect for the obstacles that many students must surmount to articulate their mathematical ideas and intuitions. Second, uncertainty or lack of conviction of the pupil in what s/he asserts is likely to be indicated by use of vague language, including modal language forms and use of hedges of one kind or another. These kinds of language can also suggest pupils' concern for their positive face.

I first identified indirect language and vagueness as significant linguistic features of mathematics talk in my own research interviews with pupils. Once sensitised to notice it, I have subsequently observed the same factors in numerous pedagogic encounters of a mathematical kind; notably when pupils have been encouraged to take an active part in their own learning, to reflect on action, and to articulate how they have made sense of it.

References

Austin, J. L. (1962) *How to Do Things with Words*, Oxford: Oxford University Press.

Brown, P. and Levinson, S. C. (1987) *Politeness: Some Universals in Language Usage*, Cambridge: Cambridge University Press.

Buxton, L. (1981) *Do You Panic about Mathematics?* London: Heinemann.
Dawson, S. (1991) 'Learning Mathematics Does Not (Necessarily) Mean Constructing the Right Knowledge', in D. Pimm and E. Love (eds), *Teaching and Learning School Mathematics*, pp. 195–204, London: Hodder and Stoughton.
Gordon, D. and Lakoff, G. (1971) 'Conventional Postulates', *Papers from the Seventh Regional Meeting of the Chicago Linguistics Society*, pp. 63–84, Chicago: Chicago Linguistic Society.
Lakatos, I. (1976) *Proofs and Refutations: The Logic of Mathematical Discovery*, Cambridge: Cambridge University Press.
Lakoff, G. (1973) 'Hedges: A Study in Meaning Criteria and the Logic of Fuzzy Concepts', *Journal of Philosophical Logic* 2: 458–508.
Prince, E. F., Frader, J. and Bosk, C. (1982) 'On Hedging in Physician–Physician Discourse', in R. J. di Pietro (ed.) *Linguistics and the Professions*, pp. 83–96, Norwood, N.J.: Ablex.
Rowland, T. (1995) 'Hedges in Mathematics Talk: Linguistic Pointers to Uncertainty', *Educational Studies in Mathematics* 29(4): 327–53.
Rowland, T. (1997) 'Fallibilism and the Zone of Conjectural Neutrality' in *Proceedings of the 22nd Meeting of the International Group for the Psychology of Mathematics Education*. Lahti, Finland.
Sadock, J. M. (1977) 'Truth and approximations', *Berkeley Linguistic Society Papers 3*, pp. 430–9. Berkeley, Calif.: Berkeley Linguistic Society.
von Glaserfeld, E. (1983) 'Learning as a Constructive Activity', in J. C. Bergeron and N. Herscorics (eds) *Proceedings of the Fifth Meeting of PME-NA*. Montreal: Université de Montréal.
von Glasersfeld, E. (1989) 'Constructivism in Education', in T. Husen and T. N. Postlethwaite (eds) *The International Encyclopedia of Education* Supplementary Volume, Oxford: Pergamon Press.
Watson, A. (1994) 'My Classroom', in A. Bloomfield and T. Harries (eds) *Teaching, Learning and Mathematics*, Derby: Association of Teachers of Mathematics.

8

COMMUNICATING KNOWLEDGE AND IDEAS

The use of language in science

Elaine Wilson

Science is about asking questions and trying to explain the world around us. Scientists involved in the search for explanations do so within scientific communities and communication is vital to the success of their work. Good communication in the scientific community is more than the simple transmission of information from one person to another; it is also about the formulation and sharing of ideas. However, whilst genuine communication is part of scientific exchanges, communication in the school science laboratory is almost always about a teacher providing answers to questions posed by a teacher. There are historical reasons and examination demands which have promoted this and the effect is to endorse a feeling in the pupil that discussion, or even ambiguity, has no role to play in the advancement of science. Observation of thirty secondary science lessons from twenty comprehensive schools which recorded the range of communication methods used by the teacher shows that the opportunity for pupils to communicate their own ideas can be limited.[1]

The results indicated in Figure 8.1 suggest that the opportunities for pupils to ask any question, let alone a scientific one, were rather limited and that talk was largely dominated by the teacher. This has significant implications for effective teaching and learning. One of these is related to the requirement of the science order for all teachers to consider ways of developing their pupils' use of language and to provide opportunities for pupils to speak, listen, read and write in a scientific context. This chapter gives an account of recent research into the communication elements of the science curriculum and describes some examples of effective practice observed in science classrooms.

Telling or interpreting?

Greater attention is now being paid to communication in the science classroom. In *Words, Science and Learning* (1992) Sutton presents an interpretation of the

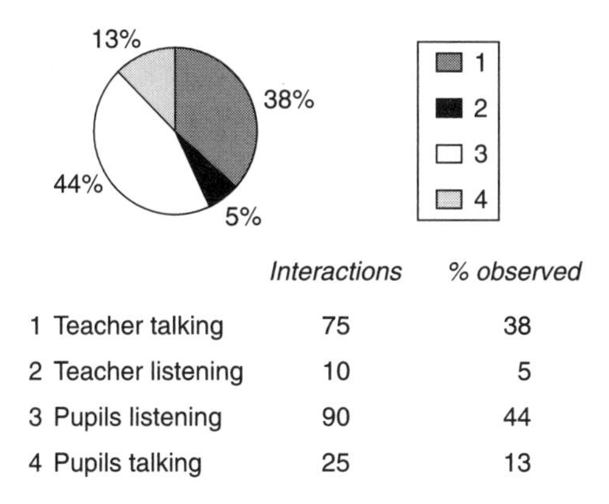

	Interactions	% observed
1 Teacher talking	75	38
2 Teacher listening	10	5
3 Pupils listening	90	44
4 Pupils talking	25	13

Figure 8.1 Classroom interactions

use of language in the science classroom which provides a useful starting point. In this he suggests that scientific language can be presented to pupils as either a labelling or an interpretive system:

1 Labelling involves:

- words which correspond in a simple way to features of the external world;
- describing, telling and reporting;
- facts coming first and then the word to describe the phenomenon;
- pupils learning by transmission of knowledge from the teacher to the pupil.

2 Interpretive systems involve:

- words steering thought and dialogue;
- figuring, exploiting, teaching, persuading, suggesting;
- active interpretation and re-expressions by the learner.

(Sutton 1992: 63)

Sutton goes on to suggest that the knowledge pupils meet in science lessons represents the culmination of a process in which an idea has developed over a period of many years. The science presented to pupils has developed through a variety of human activities before it has been accepted as scientific knowledge and been included in subsequent textbook publications. The labelling language presented to pupils in school textbooks rarely mentions the origin or the process through which scientific knowledge has evolved. Many pupils relish using this rich vocabulary, particularly in biology, and are introduced to as many new words in science lessons in their first year in secondary school as in, for example, a modern language course they would also study. The 'words' used by the textbook or the teacher are precise and intended to help pupils understand scientific knowledge. They do, however, sometimes present an intellectual hurdle for pupils too.

Wellington (1994) has classified these words into four levels:

> **Level 1 Naming words**
> These are words which denote identifiable, observable real objects or entities:
>
> 1.1 familiar objects but with a new technical name, e.g. *trachea* instead of *windpipe*;
> 1.2 new objects with new names, e.g. a living cell and its constituent parts;
> 1.3 names and symbols of chemical elements.
>
> **Level 2 Process words**
> These denote processes that happen in science. Some of these are more easily acquired than others:
>
> 2.1 processes that can be shown, e.g. distillation of ink or evaporation of water;
> 2.2 processes which cannot be shown e.g. evolution or nuclear fusion.
>
> **Level 3 Concept words**
> This is the largest category of scientific words and the one which pupils have most difficulties in learning because such words express ideas which gradually increase in their level of abstraction:
>
> 3.1 the lowest level concept words are derived from experience, e.g. the sensory concepts such as colour and taste;
> 3.2 the next level contains words which have both scientific and everyday meaning, e.g. *work*, *energy*, *fruit*, *salt*. The existence of two meanings can cause pupils difficulties and confusion;
> 3.3 concept words in the third level are used to denote abstract ideas, e.g. *element*, *atom*, *electron*, *mass*, *mole*, *valency*.
>
> **Level 4 Mathematical words and symbols**
> Chemical equations and quantitative genetics and physics fall into this category.
>
> (Wellington 1996: 170)

Wellington's word classification has obvious implications for science teachers. A common starting point for science is often through labelling. However, the practice may be ineffective for pupils to be introduced to process or concept words. If pupils are to develop a real understanding of concepts then a more interpretive approach would seem appropriate. The 'constructivist' approach offers a means of helping pupils grasp scientific concepts more readily.

The University of Leeds has undertaken a long-term constructivist research programme based on the notion that pupils construct and restructure their ideas as they learn – the Children's Learning in Science Project. This research has found that:

- learning outcomes depend not only on the learning environment but also on the prior knowledge of the pupil;
- learning involves the construction of meaning. However, a meaning constructed by pupils from what they see or hear may not be what is intended;
- the construction of meaning is a continuous and active process;
- meanings, once constructed, can be evaluated and accepted or rejected;
- teachers enable pupils to learn but pupils have the final responsibility for their learning.

Critical to this learning process, as far as the teacher is concerned, is knowing whether or not a pupil has processed a new concept or is receptive to developing another. This must be an interactive process between the pupils themselves and between the teacher and pupils. Concept maps have been suggested as a useful way in. A key word from the topic of the day is written in the centre of a page and the pupil progressively surrounds the word by other words as that pupil talks about the topic in question. The diagram thus provides the teacher with an insight into the pupils' present pattern of connected ideas. The teacher's role is vital here in deciding when a pupil has already grasped or is ready to develop a concept and which teaching style will best enable the learning process to take place. Figure 8.2 shows a typical diagram for the word *fruit*.

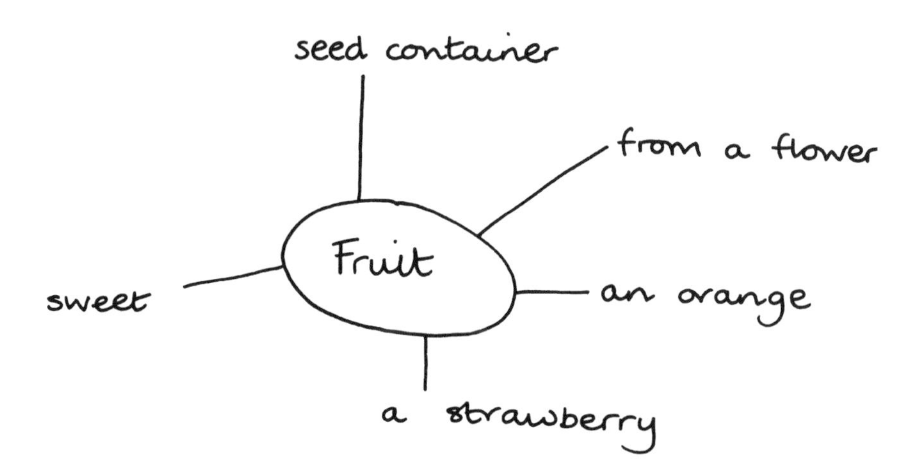

Figure 8.2 Burr diagram for fruit

As Wellington's category of concept words indicates, scientific vocabulary frequently has an alternative everyday meaning. The everyday meaning of the word *fruit*, for example, as understood by a pupil, may be different from the meaning a biology teacher would wish a pupil to hold. Sutton suggests that for each concept word there is a scientific core meaning and peripheral everyday meaning. The science teacher's task is to refine the core meaning and actively to shift the meaning held by the pupil.

When planning a lesson, particularly in the early part of Year 7 when pupils move from Key Stage 2 to Key Stage 3, teachers should know what connections the pupils have already made and the meaning, if any, that any new word being introduced holds for them. Being clear about the pupils' knowledge is a key to how to divide time in a lesson and what activities to make available. Management of the curriculum and of time are central aspects of the teacher's professional expertise. It is not easy, however, to balance these competing demands.

There has been considerable pressure on teachers' time as a result of the introduction of the revised National Curriculum, and many would argue that the addition of yet more activities is just not possible. One way of tackling this is to take a long hard look at any areas of teaching which may not be wholly effective. Many teachers are now beginning to question the effectiveness of some aspects of practical work carried out in science lessons, particularly the illustrative recipe-following type. This is quite a contentious issue and the notion of replacing this style of practical work is considered heretical by some. There is evidence, however, to suggest that the learning outcomes planned through the use of such practicals are not actually realised. Johnstone and El-Banna, for example (1986), suggest that practical work involving pupils following a set of instructions results in information overload in which the purpose of performing each step is unclear. It has also been shown that able pupils, particularly, are resentful and challenge the notion that they are experimenting with knowledge which they know to be well established in textbooks, preferring instead to investigate real problems.

Telling needs to become *interpretation*. A bridge between practical work and the process or concept being taught should be established before pupils are expected to engage in meaningful investigative and experimental work. The rest of the chapter is devoted to looking at methods used by teachers to help pupils build such bridges.

Helping pupils learn through writing

Nearly all pupils find writing more difficult than speaking. Writing in science lessons can be even more of a problem because of the nature of the writing undertaken and the limited opportunities pupils are given to carry out extended writing projects. For example, the style of writing observed in the thirty lessons mentioned earlier predominantly involved pupils writing up experiments or copying notes from another source (see Figure 8.3).

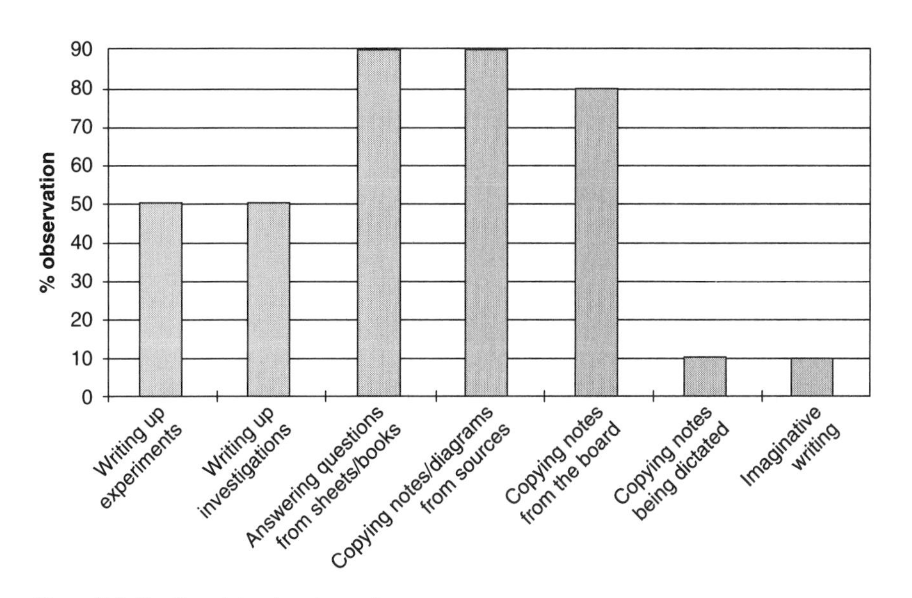

Figure 8.3 Pupils writing in science lessons

One activity observed in a Year 9 class required the pupils to read a passage of text about elements. They were then asked to complete a cloze activity filling in gaps in a paragraph of text. The pupils successfully completed the activity. Several pupils were questioned after the activity had been completed and although they were able to repeat the definition, many did not seem to have any real understanding of the concept. The pupils moved rapidly on to the next part of the lesson and did not have the opportunity to use the concept of an element further. The same subject was taught in another Year 9 lesson observed but here the pupils discussed their ideas with their teacher and the other pupils in their group. They then had to write about elements, including looking at how and why they were important to them in everyday life. They were given time to interpret their ideas before being asked to present these to their peers in their own words. Eleanor's writing about tungsten is an example of one interpretation (Figure 8.4).

The rote learning experience of the pupils in the first classroom is an example of what Ausubel (1963) described as isolated boxed learning that does not relate to anything else in the mind of the learner. Many chemistry lessons are perceived by pupils as falling into this category. The second lesson about elements observed was an attempt by the teacher to make the learning more meaningful and was probably why it appeared to be more effective. The interpretive writing did not occupy a large amount of time during the lesson and formed the basis of a consolidating activity after the lab work had been completed. The task provided follow-up homework opportunities which were considerably more challenging than simply finishing off questions – a common type of homework set following many science lessons.

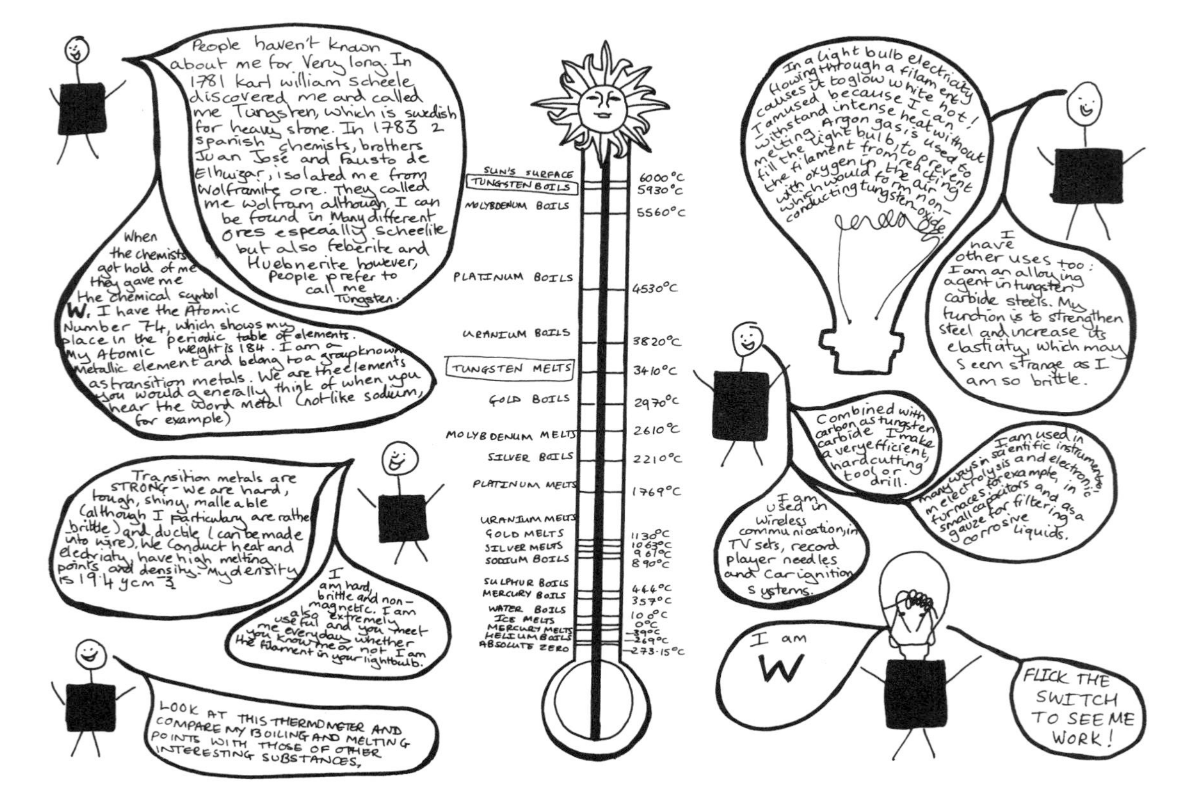

Figure 8.4 Tungsten by Eleanor, Year 9

In another lesson, Year 7 pupils were observed carrying out a practical investigation into the best conditions for cleaning muddy water, a fairly typical Key Stage 3 chemistry lesson. However, this lesson had been preceded by a visit to the local water treatment plant, followed by a short talk given by a past pupil about her voluntary work with an overseas aid agency. This work involved using local plant material to help remove very fine clay particles from muddy water. The pupils were then encouraged to work together in small groups to design, build and test suitable apparatus which would enable an African village to purify muddy water. The teacher had welcomed the inclusion in the revised National Curriculum of the development of communication skills in science and had prepared a follow-up writing activity to consolidate the ideas developed in the lessons. The follow-up task is shown in Figure 8.5.

Pupils were encouraged to use their information technology skills to word process and illustrate their work and to redraft the report. Opportunities were set up to allow access to the IT facilities over the two-week period allowed for completion of the report.

The task was completed successfully by all the pupils and some of the work produced was outstanding. The teacher's evaluation of the work attributed success to a number of points:

1. Pupils were encouraged to use technical details but could use their own usual language.
2. The content drew on the pupils' direct experience and on the hands-on activities carried out in the laboratory.
3. It had a real life purpose but also allowed the opportunity to consolidate their knowledge of concepts prescribed in the National Curriculum programme of study about filtration and solutions.
4. One part of the task report was structured so that pupils were required to use formal scientific language.
5. The reports were addressed to an audience to which pupils could relate and it had a clear real purpose.
6. Pupils had no difficulty sorting out relevant issues from those that might be considered peripheral to the investigation because the problem was something they perceived to be genuine and solvable. They were able, as a consequence, to draw pertinent conclusions because they understood the question being asked.
7. The teacher had made the assessment objectives clear to the pupils along with the task instructions and provided detailed feedback on performance with targets for each pupil (see Figure 8.6).

Having devised the assessment scheme, the teacher found that the time taken to mark the work was considerably less than that taken to mark an average class set of exercise books. Pupils took considerably more care with the work and appreciated the individual attention they were given with feedback. Other kinds

The task

You must produce two items.

1 **A technical report** aimed at the scientists and technologists at Intermediate Technology headquarters in Rugby which includes:

- your laboratory results;
- your findings from your background reading in the subject;
- your recommendations based on your findings.

2 The second piece of work will be a **short pamphlet** aimed at the local inhabitants. This should:

- use clear diagrams to illustrate you recommendations;
- recommend the use of apparatus and materials that are freely available in the area;
- the method suggested should be safe and cheap to use.

How will you be assessed?
I will be looking for evidence that you can:

- Present ideas clearly to the target audience in an organised way
- Use your scientific ideas and results from investigation
- Apply your knowledge and use other references to help with your ideas
- Work with numbers
- Choose ways of using IT to collect, store, retrieve and present scientific data
- Present ideas through the use of diagrams, graphs, tables and charts using appropriate scientific and mathematical conventions
- Use appropriate information sources to assess risks

Figure 8.5 Water task – Year 7

How clean is our water? Year 7 Assessment

You have produced two items and have submitted them on time

1 **A technical report** aimed at the scientists and technologist at Intermediate Technology headquarters in Rugby which includes:
  a) your laboratory results
  b) your findings from your background reading in the subject
  c) your recommendations based on your findings.

2 The second piece of work is a **short pamphlet** aimed at the local inhabitants and includes:
  d) clear diagrams to illustrate you recommendations
  e) recommendations for the use of apparatus and materials that are freely available in the area
  f) a method which is both safe and cheap to use.

YOUR WORK SHOWS THAT YOU HAVE ALSO ACHIEVED THE FOLLOWING:

3 Communication

2 You have presented your ideas reasonably clearly.
4 You have presented your ideas reasonably clearly and the language used is appropriate.
6 You have presented your ideas very clearly and the language is very appropriate for the target audience.

4 Using reference material

2 You make good use of the ideas developed in previous lessons
4 and you have used other sources of information
6 and you have included this reference list in your work.

5 Numeracy skills

2 You can enter data collected in your investigation into a table
4 and you can produce your own table
6 you can then go on to convert this information into a graph.

6 Investigation

a) You reached level in your planning of the investigation and you need to . . . .
. . . .
. . . .
. . . .
to move to the next stage.

b) You reached level in the doing strand and you need to . . . .
. . . .
. . . .
. . . .
. . . .
to move to the next stage.

c) You reached level in the evaluation strand and you need to . . . . . .
. . . .
. . . .
. . . .
. . . .
to move on to the next stage.

You have made a note on your script of what you now need to do to improve your investigational skills. Please include this in the space above.

7 Information Technology

2 You have word processed your work
4 You have desk-top published your work
6 and have imported graphics
8 and have used spreadsheets or databases.

Comments

Overall grade

2 3 4 5 6 8

Figure 8.6 Assessment of Year 7 water task

of expressive writing observed which appeared to engage pupils in more meaningful learning included a cartoon sequence produced by a Year 7 pupil to show the difference between melting and dissolving (see Figure 8.7) and an 'element' poem written by a Year 9 pupil (Figure 8.8).

Writing about experimental and investigative work

There is now greater emphasis on reporting and evaluating of experimental and investigative work. However, this type of writing is often difficult for younger pupils. The style required is much more formal and the content is often more abstract. It can be difficult for the pupil to decide who the reader might be and this can make the writing task more of a problem. Pupils are often unable to decide what is relevant and should be included and what is redundant and they find the evaluation stage particularly difficult. The style of writing demanded of the pupil is quite specific and most closely matches that of the professional scientist. Further to these difficulties, lack of experience of appropriate models can leave young writers floundering. Sutton (1992) showed that when pupils did not have a clear idea of the question being investigated they were unable to analyse the evidence of the results objectively or to draw accurate conclusions from the work. Many teachers try to help pupils overcome these difficulties by providing prompt sheets which structure the pupils' writing to the prescribed format. These may give structure, but can also be limiting. Examination boards have indicated that most teachers now use four or five tried and tested investigations for submission for their GCSE examination which are carried out at a predetermined time during the course. This method works well for examination purposes and with help pupils are able to achieve good enough levels to pass the course; however, the spirit of real experimental work and investigation is lost in the process

It may be felt that within the constraints of time and numbers in classes that such authentic work is really not possible. However, new materials such as those published by the Pupil Researcher Initiative or the British Ecological Society present to the teacher a range of ideas for pupils to carry out genuine investigative work which are accompanied by secondary sources. In order that pupils can write about their investigation work they must first have a working knowledge of the terminology, such as 'variable', 'value' and 'fair test', which are crucial to the report. The teacher must teach pupils to write in the language of the scientific report for this by providing examples, demonstrating how to do it and providing practice.

The first four units of the Cognitive Acceleration through Science Education (CASE) (Adey *et al.* 1989) material introduce these ideas through a series of exercises. These were observed in use in one school visited in the introductory stages of the Year 7 course. Later on, thinking skills were further developed in preparation for investigative work by using a series of activities to encourage the pupils to think critically. In an exercise to help pupils identify a conclusion they

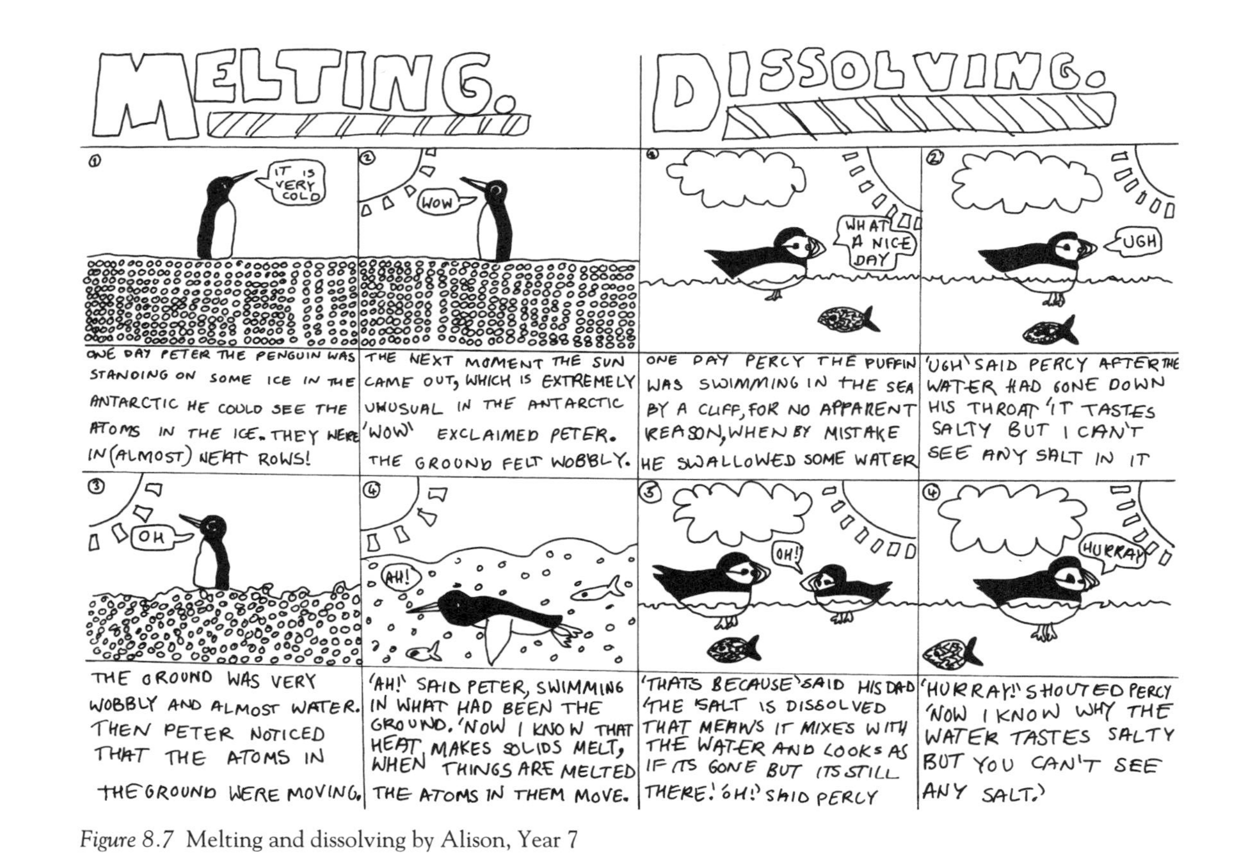

Figure 8.7 Melting and dissolving by Alison, Year 7

Mercury

I am mercury
Mad as the hatter
Just one of the 109
Wearing a top hat is a bad sign
Not Earth, Air or Fire
Thought I would make you immortal
But I am a liar
Iron will float
As gold will sink
I cannot make you think
I'm the poison in the chalice
But please don't tell Alice.

by: Stephanie Pritchard

Figure 8.8 'Element' poem by a Year 9 pupil

were given three statements which were the basis of a scientific argument but the connecting words such as *because*, *therefore* or *so* had been removed. The statements were jumbled and the pupils had to rearrange them into a logical coherent statement which would constitute a valid conclusion. In doing this they were learning how to use new strategies. What has to be remembered about these activities is that not only does the teacher need to teach the strategies but the pupils will need practice in drawing conclusions from whole investigative work.

Children learning through talk

It is a generally held belief that by talking through ideas, explaining them to someone else, the likelihood of learning taking place increases. Vygotsky wrote: 'it is the very struggle to convert half-formed ideas into articulated speech that crystallizes thought' (Vygotsky 1962: 119).

In a study of the nature of talk taking place in twenty science lessons, an analysis of the teacher–pupil talk showed that about two-thirds of this took the

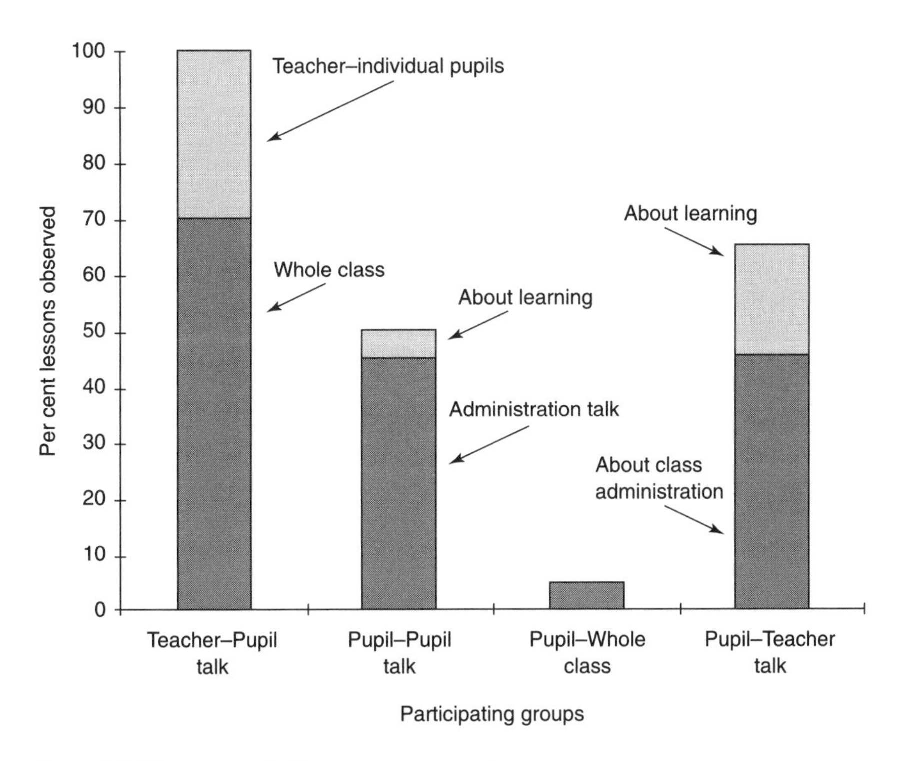

Figure 8.9 The nature of talk in twenty science lessons

form of whole class discussion (see Figure 8.9). Quite a lot of this 'discussion' matched Edwards' (1992) 'routines required of the communicatively competent pupil'. According to his portrayal the competent pupil should be able and willing to:

- listen to the teacher, often for long periods of time;
- bid properly for the right to speak, when the teacher stops talking, sometimes when competition for the next turn means balancing the risks of not being noticed against the risks of being ignored as too enthusiastic;
- answer questions to which the answer will be judged more or less relevant, useful and correct by a teacher who is seeking not to know something but to know whether you know something;
- put up with having anyone's answer treated as evidence of a common understanding or misunderstanding that the teacher will often explain something again when you understood it first time or rush on when you are still struggling with what was said before;
- look for clues as to what a right answer might be from the way a

teacher leads into a question, asks the question, and evaluates the responses – that last source of clues being often so prolific that even a wild guess may lead the teacher to answer the question for you;

- ask questions about the administration of the lesson but not usually about its content (and certainly never suggest that the teacher may be wrong);
- accept that what you know already about the topic of the lesson is unlikely to be asked for, or to be accepted as relevant, unless and until it fits into the teacher's frame of reference.

(Edwards 1992: 235–6)

When presented with this view, a number of experienced teachers agreed that Edwards' caricature was an extreme view but that it did have an unsettling ring of truth about it too. In response to this, teachers in one school decided to probe the idea further and to carry out peer observation, the focus being the effectiveness of teacher–pupil talk. For each whole class discussion of ten minutes or more the teacher-observer recorded the opportunities pupils had to contribute to the discussion, the nature and duration of their contribution and how each teacher initiated and responded to pupil talk in the class.

The observation exercise led the teachers to consider the pupil–pupil talk too. Fairly extensive research into this area of classroom interaction has already been carried out and reported in Bentley and Watts (1989). In this work, Key Stage 3 pupils' science classroom conversations were taped and analysed. The pupil–pupil talk recorded was found to be preoccupied with issues peripheral to learning, being concerned mainly with negotiating about apparatus or in talk which was not about the task in hand. Constructing meaning or talking about the issues did not occupy the pupils for much of the lesson time.

The results of the small action research project provoked the teachers to reconsider the nature of some parts of their science lessons and to work together to develop alternative activities which would allow pupils the opportunity to talk in a scientifically constructive way. It was decided that a pilot study involving planning and trialling of new lessons would be carried out with Year 9 after they had completed National Curriculum tests in early June. Each teacher planned a lesson in which pupils were required to work in small groups.

One teacher organised an activity intended to develop numeracy skills and to encourage pupils to think about ratios and proportionality. Small groups of four were asked to work on a series of problems. The groups were made up of two pupils who could confidently work with numbers and two who had less well-developed skills. Each group was asked to prepare a two-minute presentation explaining how they had arrived at the solution and every member of the group was required to make a contribution to this. The evaluation of the lesson showed in every group the talk concentrated on the problem and on the content of their group presentation. The more numerate pupils were found to be able to articulate ideas in less technical language than the teacher often used to explain the solution to the same problem. The less numerate pupils were able to contribute to the presentation quite confidently.

Another teacher planned a lesson in which pupils were asked to make decisions based on discussion. The context for the discussion was a fictitious Recycling City Council policy-making forum. The class was asked to divide into four smaller groups. Each pupil in the four small groups was given a different task. After a short period in this home group, pupils were then asked to form an expert group with all the other pupils who had the same task. After a suitable time period the 'experts' returned to their home group to represent their area of expertise in the Recycling City Council chamber. Each home group was asked to discuss the issues and to vote on the recommended course of action. The smaller home groups were reconvened into a whole class and all pupils then had the opportunity to make a contribution to the teacher-led whole class discussion.

The teacher evaluation of the lesson suggested that all pupils were involved in the expert group work because they needed to be fully conversant with the issues before returning to their home group. A pupil who was likely to distract others was selected as the Chair of each home group. The fairly onerous task of chairing a group of peers ensured that they too were always on task. The whole class discussion was easier to manage, as each pupil felt fully involved in the issues. In feedback, all the pupils said that they had also enjoyed and learned a lot from both lessons.

It seems obvious that pupils' learning in science will be enhanced significantly when greater attention is given to the development of written and spoken language. The teachers observed and reported in this chapter had taken the risk of moving outside the familiar science lesson framework. They worked with colleagues from other faculties to develop new strategies in their lesson and were rewarded by more enthusiastic pupils who seemed to have a better understanding of the key concepts introduced at Key Stage 3. Genuine communication of scientific ideas had not only raised levels of confidence and achievement in language and literacy, but also ensured that the pupils had a much firmer grasp of how science can help us ask and begin to answer questions about the world around us.

Acknowledgements:

Thanks to the teachers and pupils of the East Anglia schools who agreed to have their work reported here.

Note

1 All the data included in this chapter arise from research carried out by the author in classrooms in East Anglian secondary schools.

References

Adey, P., Shayer, M. and Yates, C. (1989) *Cognitive Acceleration through Science*, Walton-on-Thames: Nelson.

Ausubel, D. P. (1963) *The Psychology of Meaningful Learning*, Walton-on-Thames: Grune and Stratton.

Bentley, D. and Watts, M. (eds) (1989) *Learning and Teaching in School Science*, Buckingham: Open University Press.

Brook, A., Briggs, H. and Driver, R. (1984) *Aspects of Secondary Students' Understanding of the Particulate Nature of Matter*, Leeds: Leeds University Centre for Studies in Science and Mathematics Education.

Buzan, A. (1974) *Use your Head*, London: BBC Books.

Carey, J. (ed.) (1995) *The Faber Book of Science*, London: Faber and Faber.

Carre, C. (1981) *Language Teaching and Learning: Science*, London: Ward Lock Educational.

Edwards, T. 'Teacher Talk and Pupils' Competence' in K. Norman (ed.) (1992) *Thinking Voices*, London: Hodder and Stoughton.

Head, J. (1985) *The Personal Response to Science*, Cambridge: Cambridge University Press.

Johnstone, A. H. and El-Banna, H. (1986) 'Capacities, Demands and Processes – A Predictive Model for Science Education', *Education in Chemistry* 23 (3): 80–4.

Medawar, P. B. (1969) *Induction and Intuition in Scientific Thought*, London: Methuen.

Sheeran, Y. and Barnes, B. (1991) *School Writing*, Buckingham: Open University Press.

Sutton, C. R. (1989) in R. Millar, *Doing Science: Images of Science in Science Education*, London: Falmer Press.

Sutton, C. R. (ed.) (1991) *Communicating in the Classroom*, London: Hodder and Stoughton.

Sutton, C. R. (1992) *Words, Science and Learning*, Buckingham: Open University Press.

Vygotsky, L. (1962) *Thought and Language*, Cambridge, Mass.: MIT Press.

Wellington, J. (ed.) (1994) *Secondary Science: Contemporary Issues and Practical Approaches*, London: Routledge.

Woolnough, B. and Allsop, T. (1985) *Practical Work in Science*, Cambridge: Cambridge University Press.

9

DRAMA AND HISTORICAL WRITING AT KEY STAGE 3[1]

Paul Goalen

Drama is often used in progressive classrooms and at sites of historical interest to promote pupil engagement and to bring history alive. Indeed, the use of drama to promote oral work in history is now well known and widely practised, but there is less information on how drama can help develop children's historical writing. OFSTED has recently criticised pupils' writing in history at Key Stage 3, and writing has traditionally been seen in history as an end-product of learning, a means of proving that work has been done. This chapter describes a project that was designed to assess the contribution of drama to more effective learning in history, including writing used in the process of learning.

History teachers and the National Curriculum

The case for using educational drama to develop children's historical thinking is a strong one. In 1974, John Fines and Ray Verrier published *The Drama of History*, which became a source of pedagogical inspiration for history teachers in the UK. A few years later, Rogers and Aston (1977) demonstrated how the use of enactive learning on a site visit could make significant differences to children's understanding of the site. More recently Pond and Childs (1995) have shown how 'living history' events at historical sites can benefit pupils' historical understanding to a significant degree. My own research into the classroom use of educational drama to teach National Curriculum history also produced results which demonstrated that this type of learning can benefit children's developing historical understanding and knowledge to a degree that was statistically significant (Goalen and Hendy 1993). Furthermore, when this research is read alongside our growing understanding of the importance to pupils' learning of interaction and discussion (Cooper and McIntyre 1996a), and when it is remembered how many opportunities for interaction and discussion are provided by educational drama teaching strategies, then we should not hesitate to encourage our colleagues to pursue such approaches because of the way they promote engagement in the process of historical enquiry (Goalen and Hendy 1994).

However, on the face of it, the introduction of a National Curriculum for history posed a serious threat to the continuation of such pedagogical practices: an overcrowded programme of study, increased emphasis on the acquisition of historical knowledge and pressure from the Right predicted a return to traditional teaching methods. Phillips (1993), for example, reported that 90 per cent of Key Stage 3 teachers in his sample felt there was insufficient time for varied teaching and learning activities in the new curriculum. Cooper and McIntyre (1996a) also reported that history teachers feared that content overload would lead to transmission styles of teaching and an end to more engaging pedagogies. Teachers were in effect experiencing the double blow of loss of autonomy in terms of control over syllabus construction, and demotivation caused by content overload:

> To cover the content there will have to be more teacher-led lessons. More didactic teaching will result unless the issue of time is addressed.
>
> My fear is that the amount of content will necessitate 'teacher driven' delivery rather than pupil centred tasks.
>
> (Teachers quoted by Phillips 1991)

However, recent research suggests that, as teachers became used to operating within the framework of the National Curriculum, they became adept at interpreting it and so developing a sense of ownership over it (Bage 1993). Indeed, my own data derived from interviews with heads of history in a quarter of a county's state secondary schools suggest that, while many teachers did indeed experience a sense of loss and pain during the initial period of implementing the new curriculum, they nevertheless clung on to their inner core of beliefs concerning teaching styles (particularly the use of drama, about which they were being interviewed) and put such methods back into practice as soon as they felt they were in control of and had internalised the new curriculum (Goalen 1995).

The heads of history interviewed had retained their commitment to using drama to teach history through the torrid experience of implementing the centrally controlled curriculum and demonstrated to me the extent to which it was being practised in their departments. Moreover, they justified the use of this pedagogic operation in terms of the social and educational objectives which they believed drama helped to foster and which may be summarised as follows:

- the acquisition of historical knowledge;
- the development of historical skills, including empathy and interpretations of the past;
- the development of an appreciation of history through the high levels of enjoyment and engagement experienced through drama;
- the promotion of equal opportunities and the development of individual self-esteem.

(Goalen 1995)

The relationship between educational drama and pupils' historical thinking

Effective teaching and learning depends in part on the skill of the teacher in constructing a context that will support learning. The definition of that context was what concerned us in a piece of classroom research with Year 6 and Year 8 pupils in 1994, in which we took a framing model for educational drama developed by Dorothy Heathcote and adapted it for history teachers, using educational drama strategies to teach National Curriculum history. What we found was that educational drama provides the teacher with situations that help to promote discussion and to clarify ideas and points of view, whilst also enabling teachers to lead pupils to a point where they can take on the role of a historian as a commentator on, and critic of, evidence and interpretations. Our adaptation of the Heathcote model is reproduced here as Figure 9.1.

The model casts the pupils as researchers and illustrates five ways in which distance framing enables history teachers to refocus an enquiry according to the frame chosen. Each frame has a clearly defined purpose and opens up the possibility of using a wider range of educational drama strategies than many history teachers may currently be familiar with. Although not strictly hierarchical, the *questioner* and *clarifier* frames are the essential building blocks on which all pupil research must be based in order to reach the higher level skills encapsulated in the other three frames.

An essential feature of the *questioner* frame is the use of language in discussion and we noted at least three forms of discussion appropriate to this frame. The first form of discussion is teacher-directed, whole-class discussion, where a new topic is introduced or where we wish to refocus a topic in mid-session. Our technique in these introductory sessions was to make use of the overhead projector to display sources for the pupils to discuss. This approach supported a clear focus on the evidence so that the drama was based on historical sources rather than flights of fancy, and we found that pictorial sources were particularly useful for such discussion. Indeed, such discussion showed how:

> Language objectifies reality and makes possible the transmission of meaning (and its evaluation) across generations who share common concepts. It is through language that meanings and concepts are reproduced and made enduring, and it is through language that such meanings and concepts are modified or replaced, in response to social change.
>
> (Bruner and Haste 1987: 5)

A second form of discussion is undirected pupil-led discussion where groups devise dramatic scenes based on their understanding of historical evidence. An example of this kind of discussion comes from a Year 8 class we had asked to work in groups to produce three or four freeze-frames to depict one aspect of Charles I's

	Frames	*Drama strategies*	*Examples of use*
P U P I L S A S R E S E A R C H E R S	**Questioner**: the event is reconstructed because it helps to raise questions and provoke discussion	Still image Whole group-in-role Small group work Teacher-in-role Prepared scenes Mimed activities	Using a series of still images or freeze frames, small groups reconstructed an aspect of Charles I's Eleven Years' Tyranny. Through small group work, pupils reconstructed the black immigrant's view of finding accommodation and getting a job.
	Clarifier: the ideas / views of the people in the event are played in order to clarify the ideas and interpretations	Whole group-in-role Small group work Teacher-in-role Collective role-play Tunnel of conscience	The class was divided into two lines representing the Royalists and the Parliamentarians. Four pupils are chosen to walk through the tunnel. As they pass, each side must give reasons why the four undecided should join their side. Two pupils reconstruct the meeting between immigrant and factory manager. Two other pupils play their thoughts, revealing the reasons for their utterances.
	Alternating viewpoint: the reconstructed event is played from different points of view to question different interpretations	Whole group-in-role Small group work Teacher-in-role Prepared scenes Thought tracking	Whole group-in-role as MPs reconstruct two versions of the arrest of the five MPs by Charles I. Teacher describes the events as if talking to a friend or as if reporting to the king. Teacher-in-role as reporter. Small groups representing families during the Great Depression show the different viewpoints of the employed and unemployed.
	Commentator: a commentary is provided to give reasons why the event might have occurred and help make a judgement based on evidence	Whole group-in-role Small group work Thoughts in the head Hot-seating Ghosts	Individually or in pairs, pupils come as ghosts from Cromwell's past to his deathbed and give reasons for liking or not liking him. In small groups, pupils make a series of photographs to show what happened on the Jarrow march.
	Critical historian: evidence and interpretations are challenged to arrive at an informed understanding of the event	Mantle of the expert Teacher-in-role Documentary	Pupils divided into three groups at a history seminar: one group puts forward the pro-martyr theory, another the pro-traitor theory, whilst a third acts as questioners. In groups, pupils develop a documentary about immigration from different viewpoints.

Figure 9.1 History distancing frames with drama strategies

Eleven Years' Tyranny. The group whose conversation is reported below were trying to work out how to portray the Puritan reaction to Charles I's policies and they were working from a range of primary sources including a woodcut of Archbishop Laud eating Puritans' ears for dinner:

P1: How did he put the three Puritans on trial? How did he obtain the three Puritans? What did he do to get them?
P2: We got the Puritan church, the torture.
P1: Yeh, but I just want to know how did he get them to cut off their ears and stuff?
Teacher: You mean how he caught them?
P1: Yes.
Teacher: I don't know. Possibly by some sort of trick.
P3: Are we doing the church with them all listening?
P4: Are we doing the Puritan church or are we doing the Catholic church?
P1: Puritan.
P2: The boring one.
P4: So we are all going like that and listening.
P3: And someone comes in and chops your ears off, yeh?
P1 No!

Here the *challenge of drama* (Goalen and Hendy 1992: 26) was forcing this group into grappling with issues they might well have left to their more articulate classmates in a more formal setting, and the undirected discussion helped them sort out some misconceptions before they devised and presented their *freeze-frames* to the rest of the class.

The third form of discussion we identified is perhaps the most important in terms of developing children's historical thinking because in the plenary discussions that followed the drama we were able to explore issues raised through the drama and deal with the questions it provoked in the minds of the pupils. Sometimes the results were quite striking, as when we taught the Aztecs to a Year 5 class, some of whom were able to operate at levels 6 to 8 in the pre-Dearing levels of attainment for history. For example, when discussing the death of Montezuma, the Aztec emperor, we raised the issue of motive and in whose interests it was to pin the blame for Montezuma's death on either Cortes or the Aztecs:

Teacher: Who might have wanted us to believe that Cortes killed Montezuma?
P1: The Spaniards because they wanted him to be great.
P2: Cortes might have done it, if he was paid for it; if someone wanted him dead . . .
P3: The Aztecs because they wanted Cortes to go to prison.
P4: In all the [versions of the story] it was Cortes who set Montezuma up so it was actually his fault.

P5: The Aztecs because they wouldn't want people to think that they killed Montezuma.

Teacher: So in whose interests is it to put the blame on the Aztecs? Who might have wanted us to believe that it was the Aztecs who threw the stones that killed Montezuma?

P6: Cortes because he doesn't want the blame.

P7: The Aztecs would want to put the blame on Cortes because they would be afraid that the gods might be angry with them.

These children were beginning to make judgements about the reliability and value of historical sources by reference to the circumstances in which they were produced, because they had just enacted four different versions of Montezuma's death. Such high-level thinking from Year 5 children suggested to us that drama was providing a very favourable context for the development of pupils' historical thinking since it helped to make the sources accessible to them and raised issues for historical debate.

We also discovered that the pupils found that drama helped to clarify issues and ideas that they were studying. For example, we used the *clarifier* frame with the Year 8 class, to introduce some of the political ideas of the Puritan Revolution by dividing the class into four groups, each of which had to take on the role of either Levellers, Diggers, Fifth Monarchists or Women.[2] The ideas of each group were then exposed to question and comment by the rest of the class and the pupils found this helped them to understand the history: *It was quite fun doing that because we had to decide what to do and think about what to say* (Year 8 pupil). In addition, they claimed it helped them with their homework and the following example of a pupil's written homework shows how the drama had helped in handling abstract concepts and making historical judgements:

> There was a time in the mid-seventeenth century when people say the world was 'turned upside down'. Of course this didn't happen physically but at the time there was a big muddle as to how England could be made into a perfect society.
>
> Many people believed that the execution of Charles would establish a perfect society, but this was not achieved. It only sent up an uproar and really it caused the big muddle. But I think it was still a good thing that Charles was killed, because Cromwell was, in my opinion, a better leader and if Charles wasn't killed I hate to think about where we would be now.
>
> (Year 8 pupil)

Drama and pupils' historical writing

Much work has therefore been done to show how drama may help to develop historical thinking. In the main, this research has focused on oral responses, so this chapter focuses on pupils' writing. For, if writing is built into the active learning programme and incorporated within a coherent framework of whole class teaching, small group work, drama learning frames, discussion, and written homework assignments, then drama can indeed be said to help to develop historical writing.

OFSTED's report on school history based on the inspection findings of 1993/4 drew to the attention of the history teaching profession that pupils' standards are often higher in oral work than in written work (OFSTED 1995). This weakness was noted in Key Stages 2 and 3, for only in Key Stage 4 were pupils found to be doing much extended writing:

> In a significant number of lessons, even where standards were in other ways satisfactory, poor achievement was characterised by responses which lacked factual detail, were directly copied from the textbook or other reference books, or which did not go beyond the literal comprehension of sources. In a number of cases where pupils achieved high standards orally, this was not replicated in written work. Extended writing, and particularly writing in response to investigation or open questioning, was infrequent – particularly at Key Stage 3.
>
> (OFSTED 1995: 7)

Whilst researching the development of pupils' historical writing, I found it useful to keep in mind Bruner's three modes of representation as well as the history distancing frames we had developed in the earlier research. Bruner defines *ikonic*, *enactive* and *symbolic* modes of representation and suggests that mastery of all three is integral to intellectual development (Bruner 1966). My method was to begin each session with a discussion of the relevant historical sources with a focus on the pictorial (ikonic) evidence, which is often more accessible than written sources and therefore useful for introductory classroom discussion. This evidence was presented on overhead transparencies so that the pupils could gather round the screen to discuss clear and enlarged images of the relevant painting or print, and written sources could be fed in when the discussion or pupils' questions made them relevant. I would then introduce some drama learning frames to provide a context for them to explore their own and each other's understanding of the sources we had been discussing, at which point they would be working within Bruner's enactive mode. Finally, I would set a written homework which challenged them to operate within Bruner's symbolic mode by exploring through writing specific historical questions and issues. Figure 9.2 presents an outline plan of this process leading to a homework on the Peasants' Revolt which required the pupils to write a speech for John Ball on the causes of the revolt.

This homework produced some delightful empathetic responses from the pupils who were expected as part of the assignment to think about the distinction between long-term and short-term causation as well as how to present the

Drama learning frame or activity	*Drama strategies and resources*	*Description of activities*
1 **Teacher directed discussion** on the causes of the Peasants' Revolt	OHTs on the causes of the Peasants' Revolt	Emphasise in the discussion the long-term causes and short-term causes paying particular attention to the Poll Tax.
2 **Questioner**: the event is reconstructed because it helps to raise questions and provoke discussion	Whole-group-in-role Teacher-in-role	Villagers meet to discuss the expected arrival of royal commissioners collecting the Poll Tax. They listen to an itinerant preacher who has news of the collection from elsewhere; they ask the friar questions about tax collecting in 1381.
3 **Clarifier**: the ideas/views of the people in the event are played in order to clarify the ideas and interpretations	Small group work Prepared scenes	In groups of four, pupils discuss how to prepare the scene where the commissioner arrives to assess the Poll Tax at the village. Pupils rehearse their scenes.
4 **Alternating viewpoint**: the reconstructed event is played from different points of view to question different interpretations	Teacher-in-role Playback prepared scenes with some improvisation	The teacher-in-role as the tax collector interviews the groups who have prepared how they will receive the tax collector. Out-of-role discussion on the different interpretations enacted by each group.
5 **Commentator**: a commentary is provided to give reasons why the event might have occurred and help make a judgement based on evidence	Hot-seating Teacher-in-role	Pupils hot-seat John Ball, the leader of the Kent rebels, just before his execution. Then try to find out more about the causes of the rebellion and the events of the rebellion itself, while John Ball offers a commentary on the rebellion with the benefit of hindsight.

Figure 9.2 History through drama: planning grid

material in a lively and fresh format. The requirement to shape and use their knowledge of the period was made explicit and although not all the pupils were able to meet all the expectations, the challenge of producing a speech was met by the whole class with some striking successes, as the following example shows:

> Friends, I have come to address you for the very last time. By this time in a few days I will be dead from being hung, drawn and quartered. A horrible death, as I'm sure you'll agree. And what for? Why did we waste our efforts just for our leaders to die gruesome deaths? I'll tell you. It was because we, the serfs, wanted equality, the right to be the same as everyone else. All our lives we have lived in squalid, cramped conditions, and why? So people like the hated poll tax collectors can live in luxury and eat fine foods from silver platters, drinking fine wines, while we have to make do with coarse black bread, wooden plates and water. [The poll tax collectors] who, as you know, were another reason for the revolt by trying to extract every last coin from us. The amount was too high, it was unfair, they came too often. Are these the actions of fair men? We have had a bit of a hold over the rich, especially after the Black Death, when there was only a few peasants to work. Then we could demand payment or threaten to move elsewhere. The Statute of Labourers was too outrageous. They said they were angry because we wouldn't work for free! We were probably more angry than them though. To try and make us work for less than 2d a day! To try to treat us like the dogs in their manors! We foiled that plan however. Also the King said he would lead us in the place of the valiant Wat Tyler, who suffered so horribly under the cruel blade of the Mayor of Smithfield, taking us back to our villages, only to send his men to capture the so-called 'ringleaders'! He who we trusted above all others. I ask you, I plead with you, to carry on the revolt after my death. Farewell, and thank you.
>
> (Morag, Year 7)

In this passage Morag successfully uses her knowledge of John Ball's sermon to the peasants at Blackheath, the Poll Tax, the Statute of Labourers, and the events of the rebellion itself to put together a lively and informative speech which was also honest to the historical record as revealed to the pupils. The writing is clearly imaginative but it is also firmly rooted in the evidence that was available to them for study; and crucially, in between the first examination of the sources and the writing had come the educational drama which had been used not for filling gaps in the evidence or for flights of fancy, but in order to illuminate the historical record and to make the sources meaningful and accessible to the pupils.

Levine suggests that more advanced historical writing depends on the ability to classify information by searching for themes and ways of grouping information, and then organising these themes and groupings into paragraphs (Levine 1981). Some shaping of the material has of course taken place in Morag's work above, but I also set several homeworks which were designed to encourage pupils to analyse the sources in a more formal way. Once again the same process was adopted of introductory whole class teaching with a focus on pictorial evidence, followed by small group work, drama learning frames, plenary discussion and written assignments for homework, and I then set about gathering evidence for pupils' extended writing, probabilistic reasoning, and extensive commentary on the evidence in answer to a particular question (Goalen 1996).

One of the homeworks on the Black Death encouraged the pupils to go beyond the factual content of the sources to make some assessment of the likely impact of contemporary ideas on prevention and cure. They were asked:

- How did those who lived through the Black Death try to prevent and cure the disease?
- How successful do you think they were?

Many pupils responded by describing the various methods adopted for prevention and cure and it was refreshing to see how few of them followed the wording of the sources and how some were able to clearly shape the material into the themes of prevention, cure and success. The following example shows a pupil organising the material well and commenting on the likely success of the measures employed as she wrote, rather than with a summary comment at the end:

> Some doctors said the lumps on the groin and armpits should be burnt off like ulcers or softened with figs and should then be rubbed with a mixture of onions, butter and yeast. One doctor tried this and survived the plague. . . . Many people burnt attractive flowers and sweet smelling wood in the hope that the smell would drive away the disease. As a precaution many people took a sweet smelling apple out with them. . . . People with power often ordered the streets of a town to be cleaned up. This was very effective as all the rubbish could be traced down to the cause of the plague.
>
> (Katie, Year 7)

This extract from quite a long answer, together with other quality answers in the data, suggests that teachers should not be frightened into abandoning active learning when OFSTED implores them to set more assignments that require extended writing. On the contrary, the adoption of a more restricted diet of formal teaching strategies could quickly result in sterile responses lacking in both historical imagination and analytical skill as pupils opt out intellectually from the learning process. Drama, on the other hand, when it is included as part of a coherent teaching strategy which is both intellectually honest and challenging, enables pupils to engage with the issues and evidence in a manner which enhances both oral competence and writing skills.

Conclusion

Recent research by Wallace (1996) reminds us that work for Years 7 and 8 pupils needs to be intrinsically interesting because the instrumentalism of Years 9, 10 and 11 seems a long way off to the average lower secondary student. Drama helps to provide this interest by engaging the pupils in the learning process and introducing them to new sources, ideas and concepts with which they can grapple at their own level in pairs and small groups. Indeed, by providing opportunities for small group discussion, drama helps pupils to come to terms with new meaning:

> In practice, of course, we do not simply listen to the words and derive their meaning from these alone. We try to make sense of them by treating them to memory, knowledge and association. We make them 'mean' by locating them in our known world.
>
> (Bruner and Haste 1987: 15)

Furthermore, the success of drama in developing historical thinking and writing must in part be due to the transactional nature of drama, to the fact that control over the content and direction of lessons is shared between pupils and teachers in different ways (Cooper and McIntyre 1996b), for pupils in drama do make real contributions to the lesson and help to lift sessions that might otherwise be taught in a mundane or routine way through transmission styles of teaching. Indeed, Cullingford (1991) found that pupils saw much of the secondary curriculum as routine and that subjects like history and geography failed to make the impact that practical subjects made because they did not have the same level of engagement. Teaching history through drama provides that level of engagement which enables pupils to master new forms of knowledge in an exciting and thought-provoking arena.

Notes

1 Some passages from this chapter were printed in an earlier paper: P. Goalen (1996) 'The Development of Children's Historical Thinking through Drama', *Teaching History* 83: 19–26.
2 For a discussion of the other history distancing frames see Goalen and Hendy (1994).

References

Bage, G. (1993) 'History at Key Stage 1 and Key Stage 2: Questions of Teaching, Planning, Assessment and Progression', *The Curriculum Journal* 4(2): 269–82.

Bruner, J. (1966) *Towards a Theory of Instruction*, Cambridge, Mass.: Harvard University Press.

Bruner, J. and Haste, H. (1987) *Making Sense: The Child's Construction of the World*, London: Methuen.

Cooper, P. and McIntyre, D. (1996a) *Effective Teaching and Learning*, Buckingham: Open University Press.

Cooper, P. and McIntyre, D. (1996b) 'The Importance of Power Sharing in Classroom Learning' in M. Hughes *Teaching and Learning in Changing Times*, Oxford: Blackwell.

Cullingford, C. (1991) *The Inner World of the School*, London: Cassell.

Fines, J. and Verrier, R. (1974) *The Drama of History*, London: New University Education.

Goalen, P. (1995) 'Twenty Years of History through Drama', *The Curriculum Journal* 6(1): 63–77.

Goalen, P. (1996) 'Educational Drama and Children's Historical Writing: Process and Product', *The Curriculum Journal* 7(1): 75–91.

Goalen, P. and Hendy, L. (1992) 'The Challenge of Drama; An Historical Investigation', *Teaching History* 69: 26–33.

Goalen, P. and Hendy, L. (1993) 'It's Not Just Fun It Works! Developing Children's Historical Thinking through Drama', *The Curriculum Journal* 4(3): 363–84.

Goalen, P. and Hendy, L. (1994) 'History through Drama: The Development of Distance Framing for the Purposes of Historical Inquiry', *Curriculum* 15(3): 147–62.

Levine, N. (1981) *Language Teaching and Learning: 5. History*, London: Ward Lock Educational.

OFSTED (1995) *History: A Review of Inspection Findings 1993/4*, London: HMSO.

Phillips, R. (1991) 'National Curriculum History and Teacher Autonomy: The Major Challenge', *Teaching History* 65: 21–4.

Phillips, R. (1993) 'Change and Continuity: Some Reflections on the First Year's Implementation of Key Stage 3 History in the National Curriculum', *Teaching History* 70: 9–12.

Pond, M. and Childs, A. (1995) 'Do Children Learn from Living History Projects?' *The Curriculum Journal* 6(1): 47–62.

Rogers, P. J. and Aston, F. (1977) 'Play, Enactive Representation and Learning', *Teaching History* 19: 18–21.

Wallace, G. (1996) 'Engaging with Learning' in J. Rudduck *et al.* (1996) *School Improvement: What Can Pupils Tell Us?* London: David Fulton.

Part 4

DEVELOPING A CRITICAL EYE

> What is needed is a judicious attitude: scrupulous to understand, alert to probe for blind spots and hidden agendas, and finally, critical, questioning, skeptical.
>
> (Scholes 1985: 16)

Many adults would agree. Any nation wants its young people to become citizens who will not accept things blindly. However, there is a gap between those wishes and the ways schools and curricula operate. Evidence from OFSTED suggests that there is still too much dependence on a 'transmission' model of teaching and learning. If 'knowledge' is seen as fact-gathering and success is determined by the extent to which a pupil can re-tell the content of the curriculum, then the possibilities for developing alert, judicious and critically literate young people is put seriously in jeopardy. This part of the book builds on all the issues which earlier parts have identified as significant factors influencing the development of robust and versatile language users. To adopt a judicious point of view means coming to know that language is not value-free – and being able to debate values through language. The ability to remain alert to hidden messages and gaps in texts – both spoken and written – is the result of thoughtful teaching. Classroom methods, which acknowledge the active ways in which young people already use the language of home and community, offer a firm foundation for building critical literacy. In their turn, school managers have to make it possible for teachers to work on developing teaching approaches which use language as a process towards constructing knowledge. This means affording time for teachers to reflect on their practices and professional aims. The development of proper scepticism in pupils can only come about if teachers and pupils alike have opportunities for reflection.

There are connections between the ways in which adults and children learn. All learners – whether teachers or pupils – need to start from a position of assurance before they can first develop a critical view of other people's ideas, but then have the confidence to turn the critical eye inwards. This returns to some of the preoccupations of the contributors to Part 3 and to one significant difference between the position in secondary schools of the Bullock era and today. Current attention to language and literacy practices now focuses much more on methods of teaching. As far as teachers are concerned, though, developing a critical view is not a straightforward matter. There can be no single 'best' way of teaching, just as there are many different ways in to learning. At times whole class instruction is necessary; at others, paired or group work will help make the learning take root; at others individual reflection or evaluation is best. Variety of approach is essential if teachers are to cater for the variety of curriculum demands and the diversity of pupils who enter their classrooms. However, the necessary moves towards more varied approaches in the organisation of teaching and learning can seem threatening to classroom order and discipline and to endanger getting through the curriculum. A closer look at methods is essential in finding ways of raising standards of achievement both in learning in general and in pupils' versatility with language.

Recently there has been a shift towards considering how pupils learn, rather than simply considering how teachers should teach. This has led to a much more analytically constructive approach to managing the ways in which learning goes on. Teachers who have set out deliberately to develop more effective teaching and learning practices in their own subject areas comment on the role of language in learning. Whether starting by looking at learning and finding language pivotal, or starting with language and developing theories of learning, it has become clear that the two operate reciprocally. The Use of Language documents trace links between the different modes of language and what pupils learn:

> All lessons include, and largely depend on, oral and written communication. The teacher's role in explaining, questioning, describing, organising and evaluating in the classroom is mostly conducted through talk, and sometimes writing. Pupils are often answering, discussing and working out ideas through talk, and they commonly write in order to record, summarise, note, show evidence of understanding and develop ideas and arguments. To be successful learners, pupils need to read in order to gain access to information and ideas from a range of texts and sources and to evaluate them.
>
> (SCAA 1997a: 6)

This somewhat instrumental view of the relationship between language and learning points to the role which language plays in learning. SCAA firmly links subject teaching with the development of language, asking two questions:

> In what ways can work in other subjects help develop speaking, listening, reading and writing skills?

> How can pupils' understanding of English be enhanced by their work in other subjects?
>
> (SCAA 1997b: 1)

In order that their pupils can learn successfully, teachers need to pay attention to English. Paying attention to English directs teachers' attention towards the ways in which learning takes shape through language. This means that methods of getting to grips with the content of different subjects become more like scaffolding learning than the traditional transmission model. In other words, when teachers get to understand just how language contributes to learning, they take a more 'constructivist' view of teacher intervention. Attention to language can bring about more systematic approaches to the processes of learning and to ways in which the different texts involved in the separate subject areas can best be understood.

Opportunities for reflection

Teachers commonly identify *having the chance to reflect on practice* as a significantly valuable aspect of inservice work or school-based professional development. Such experiences can help to quiet the twin fears – about content and control – which teachers express when challenged to change their practice. As part of their work for the National Oracy Project, one group of teachers in Mid Glamorgan used video evidence from their own classrooms as a basis for reflecting on practice. Philip Jackson, the project co-ordinator, describes the teachers' initial fears about collaborative groupwork in classrooms:

> There is clearly much enthusiasm here and a belief that this is a valid way in which to operate, and yet, maybe two basic, and recurring inhibitions get in the way:
>
> **Content**
> How do I manage to deliver the content of my course in the allotted time, and most effectively?
>
> **Control**
> Will children deflect from the task, mess about, waste time etc . . .?
>
> (Jackson 1991: 16)

An extract from a transcript shows one teacher's view:

> When I came back from our meeting last time I sat down and asked myself 'What is groupwork all about?' If I'm going to do group work what am I looking for?' And I came up with the idea, that was very definite in my mind, that instead of the teacher giving the information, by a groupwork process they had to come up with the information for

> themselves, by helping each other, and supporting each other, and managing their own group. . . . And really all you're doing is supporting, and giving them as much confidence as you can. Now, when you look at the video, it's obvious to me that I have not given them enough freedom to go on and do it; I'm continually guiding and calling them back to me . . . I found it very difficult to let go.
>
> (Jackson 1991: 14)

This very honest appraisal of her own teaching captures a moment of reflection about language – the group are looking at talk in their classrooms – which in fact leads to the much wider consideration of teaching and learning approaches. What this group found was what contributors to this book have already indicated, that learning is, in fact, more likely to take root if pupils have the chance not only to build their own knowledge but to reflect on it too. One humanities teacher commented about a Year 7 class:

> There was an incredible amount of discussion and constructive argument. When I brought them together again we heard the final versions, but each was followed by a class evaluation of how well the evidence had been used, and each group was allowed a right of reply. . . . Any worries I might have had about children opting out had gone . . . all the groups were working well together adding details to accounts . . . many of the children seemed to grow in confidence . . . strict timing and clear structure seem important to the success of much groupwork.
>
> (Jackson 1991: 16)

This is not to suggest that developing more opportunities for reflection will magically transform classrooms into productive, harmonious working environments. However, what is clear, as Part 3 outlined, is that attention to language is deeply bound up with more dynamic and developmental models of teaching and learning. Further to that, an essential part of a developmental model of learning is the importance of reflection. The process of learning – both for teachers and pupils – depends on being able to see where we have been. As Jerome Bruner puts it: 'Much of the process of education consists of being able to distance oneself in some way from what one knows by being able to reflect on one's knowledge' (Bruner 1986: 127).

How can teachers create that distance? In explaining work on structuring learning, Peter Forrestal gives sensible warnings about apparently straightforward sequences being more complex than a list suggests. He offers the following model of the learning process: Engagement, Exploration, Transformation, Presentation, Reflection. Whilst, of course, the first four components of learning are important, Forrestal emphasises the value of reflection, which he stresses *can come at any stage of the learning process*. Pointing out that 'reflection may well become the starting point for a new cycle of learning', he comments:

> Reflection has a significant part to play in the learning process, if teachers are concerned with pupils accommodating new information into what they already know. Reflecting on what they have learned and the way in which they have handled the learning process will help pupils deepen their understanding of the process of learning.
>
> (Forrestal 1992: 164–5)

Reflection aids both teachers and pupils as they turn an interrogative eye on their own teaching and learning. This part of the book examines how opportunities for reflection might be built in to the fabric of regular learning. However, reflection alone is not enough to develop the probing, sceptical citizens of Robert Scholes' depiction. A further question needs to be asked: when does reflection become critique?

Looking critically at texts

How do pupils learn to talk or write critically about learning? One of the first steps is for them to take on a vocabulary of evaluation and this has to be introduced to them. The development of a metalanguage – a way of talking about language – depends on learners being introduced to specific vocabulary and evaluative processes.

A properly critical approach to text needs to be built up through deliberate planned teaching. Development of a judicious attitude depends on pupils' experience of both the texts and processes of language. The model of English on page 6 illustrates the integration of these in language and literacy learning. In order to increase knowledge of the systems and structures of language and texts, learners have to become adept at taking in and communicating information and ideas, but most particularly they have to move steadily towards developing a more discriminating view of the texts they confront or are confronted with. Both Richard Hickman and Liz Mellor in Chapters 10 and 11 identify the move towards a vocabulary of discrimination as essential to learning – in their two cases, of learning in the arts. However, as Liz Mellor points out: 'the language of evaluation goes beyond the vocabulary of the subject.' Becoming properly critical is a genuinely cross-curricular process.

Language moves learning forward. As Richard Hickman points out in Chapter 10: 'Language helps us to make our ideas real; by voicing our thoughts and by writing them down, we are able to realise them and place them into our existing conceptual matrix and reflect upon them.' Importantly, the reflective and evaluative functions of language move learning from mere acquisition towards understanding. A traditional approach to learning as fact-gathering can lead to an over-emphasis on the cognitive aspects of learning, or a too technical or sanitised view of language. Liz Mellor indicates the dangers of this kind of approach, pointing out that 'language not only describes and labels, but also generates knowledge and understanding'. Learning the vocabulary of criticism does not end when a learner can name all the elements of music, art or any other subject. In Liz Mellor's words, *naming is not knowing*. Both Hickman and Mellor see the teacher's role as pivotal in moving young people through newly learned terminology towards discriminating judgements. However, concepts and information are rarely developed without some personal commitment to learning – a link between the cognitive and the affective. Recent attention to the processes of learning has also stressed the significance of experience, both a learner's past experience and the validity of active engagement with learning – *experiential* learning. The chapters in this part of the book focus on reflective and evaluative approaches as a means of examining the importance of experience as well as the affective and cognitive domains of learning.

The documents *Art and the Use of Language* and *Music and the Use of Language* make links between the affective, cognitive and experiential aspects of learning. Both see reflective uses of language as a way of 'making pupils' understanding explicit' (SCAA 1997c: 1; 1997d: 1). In many subject areas, the use of a work log or journal serves to give the teacher insight into the pupils' processes of thinking as well as being the means for the learners to work out their own developing ideas and find out what they know. This can be particularly enlightening in those subjects where writing is not seen as a usual element of the regular work. One teacher who used diaries as part of his PE teaching in a secondary school wrote:

> The diversity of pupil response has been enlightening and has led me to question some of my practice and be self-critical. It has made me aware that there is plenty we can do to improve our teaching. Pupils' and teachers' perceptions often differ as to what they think they have been doing. In my case it has led to wider use of a variety of teaching styles, with greater emphasis on pupil input and response in lessons.
>
> (North 1989: 50)

Reflections and evaluations of learning not only give a window into the process of a pupil's learning but also help teachers in planning for future work. In journals where the teacher writes a response, there is the opportunity to give individual feedback on a pupil's learning. Reflective evaluation can also help teachers in the assessments they have to make. Nevertheless, the use of reflective writing – or talking – is problematic. Phil Jackson outlines the dangers of assuming that all teachers will have the same view of what 'reflection and evaluation' mean:

> For example, the English teacher who is co-ordinating the Language and Learning initiative may have a pretty clear notion in her/his head about what is meant by 'reflection' and the kinds of language behaviour to accompany the process. Ideas of respect for others' ideas, and quietly challenging debate about a range of equally valid options, for example.

> Possibly, one is thinking of pupils having the opportunity to write, or speak, in an almost confessional mode, about how they felt while undertaking an assignment, or what they felt they have learned in an inward sense. But are such notions compatible with what technology calls 'evaluation'? Not necessarily . . . [1]

One way of establishing shared understanding about reflection and evaluation is through teachers themselves using writing to reflect on teaching and learning. To Ian Terrell and Gill Venn, 'the key to understanding achievement is through staff development'. They outline ways in which reflective evaluation can form part of a process of professional development.

In examining the elements of successful learning, the contributors to Part 4 add another important ingredient to the cognitive, affective and experiential – the cultural aspects of learning. These include not only giving value to the cultural experience and knowledge which pupils bring from home, but of understanding the importance of peer culture, seeing how teachers' and pupils' cultures interact and acknowledging the power of classroom and school cultures. If information is to become understanding through the process of learning, reflection and evaluation, then the friction of negotiations, accommodations – or agreements to differ – is essential.

Future citizens need to be in a position where they can genuinely develop a critical eye. They need to understand that all texts are composed by people who hold opinions, even if these are well hidden. For this they need the experience of hammering out views and values, not just gaining access to information and evaluating it, but making their own knowledge and understanding and in a process of rigorous scrutiny being able to justify, defend – and, if necessary, reject – it. For pupils to be able to do this they need to follow the models and examples of teachers who have also developed a critical view of their own practice.

Note

1 Phil Jackson, personal communication whilst thinking through some of the inservice issues for Use of Language/Language and Learning initiatives.

References

Bruner, J. (1986) *Actual Minds, Possible Worlds*, London: Harvard University Press.

Forrestal, Peter (1992) 'Structuring the Learning Experience' in Kate Norman (ed.) *Thinking Voices: The Work of the National Oracy Project*, London: Hodder and Stoughton.

Jackson, P. (ed.) (1991) *'We only talked . . . ': Groups and Collaborations and Talking about Reading*, Bridgend: Mid Glamorgan Oracy Project.

North, Charles (1989) 'Profiling in PE' in National Writing Project *Writing and Learning*, Walton-on-Thames: Nelson/National Writing Project.

Scholes, Robert (1985) *Textual Power*, London: Yale University Press.

School Curriculum and Assessment Authority (1997a) *Use of language: A Common Approach*, London: SCAA.

School Curriculum and Assessment Authority (1997b) *English and the use of language requirement in other subjects*, London: SCAA.

School Curriculum and Assessment Authority (1997c) *Art and the Use of Language*, London: SCAA.

School Curriculum and Assessment Authority (1997d) *Music and the Use of Language*, London: SCAA.

10

REACT, RESEARCH, RESPOND AND REFLECT

Language and learning in art

Richard Hickman

The 'language of art and design' is a phrase which is sometimes used to refer to the various conventions which are used in the visual arts in order to communicate and convey meaning. We might, for example, refer to the vocabulary, grammar, syntax and rhetoric of art, but these terms are used metaphorically. It could be argued that the teaching and learning of art concepts can be achieved purely through visual language; however, in a school context it is often necessary to use what might be considered to be a more reliable and accurate mode of communication and indicator of learning, which in this instance is verbal language. While some might argue further that thinking goes beyond the limits of discourse, there is little doubt, in my mind at least, that language facilitates and crystallises thought and both are bound up with perception. Art making is not a below the wrist activity; both the making of art and the understanding of art are cognitive activities and as such are concerned with both language and perception.

We all deal with thousands of bits of knowledge and information every day; in order to make some sense of it we need to reflect upon it and sort it out. Pupils in schools need to do this, but they have precious little time for reflection. Secondary schools can be fairly chaotic and at best pupils get discrete bits of information which occasionally make some sort of sense as a whole. We make sense of concepts through language, but imagine the potential for pupils' confusion if they have just come to the art room from biology where they were examining the scales of a fish, or from home economics where they were using scales, or even PE where they were asked to scale a wall frame, and then they are asked to pay attention to the scale of the image in their drawings. When some of them are confused, we might think that they have trouble with the word *image*. This kind of confusion is a common problem, and while most pupils would have little difficulty in distinguishing between *flat* as in a flat battery and *flat* as in a horizontal surface, the application of the word to the quality of a colour might present more difficulty, particularly if the pupil equates a flat colour with the colour of an apartment block! These examples, and there are many more, point to the need for art teachers to be not only aware of the language they are using, but to induct pupils in an active way into both the specialist vocabulary of art and the whole discourse associated with art. When we examine the nature of art and art learning, it becomes clear that art teaching depends to a remarkable extent upon all aspects of language.

There has been a move in western art education over the past generation to introduce elements of critical and contextual studies into the art curriculum in addition to practical work. In America this has taken the form of discipline-based art education (DBAE) which emphasises the interrelatedness of the four disciplines associated with art: art history, art criticism, aesthetics and studio art. Since the implementation of the National Curriculum Orders for art, teachers in English schools are required to teach pupils at Key Stage 3 'to express ideas and opinions and justify preferences, using knowledge and an art, craft and design vocabulary'. In England, the National Curriculum Attainment Target of Knowledge and Understanding in art has brought to the fore the use of critical and contextual approaches to complement and inform practical work. This has meant an increased awareness of verbal discourse, with pupils talking about their own art work and the process of art making, as well as dialogue and discussion about the work of others. The importance of talk extends to pupils' own practical work and is especially useful for addressing the need for them to review and modify their work as it 'progresses in the light of their own and others' evaluations' (DfE 1994: 7). More recently, the School Curriculum and Assessment Authority (SCAA) has published guidelines on language use in art which underline the recognition amongst art educators of the central importance of language use in the assessment of pupils' art work (SCAA 1997). The SCAA guidelines illustrate the link between language and work in art and attempt to address two aspects of art and the use of language in schools. These two aspects are related to the complementary notions of learning through art and learning about art; learning through art by looking at ways in which work in art can develop speaking, writing and listening skills and about art by looking at ways in which pupils' understanding of art can be enhanced through language.

Raising awareness – the role of language

A fundamental aim in art education is that of heightening aesthetic awareness; to do this, we must make art and the language of art meaningful to pupils, and shift the focus of aesthetic response back towards the learner. It is through having a meaningful dialogue with art that any learning in the field of art is made worthwhile. David Hargreaves has put forward the traumatic theory of aesthetic learning (Hargreaves 1983). Such learning was described as having four characteristics: concentration of attention; sense of revelation; inarticulateness and, finally, arousal of appetite. Time needs to be put aside so that pupils can engage directly with art works and interact in their own way. An important outcome of such an approach is to allow pupils to be affected by art works so that they may seek further experiences, and participate in an active and involved way in learning about art. The central aspect of this approach to aesthetic learning is the importance attached to individual and personal aesthetic experience, which acts as a catalyst for further exploration and learning. One of the teacher's principal tasks is to facilitate this learning and bring the pupil's personal interaction with art into the public domain; this is best done through verbal discourse.

As educators we need to remind ourselves from time to time about the essence of our subject area. In art, this would include acknowledging the importance of personal aesthetic experience; in our teaching, this would be reflected in focusing upon our pupils' initial reactions to art, and using these as a starting point for the development of aesthetic understanding. In my own experience, aesthetic responses to natural phenomena have been similar to those felt when viewing art; art forms differ from natural forms in that they are created for the specific purpose of aesthetic apprehension. In broad, general terms with regard to both art and nature, I would have had an initial reaction which caused me to investigate further, wanting to find out the name of the artist or the species of plant, researching by examining the phenomenon more closely, looking in books and perhaps asking other people. Then I would look at it in a new light, I would know what to look for and my perception would be sharpened through knowledge. The experience gained would then be internalised and personalised and could be reflected upon in terms of my knowledge and understanding of wider issues. This process can be abbreviated as reacting, researching, responding and reflecting.

I can illustrate this process with reference to a particular episode which in many ways was my initiation into the realm of art. . . . As a boy, I collected fossils and I heard that one could take them into Birmingham museum to have them expertly identified, so, with a fossiling chum, I climbed onto the (steam!) train to New Street and we made our way to the palaeontology department. To get there, we had to pass through the museum's collection of Pre-Raphaelite paintings, in so doing we passed by Holman Hunt's *The Finding of the Saviour in the Temple*. I was transfixed by it. I could not understand how it was possible to paint such bright colours, exercise such control and execute such detail. I suppose my attention was captured and I was rendered inarticulate: my appetite was certainly aroused; I was more interested in finding out about the artist than in identifying my trilobite. Subsequently, I read a little and found out about Holman Hunt's approach to painting and the contexts in which he painted, about his contemporaries and how his paintings were received at the time. I was particularly intrigued by his insistence on *truth to nature* and the lengths to which he would go in order to achieve veracity. The next time I viewed the painting, armed with some background knowledge, I noticed more detail and had greater insight – for example, the small ear of wheat on the temple floor which, according to one book I read, was symbolic of the Jewish feast of first fruits, and the positioning of the bird directly over the young Christ's head, prefiguring his baptism, and in the background, a lamb being taken to slaughter, prefiguring his crucifixion. I shared my new-found knowledge to my fossil-collecting friend; talking to my friend about the painting was a considered response, arising out of research into it, and built upon an initial reaction. I have of course had plenty of time since then to reflect upon this first real engagement with a real painting and have continued to learn more about that painting in particular and art in general. This has occurred through my own art practice and through interaction with the art work of others; in both cases my own understanding of art and the art making process has been facilitated by language, whether through reading, listening, internal dialogue or public discourse.

The purpose of this anecdote is to illustrate further the rationale behind an overall general strategy for guiding learning in art. Such a strategy should be a synthesis of pupil-centred and subject-centred approaches, based on the areas of reacting, researching, responding and reflecting. Characteristics of these '4Rs' are as follows:

React – an initial affective response to the art work (*How do you feel about it? What does it remind you of? How do you 'relate' to it?*). It is commonplace to have a piece of contemporary art greeted with cries of *That's crap!* or My *dog could do better than that!* but even if the responses are positive (cool, brill or wicked in '90s adolescent language), there are opportunities to go further and develop critical language and by doing so the level of understanding.

Research – a systematic enquiry (a) within the art work: examining the formal elements, the art work's content, and the processes which the artist went through in order to arrive at the product under scrutiny; and (b) enquiry without the art work: investigating the artist's intention; looking at the relationships between the content and process and the social/historical/cultural and technological contexts in which it was produced; considering the theoretical and philosophical issues which may have influenced it. This relationship (between content and process) is reflected in the nature of language in that we use language as the process to make clear the content. The research aspect is inevitably language-based, but need not be confined to browsing through books; keywords relating to the art work could be entered into an Internet search, or CD-ROM images and text could be downloaded and discussed in small groups.

Respond – a considered response, based on what has been discovered through systematic enquiry (*Having found out about the artist and her/his circumstances, how do you now feel about the art work?*). This is an opportunity for pupils to talk in an informed way about the art work, and to engage in meaningful dialogue.

Reflect – an opportunity to think over and contemplate the meaning and nature of the art work in the light of the above (*What does it mean to you? How does it relate to issues which concern you?*). It is important to let things sink in, to give time for pupils to consolidate their learning and reflect upon their interactions with art objects. After all, art works are often made to have a significant, profound and moving effect upon those viewing them.

These areas form a framework within which pupils can operate in a structured way, drawing upon and informed by the specialist language of art. By focusing on the language used by the pupil in each of these phases, the teacher can help the learner in a way which facilitates both conceptual understanding and perceptual awareness. If we have a rich and varied discourse involving the visual elements in art, i.e. relating to colour, line, form, shape, texture and other sensory qualities, then we are more able to discover those qualities and discern their meaning in art objects.

Learning is made easier when there is an existing conceptual base to work from, in this case the pupil's initial affective response (together with the pupil's existing linguistic framework) and where there is a combination of visual, oral and written stimuli. Language helps us to make our ideas real; by voicing our thoughts or by writing them down, we are able to realise them and place them into our existing conceptual matrix and reflect upon them. The *research* component allows for investigations to be undertaken which are appropriate to pupils' abilities, needs and aptitudes. Additionally, structured teaching and learning may take place within the overall pupil-centred framework. There are several tried and tested strategies for getting pupils to investigate art in a structured way. Perhaps the most well known is the four-step approach described by Feldman (1970); for reference, the steps may be summarised as follows:

Description: make an inventory of the content of the art work – its subject matter and visual elements.
Analysis: determine the relationships within and between the visual elements and the subject matter.
Interpretation: determine possible meanings of the art work as a whole: *What are the artistic problems which may have been dealt with? What do the iconographic (symbolic) aspects of the art work represent (if present)? What are the emotional and/or expressive qualities which the art work is trying to convey (if any)? What is the art work trying to tell us – what is its message (if any)?*
Judgement: evaluate the art work as a whole, using particular criteria.

This strategy is largely dependent upon pupils' verbal skills, but if used sensitively, with appropriate guidance, can help pupils develop such skills; its weakness lies in the fact that it is concerned almost entirely with the formal elements of art, with little regard for its social context and gives little opportunity to build upon pupils' existing understanding of art. Other approaches to engaging with art in the classroom have been formulated which have refined and developed Feldman's suggested approach, but they have tended to be rather complex without addressing the issues noted here. In the UK, Rod Taylor has done much to promote critical studies in art education, and has produced several publications arising from his work in Wigan (e.g. Taylor 1986 and 1992). He described a simple approach to looking at art works which encapsulates many of the elements described above, but with a different kind of emphasis. He suggests that there are four fundamental standpoints from which art objects can be approached: *content*, *form*, *process* and *mood*. Each of these four aspects can be used to elicit discourse about the art object. A discussion of the content of an art work might focus on the question *What is the work about?* Form is concerned with how the various elements in the art work have been arranged, eliciting questions such as *How has the artist used colour and shape to depict space?* On the other hand, questions relating to process might include *What materials did the artist use to get the effect of scale?* The mood aspect is an area which gives opportunities for pupils to talk about how the work affects them. Taylor's approach can be seen to be less art-centred than Feldman's, taking more account of pupils' personal, affective responses, but it too tends to focus on the formal elements of the art object. If we are to value pupils as individuals, it is appropriate to take account of their initial reactions to adult art and to encourage discussion and debate. The approaches to structured teaching and learning decribed above can all be used as frameworks for assisting research into art works, but they need to be put into an overall context of learning.

The 4R framework gives both formal and affective learning a context; it acknowledges the validity of pupils' personal engagement with art and recognises the importance of the relationship between the observer and the observed. It provides a strategy for both structured teaching and heuristic learning: the teacher can coach, direct and guide as appropriate, and learners can research at their own pace, discovering for themselves the properties of materials and the secrets of art objects. Both the *react* and *respond* stages help evaluate pupils' learning and determine the extent of the development, from naive to sophisticated, of pupils' dialogue with art, and could form the basis for developmentally referenced assessment. The proposed framework is not intended to be seen as a linear model; the *reflect* aspect can and, in my view, should be encouraged at every opportunity, particularly with regard to personal aesthetic experience. Language enters at every stage: reflective activities are internal, private and personal but might nevertheless be facilitated through the medium of verbal language; the activities of reacting, researching and responding occur in the public domain and are characterised by interaction through dialogue. It is important that learners articulate their personal responses and that educators facilitate dialogue to ensure that learners have learnt and understood.

Making connections through language

Learning in art is much the same as learning in other areas of human endeavour, but art can offer something special. This 'something special' has been examined by David Perkins, working alongside people such as Howard Gardner on the Harvard Project Zero (Gardner 1983 and 1990). Perkins, in *The Intelligent Eye*, referred to three different kinds of intelligence: neural intelligence, which is associated with the inherited mechanics of the brain and its networks, experiential intelligence, which is derived from learning, and reflective intelligence, which is concerned with the ability to stand back and make sense of learnt information (Perkins 1992). If we use a combination of experiential and reflective intelligence, we can then make creative connections in an art work and this helps us to develop our thinking skills in a more general way. According to Perkins, art objects are particularly suited to this approach for a number of reasons:

1 Sensory anchoring: art works provide an anchor for attention over an extended period of exploration and research. If we are talking about a particular art concept, an art object allows us to focus and acts as a reference point.
2 Instant access: you can check something with a quick glance or you can point to it in the art work and say *this bit here*. The picture is here and now; it's not like trying to tell a story about last night's revelries and you forget the bits that made it funny or worth relating in the first place.
3 Personal engagement: works of art beckon you to become involved with them – we are rarely neutral. Pupils often have a strong affective response to a given art object and this kind of engagement is an excellent starting point for active discussion.
4 Dispositional atmosphere: art can provide a context which facilitates or cultivates a range of positive thinking dispositions; thinking constructively and clearly helps learners communicate constructively and clearly.
5 Wide-spectrum cognition: through thoughtful looking at art, we can use many different styles of cognition, including analytical thinking, visual processing and testing hypotheses, all of which are facilitated by language.
6 Multiconnectedness: Perkins asserts that a typical feature of art works is that they allow us to make connections between a great variety of things, which can include 'social themes, philosophical conundrums, features of formal structure, personal anxieties and insights and historical patterns' (Perkins 1992: 5). Such connections emphasise the role which language plays in cross-fertilisation of ideas throughout the whole curriculum. The important point in all of this is that we need to give time for reflection and for thoughtful and organised looking, which, to use Perkins' words, should be 'broad and adventurous' and 'clear and deep' (ibid.: 5).

There is great potential for art to contribute to the wider school curriculum – not only to basic skills of reading, writing and listening, but in a significant way to thinking skills. According to developmental psychologists, learning develops in stages, but the higher stages cannot be reached without structured teaching (Parsons 1987). Art and design teachers can provide an environment which facilitates 'natural' learning, but this is not enough. In addition we need to direct, guide and instruct in a focused way, a way which focuses on both the learner and that which is to be learnt. Many teachers have found it useful to plan their lessons around 'key concepts' and associated vocabulary; it is useful to identify the concepts which underpin the activity and to list specialist terms. It is particularly important to identify those words which have subject-specific meanings, such as tone, which has a similar but distinctly subject-specific meaning in music.

Noting the potential difficulties associated with the concept of tone leads me into a general discussion of colour terms. An area fraught with potential for confusion is that of colour, or more precisely, the vocabulary associated with colour. It is not only complicated by the difference between English and American terms (tone/value, hue/chroma) but also by the vagueness and interchangeable use of terms such as *brightness*, *brilliance*, *intensity* and *saturation*. I saw a specific problem with the concept of light on one occasion: the lesson was about different conventions for representing distance, such as aerial perspective. The teacher mentioned that some painters make objects in the distance appear *lighter* and one pupil took issue with this, saying that distant objects do not appear lighter, asserting that this was a characteristic of objects in the foreground. It turned out that the confusion was not to do with differences in perception, nor to do with the quality of illumination nor indeed to do with the distinction between *light* and *heavy*, but the pupil understood *light* to be the same as *bright*. This illustrates the need to be very specific in our use of terms. As far as colour is concerned, the teacher in this case, in dealing with attributes of aerial (or *atmospheric*!) perspective, could have avoided problems by ensuring that all pupils understood the terms associated with three principal attributes of colour – *hue*, *tone* and *saturation*, then the pupils could have learned that aerial perspective is based on distant objects appearing to be cooler in hue, paler in tone and less intense in terms of saturation. Of course, teaching is never as simple as just telling someone a fact which they then learn. There is something to be said for the old adage *Say what you are going to say, say it and then say what you've said*; but in addition, there is a need for what we might call 'supporting contextual material'. This material should be visual and/or tactile and might include examples of art work which illustate a particular concept. Pupils engaged in producing their own art work will also learn to make conceptual distinctions and connections.

In addition to visual support, other contextual support is also of importance in developing art concepts. It has been found that abstract words need a considerable amount of contextual support to be understood as easily as concrete words (Schwanenflugel 1991). It follows, then, that contextual support, in the form of, for example, paintings or sculptures, would facilitate learning of art concepts at sophisticated (i.e. more abstract) levels. Other research has been based on showing a reproduction of Marc Chagall's painting *The Birthday* to 120 undergraduate students, together with different 'supporting art contexts' in order to find the effects of contexts and verbal cues on students' level of response to the painting (Koroskik *et al.* 1992). The supporting contexts involved using different situations in which the key art work was shown: with other paintings by the same artist; with paintings depicting the same theme; with works in other art forms (a dance, a lithograph and a poem). One group of students was given verbal cues which related the key art work to its comparative context, a second group received no specific verbal support. They found that the students who showed greater understanding of art works were those who were given 'explicit verbal cues about the artworks' shared characteristics' (Koroskik *et al.* 1992: 164). Further to this, it was extrapolated from their findings that it is 'wise to base art comparisons on key ideas that have some relationship to pupils' existing knowledge' (ibid.: 164). This is likely to involve the transference of concepts learnt elsewhere to a new (art) context, thus expanding the pupils' understanding of those concepts.

Learning about the principles of colour through a combination of practical activities, visual exemplar material and accurate verbal instruction has implications for increasing perceptual awareness. If we know the terms for different kinds of blue for example, such as cerulean and cobalt, then we will be more able, literally, to see those colours. If a pupil knows the appropriate words, then further learning can occur by building upon this conceptual framework; a pupil can be advised to modify the hue in a painting, to make it cooler and will know that, for example, cobalt is a cooler hue than ultramarine – it is not simply a different colour as they are both blue. This illustrates to some extent the centrality of language in practical art work.

Concluding remarks

There has been much interest in recent years on the role of language in art education. A number of dissertations for higher degrees in the years leading up to and immediately after the implementation of the National Curriculum in England and Wales have focused on this topic (Dunning 1982; Hickman 1985; Northing 1989; Jackson 1995). All of them have recognised the importance of developing language alongside practical art skills as a way of developing pupils' understanding of art and the art making process. Jackson (1995) questioned a range of people directly involved in art education (inspectors, advisers, lecturers, teachers and students) about the role of language in art education and came up with a considerable amount of support for the notion that developing a critical language and art vocabulary should be central to pupils' learning in art in secondary schools. Amongst the responses given were several asserting that learning a specialist (art) language aids learning in art and enhances cognitive and perceptual understanding. Others felt that 'teacher talk' is essential for teaching and evaluating, while others flagged up the importance of pupil-to-pupil talk as well as dialogue between teacher and pupil. It was also felt that other language-based activities such as reading and writing have their place in the secondary art classroom; reading is an essential part of research-based activities, it reinforces learning, and can stimulate the imagination, while writing was considered to be essential for pupils' self-evaluation.

It has taken many years for art teachers in the classroom to take on board the notion that the 'language of art' need not be confined to the elements of visual form but can be enriched and enhanced by focused and informed use of appropriate verbal language in a variety of contexts: 'a well developed vocabulary of specific nouns, verbs, adjectives and adverbs is essential to comprehending art and teaching it' (Chapman 1978: 73). It is not in the best interests of pupils for art teachers to be protective of their subject by excluding elements from other disciplines. Moreover, it is clear that art can offer much of value to other curriculum subjects. We should not lose sight of the fact that we are teaching pupils, not subject areas; art teachers may teach about art, but with attention paid to the fundamental role of verbal language they may also develop pupils' potential as sensitive and aesthetically aware human beings.

We all learn by building upon our existing conceptual framework. To make art understandable and meaningful to pupils, it makes sense to teach through building upon pupils' initial affective reactions to it, through language. Like great works of art, classrooms and therefore art classrooms are complex and multi-layered; it is up to the art teacher to ensure that the layers are meaningful and the activities which take place are worthwhile with due regard for reflection – giving pupils space and time to research, respond and reflect. The 'centrality of language' has been recognised by many working in art education (Buchanan 1995). This recognition provides a sound basis from which to develop exciting and worthwhile projects which help pupils learn about art through talking, listening, reading and writing about art as well as through making art.

References

Buchanan, M. (1995) 'Making Art and Critical Literacy: A Reciprocal Relationship' in R. Prentice (ed.) *Teaching Art and Design*, London: Cassell.

Chapman, L. (1978) *Approaches to Art in Education*, New York: Harcourt Brace Jovanovich.

Department for Education (1994) *The National Curriculum Orders for Art*, London: Her Majesty's Stationery Office.

Dunning, R. 1982 'Language in Art Education', Ph.D. thesis, University of London.

Feldman, E. B. (1970) *Becoming Human through Art*, Englewood Cliffs: Prentice-Hall.

Gardner, H. (1983) *Frames of Mind: The Theory of Multiple Intelligences*, New York: Basic Books.

Gardner, H. (1990) *Art Education and Human Development*, Santa Monica: Getty.

Hargreaves, D. H. (1983) 'The Teaching of Art and the Art of Teaching: Towards an Alternative View of Aesthetic Learning' in M. Hammersley and A. Hargreaves (eds) *Curriculum Practice: Some Sociological Case Studies*, London: Falmer Press.

Hickman, R. (1985) 'An Investigation into Language Use in Art and Design Education', MA dissertation, De Montfort University.

Jackson, D. (1995) 'The Use and Development of Language in Art and Design Education', MA dissertation, Brunel University.

Koroskik, J. S., Short, G., Stravopoulos, C. and Fortin, S. (1992) 'Frameworks for Understanding Art: The Function of Comparative Art Contexts and Verbal Cues', *Studies in Art Education* 33(3): 154–64.

Northing, C. (1989) 'A Consideration of the Place of Conceptual Development and Language in the Study of Art', M.Phil. thesis, University of Leeds.

Parsons, M. (1987) *How We Understand Art: A Cognitive Development Account of Aesthetic Experience*, New York: Cambridge University Press.

Perkins, D. (1992) *The Intelligent Eye – Learning to Think by Looking at Art*, Santa Monica: Getty.

School Curriculum and Assessment Authority (1997) *Art and the Use of Language*, London: SCAA.

Schwanenflugel, P. J. (1991) 'Why Are Abstract Concepts Hard to Understand?' in P. Schwanenflugel *The Psychology of Word Meanings*, London: Lawrence Erlbaum.

Taylor, R. (1986) *Educating for Art: Critical Response and Development*, London: Longman.

Taylor, R. (1992) *The Visual Arts in Education: Completing the Circle*, London: Falmer Press.

11

THE LANGUAGE OF SELF-ASSESSMENT

Towards aesthetic understanding in music

Liz Mellor

I live in music
live in it
wash in it
I cd even smell it
wear sound on my fingers
sound falls so fulla music
ya cd make a river where yr arm is and
hold yrself
hold yrself in a music

These words are part of a poem written by American musician and novelist, Ntozake Shange (1994). The poem captures how one individual defines herself through what she perceives and values in music. Maybe, when we listen to music in our own lives we are driven to write poetry, maybe not. But when we do listen to music we often respond through movement, dance, images in our mind and through language – our own thoughts and words, as we seek to communicate something of the sense of what the music means to us and for us. In the course of this chapter I shall consider how young people responded to their own music compositions by referring to a research project which I undertook as part of my own teaching at Key Stage 3. The examples show that the role of language not only describes and labels but also generates knowledge and understanding. I shall then go on to consider the teaching approaches which foster genuine reflective language in promoting aesthetic understanding in music education and the wider implications for assessment.

Here are several statements written by pupils in response to the same piece of music composed by one of their peers.

I like the beat, nice ending
brilliant
hardly any tune and boring

unoriginal and repetitious
a good sharp tune
not much happened
notes go well and fun

Different thoughts may strike us about these statements: their diversity of opinion, the value judgements expressed in terms of *I like*, *nice*, *boring*, *brilliant* and the musical language: *beat, tune*. Other statements raise some interesting questions regarding the use of language. For example, what sense do we make of the statement *a good sharp tune*? On one level of musical understanding, *sharp* is a quality which is aligned to pitch. A note can be sharp or flat. But in the context of this statement the word *sharp* may function linguistically as a metaphor to describe a quality in the music equated with *sharp* as in knife – *cutting, incisive*. Equally, the term may be borrowed from visual perception to mean *sharp* in the sense of *in focus*. Whatever the literal meaning of the word *sharp*, the personal understanding suggests that '*sharp*' = good. What about *repetitious*? We might assume that to make this statement the listener can discriminate between musical ideas which are similar, different and those which are repeated. Is this an objective technical observation or does it carry some subjective weight and value? The last statement *notes go well and fun* shows understanding in another dimension, that of a pleasurable feeling or mood evoked by the music. Does the meaning of *the notes go well* belong to some sense of structure, pitch relationships, the way it was performed or a sense or feel for the tune as a whole? Can we say that here is an insight into the pupil's aesthetic experience of a piece of music?

These examples serve to illustrate that this is a highly problematic and complex area. It can be argued that any subject discipline has its own subject vocabulary and discourse. The end of Key Stage 3 descriptions for music state that pupils are expected to:

> Respond to music, identifying conventions used within different styles and traditions . . . analyse changes in character and mood, and evaluate the effect of the music . . . critically appraise their own work, taking into account of their intentions and the comments of others . . . compare music across time and place recognising those characteristics that stay the same and those that change . . . use a music vocabulary appropriately.
>
> (DfE 1995: 9)

In a sense these statements define the discourse of musical understanding in terms of the knowledge content: *conventions*, *styles*, *traditions*, *times*, *places*, *characteristics* and the processes: *responding*, *identifying*, *recognising*, *analysing*, *justifying*, *evaluating* and *critically appraising*. It follows that acquiring an increasingly refined music vocabulary may enable an individual to make increasingly discriminate judgements about a piece of music. More recent documentation, for example

Exemplification of Standards, Music: Key Stage 3 (1996), sets out some ideas of how teachers might interpret pupils' verbal responses as evidence for assessment, and *Music and the Use of Language* (SCAA 1997) suggests ways of developing links between language skills and music. The issue of musical response extends much further into the arena of aesthetic perception. Some people would argue that there are two identifiable types of aesthetic response to music. One is ascribed to an awareness of form and might include an appreciation of technical features in the music such as the effect of repetition, the way the notes are used. The other type of response denotes how we understand music as it affects us. In its heightened form this type of aesthetic encounter is sometimes called the 'eureka' experience, a moment of revelation, clarity and insight, when we realise that we have made a new sense of organising our world: 'This in itself is a new experience, and one which is very much more profound and stirring than the individual experience of which it is composed' (McLaughlin 1970: 108). So, whether it is the spine-tingling sensation at a classical concert, the wave of 'techno' at a rave, or the soul-searching song composition of a friend in class, we can be in no doubt that, as an experience, music can be totally absorbing, taking us into a dimension beyond our present reality: the aesthetic dimension.

Clearly, words play their part in articulating these types of aesthetic experience. By the time young people come to secondary school they already have a musical life outside the classroom, where they are developing both an interest and an expertise in talking discerningly about music (Willis 1990; Balding 1995; Ross and Kamba 1997). I would like show how this aspect can be integrated into the teaching of music at Key Stage 3 in two ways: first, by looking at a range of verbal responses which pupils gave to their own compositions and those of their peers and second, by examining how these statements were used by the pupils as a means to reflect on their own learning.

What makes a good tune? research project

The examples cited in this chapter were selected from a research project where I participated as both teacher and researcher. Initially, the pupils had performed and recorded their own electronic keyboard compositions onto audio-tape. Their compositions were commissioned to demonstrate their musical understanding of *What makes a good tune?* As a class we listened to the taped recordings and each pupil filled in a standard response sheet which was used as the basis for discussion. As the teacher witnessing this discussion, I was party to the class creating dynamic dialogue using their comments as a starting point – first in pairs, then in larger groups and finally as a full class. Essentially, they were using language as a means of discovering meaning in their music. The discussion was characterised by each pupil's sense of involvement, willingness to share their own experience of making music and readiness to listen and draw conclusions for their own learning. By setting out a series of signposts which helped the learners reflect on their own language use, the class arrived at the following statements, which described their discoveries about the use of language and music as follows:

- We can make different statements about the same piece of music;
- Some of us use 'music' words;
- We use words in different ways to describe music and we have our own language code to express value;
- Boys and girls use language in similar and different ways;
- What we say depends on how we feel about ourselves as we make, share and reflect on our music;
- What we say is influenced by our musical backgrounds, experiences, and by our relationships in class.

Each of these learning statements offers a way of structuring the case for how pupils' aesthetic awareness develops through language and for the assessment of their musical knowledge and understanding.

We can make different statements about the same piece of music

Young people are enthusiastic about sharing their ideas and opinions about their compositions. The kind of experience that this offers is guided by procedural principles rather than conceived in terms of precise outcomes. In other words, there is enough space to allow individuals to respond and determine what they will take away from the learning. At this stage of the learning process it is enough that all young people participate. They are taking enough of a risk to trust the group in 'putting their cards on the table' – there are no right or wrong answers, just the perspective that a multiplicity of views can be held. In this climate young people gain a sense of ownership as they share comments about their own and others' work. Here new meanings may be contemplated. On the table, so to speak, are some examples given by the same class to a piece of music composed by one of their peers which illustrates a varied and dynamic use of language:

it's got good rhythm
it's got liveliness
I love the way she does lots of notes
nice and completed
it has a good slinky style

Sometimes we use 'music words'

When the young people involved in this unit of work were invited to reflect on the *types* of language they used, they noticed that some people used a special 'music words' or technical music vocabulary. For example – *rhythm, beat, repetition.*

The National Curriculum for Music sets out the expectations at each of the three Key Stages which suggest a sequential progression towards increasing knowledge and understanding through the elements of music. The musical elements are *pitch*, *duration dynamics*, *tempo*, *timbre*, *texture*, *structure*. Thus:

Key Stage 1	Pupils should be *recognising* the musical elements
Key Stage 2	Pupils should be *distinguishing* the musical elements
Key Stage 3	Pupils should *be discriminating within and between* the musical elements

A reading of the Music National Curriculum expands the progression for each musical element. In the perception of pitch, pupils would first talk about *loud*, *quiet* and *silence* before recognising levels of volume, and accent before recognising subtle difference in volume. This implies that conceptual understanding is developed through an increasingly discriminating vocabulary based on the principle of quantitative addition.

The danger with this approach is that teachers may be seduced into introducing such elements in a purely systematic way. In the secondary school, many schemes of work are based simply on the statements in the National Curriculum and as the OFSTED (1996) Key Stage 3 inspection findings report, the music curriculum may be too closely tied to published schemes which model learning in this way. Unfortunately, a 'check-list' mentality results in mere verbal training in musical terminology rather than musical knowing. The music curriculum gets littered with evaluation sheets where the learners are asked to name musical elements without actually handling music concepts. Consequently, the ability to write about musical terminology becomes equated with music knowledge and understanding.

However, the role of language in building conceptual understanding is more than verbal training. One of the keyboard tunes composed by the pupils received a diverse number of responses. From a technical point of view the piece experimented, using the chromatic black notes of the keyboard. This piece stood out from everyone else's as something different. What was the response? Here are some of their comments as they search to find meaning through words:

Went on a bit.
Good tune but quite a few mistakes.
Did not like it much, it was a bit random.

It was out of tune.
It was a bit muddled but nice.
It was Egyptian-like.
It doesn't go well.
It sounded like an old man walking.
It could be described as sad.
It was a bit creepy. She got some notes wrong and that sounded good.

Clearly, the music presents a listening challenge which is difficult to make sense of. Some responses show a critical stance: *went on a bit, a bit random, it doesn't go well.* Some language choices reflect mood responses: *sad, creepy.* What is interesting from a language point of view is that metaphorical language is used to reflect the quality of movement in the music: *it sounded like an old man walking.* Another shows a stylistic reference; something in the music is associated with the listener's experience of a quasi-oriental 'Egyptian' style. A development in conceptual understanding is revealed in the way that some responses present two ideas alongside each other. On the one hand, this tune appears to break musical rules yet, on the other hand, appeals to the listener: *It was a bit muddled but nice; She got some notes wrong and that sounded good.* Although these statements lack technical vocabulary we certainly get a sense of the music. Interestingly and typically, the only technical statement, *It was out of tune*, is adopted inappropriately. Whilst the tune may appear 'out – of something', technically speaking it is not out of tune. Quite often pupils adopt these terms of reference without real understanding, which can mean that musical concepts get muddled. *Out of tune* could mean *out of key*; out of tune might also mean *out of time.*

In my experience, secondary-trained teachers of music have internalised a highly technical vocabulary. The value they place on this language arises from a specialised training. Embedded in this 'language of the expert' is power. It is easy to see how learners can become dispirited if the teacher responds to their compositions, albeit without awareness, by using a battery of technical terms which the pupils do not yet understand. This gives a message that other responses, which perhaps don't have the sophistication of 'music-speak' or which allude to feelings, are not valued. A teacher's view of achievement in music can become equated with an overemphasis on the acquisition of a technical vocabulary and this is both affirmed by and perpetuated through a traditional model of assessment. It is not enough to use written listening tests or self-evaluation sheets which encourage labelling in technical terms. The long-term effect is that the learner buys into the 'game' of verbal training, the real music learning is lost and, most important, the pupil's authentic voice is compromised. The language of evaluation should go beyond the vocabulary of the subject.

We use words in different ways to describe music and we have our own language code to express value

In sharing their language responses with the rest of the class, young people recognised that their comments not only revealed a range of individual diversity but also they appeared to make references to a range of different aspects of the music beyond the language of musical elements. The field of experimental aesthetics in psychology has investigated the composition of pupils' verbal responses to music (Hargreaves 1982), as have other studies in aesthetic education (Gilbert [now Mellor] 1990). What seems to emerge is how young people demonstrate their aesthetic profile through their choice of language. The study which I undertook within the school involved responses by 156 pupils – 68 pupils at Key Stage 3. The responses were analysed in both quantitative and qualitative ways. For the quantitative part of the study the written responses were coded into five categories. The study recognised that quite often the language used defied a simple categorisation, for example the comment 'jazzy' could quite easily sit within the category of style, mood or evaluation of composition. Examples of responses in each category are as follows:

I	Musical elements	*it was loud* (dynamics)
		the notes went up and down (pitch)
		it had a nice hollow sound (timbre)
		it repeated (structure)
II	Style	*it sounds classical*
		it sounds Japanese
III	Mood	*it made me feel happy*
		it was depressing
		it was spooky
IV	Evaluation of composition	*it was good*
		it was well put together
V	Evaluation of performance	*it was played well*
		he missed a note

The results of the statistical analysis showed that the category which contained the most frequent verbal references was category IV: Evaluation of composition. This category contained significantly more statements which communicated the young people's sense of *value* for the music compositions. Second came statements containing references to musical elements. In third and fourth places came statements referring to Mood and Style. In last place came the category which referred to how the compositions were played.

Whilst the quantitative analysis demonstrates general trends, the qualitative analysis uses results to illustrate the ways in which young people show, through their use of language, the ability to move from unsubstantiated value judgements towards modes of aesthetic discourse. Many pupils express their first views about music in simple terms of personal preference: *brilliant, boring, nice, I like it, my kind of tune.* It is often at this stage that the peer language has its own code. When I was at school good music was 'cool' or 'wicked'. At the time of collecting this data, pieces of music valued very highly by the peer group use words such as *sweet, cute, scary, strange, weird* and *unreal.* This coded language may vary from class to class, year to year, school to school. How far words are coined within the social group, or created and perpetuated by media forces, is debatable. What is apparent is that part of being accepted into the peer group at this age involves using these value-laden words. In this cultural setting, it is just as likely that a music composition can be as 'scary' as a new pair of trainers.

As the process of discrimination evolves, value judgements become qualified, for example *quite nice, really good.* Value judgements then become attached to one musical element: *good tune, too short.* Concepts function in webs of interrelationships, deriving meaning from the human activity in which they are embedded – be it making music, movement to music, association with music. Evidence of this is illustrated when young people qualify more than one musical element in the same expression: *nice sound, good rhythm.*

A further interconnectedness appears when the listener seems to respond to the piece as a whole and not just to its constituent parts. This stage is characterised in several ways. When the interconnectedness of one aspect of the music is expressed as having an effect on another, for example *the cathedral sound and the beat don't go, the nursery tune doesn't fit the low sound, good considering the end was improvised.* Sometimes this sense of the whole is expressed in terms of the narrative structure of the music. Just as a story has a narrative structure, for example *In the beginning,* so too has music. Responses seem to emerge in terms of the narrative of the music: *beginning good but the end spoilt it a bit, the end was so good nothing happens, it did not lead anywhere, you sort of knew which note would come next.*

Other perspectives which consider the piece as a whole do so in terms of the perceived thinking behind a piece: *well thought out, well organised* or in terms of its originality, *good because it is different, it's a copy of Aimi's, beginning a bit familiar, he nicked it off the TV.* Other order statements discern a properness about the music: *no proper rhythm like a proper piece, it sounded like a real piece, I just enjoyed it so much, it was getting to the point of a piece.* On another level of perception, pupils express the quality of a piece of by using metaphor: *I like the downhill effect, it was like rain dropping, like a fairy dancing.* Some might argue that younger children use this type of expression to describe music in the absence of a more precise technical language. Others might argue that metaphorical language is more capable of capturing the essence of the music.

The language choices that learners use at any one time provide a snapshot of their 'aesthetic profiles'. Different pupils demonstrated different profiles made up of a range of language choices. For example, some pupils demonstrated responses which were dominated by personal preferences, others by references to the musical elements. Whilst the full extent of the research cannot be reported here, it showed that a more developed aesthetic profile seems to show a balance between the types of response given above. Aesthetic understanding may be demonstrated not simply as successive analytical discriminations within each musical element in turn, nor between the musical elements, but when a young person can demonstrate relationships and connections across all categories of perception.

When teachers are attuned to the language which pupils use and encourage them to make language choices beyond their 'typical' profile, learners can move through both objective and subjective modes of discourse. This means that teachers can help learners to develop both a voice of the inner critic, which belongs to an understanding of their music in personal terms, and a public voice, which enables learners to contribute to the wider debate of what constitutes aesthetic value in music. Such might be the educative role of language in music: building a vocabulary which can support a metalanguage. In this way genuinely reflective language can lead to metacognition and, in this process, whereby individuals become aware of their own thinking, lies the relationship between metacognition and aesthetic development.

Boys and girls use language in similar and different ways

When the young people in this study discussed their responses to their peers' compositions, they agreed that the girls and boys used language in both similar and different ways. In a piece of experimental research Green (1993) reveals some important considerations for teachers' attitudes towards young people as music listeners. For example, 67 out of 78 secondary teachers participating in Green's study thought that girls and boys responded equally to listening activities in the music curriculum; 11 thought girls achieved better; no teachers thought that boys achieved a greater success in this area. Girls were believed to be better at listening because they could listen in a more sustained way, could concentrate more easily, were more aware of what they were listening for, were better prepared and appeared to think more carefully about the presentation of their ideas. Conversely, boys appeared to be restless, less prepared and not able to listen carefully enough for most of the time. The findings also showed that some teachers believed that boys were more likely to move to the music as a way of responding. This seems to corroborate one gendered view of music making in school – that boys appear to be more active whilst girls are more passive. The corollary follows that listening to music and talking about it is the girls' domain whilst playing music is that of the boys (this has been debated otherwise in O'Neill 1997). Other beliefs made explicit in Green's report assert that open-mindedness, along with feelings and perseverance are assumed to be more characteristic of a female attention style in listening to music.

My quantitative analysis of the pupils' written responses to their peers' music appears to bear out some of these assumptions exposed by Green. Girls produced significantly more responses than the boys at Key Stage 3. Further analysis between the categories of perception revealed more significant gender differences. For example, girls made more use of music vocabulary in the category 'Musical elements'. Girls also produced marginally more statements referring to Mood than the boys. In the category Evaluation of composition girls also made significantly more evaluative statements about their classes' compositions than the boys. In both the Style and Evaluation of Performance categories there was no significant difference in the number of references made by the girls and boys.

There was also evidence to show the gendered use of language. For example, whilst the girls and boys made similar statements about tempo: *boring and slow*, *it's faster and more interesting*, boys make *more* verbal references to tempo than the girls. The pupils' evaluations showed that language preferences which can be recorded through speaking and writing about music can help both the teacher and the learner understand what boys and girls value in each other's music. They can also prompt thoughts about how these perceptions come to be created and perpetuated in the social climate of the classroom. The implications for teachers would be to encourage all pupils at some time to focus on mood, for example, or to encourage the boys' verbal repertoire beyond the perception of tempo. In this way, learners' language need not be limited by any gender boundaries which may exist.

What we say we value is influenced by our musical backgrounds, experiences and by our relationships in class

One of the striking dimensions of the initial feedback sessions was how young people in secondary school shape their sense of personal aesthetic in terms of their lived and shared experience. We cannot assume that their language choices are voiced independently from peer group issues of perceived musical expertise, status, friendship and competition, for example. Whilst on the one hand independence in learning might be characterised by the ability to distance oneself from the pull of the group', on the other hand, young people's language choices reflect their continually evolving autobiographies.

For example, the experienced pianist speaks with voice of expertise: . . . *could have practised more, original and good for someone who doesn't play the piano.* And the saxophonist with experience of playing jazz comments on a peer's composition: *doesn't make the most of the rests, needs to sit back on the beat.* For these young musicians, their individual experience feeds their ability to evaluate. There are not only different responses according to personal experience, however; shifts occur when pupils work in group settings.

A significant example of group dynamics influencing evaluation happened in response to Bruce's composition. In a class of 22 children, 21 responded positively. Bruce not only had 'street-cred' as an individual in the class, he also had piano skills and produced an upbeat pastiche blues tune. Only one 'high status' girl challenged this in the statement *a nice tune, but it wasn't original.*[1] In the same class, Caroline was also a competent piano player and produced a well-played pastiche tune. However, she had low personal status in the class. Whilst some of her friends gave her credit in statements such as *it's a real piece, I like the tune and the beat*, many discredited her composition in terms such as *not very interesting, like music for children* and *it's copied*. Some typical examples of language used as peer putdowns or to demonstrate group allegiances were:

It's a soppy tune	(high status girl about low status boy's composition)
Unoriginal	(high status girl about low status girl's composition)
It's babyish	(high status girl about low status girl's composition)
Catchy tune but not as good as Jenny	(girl friendship and regard for Jenny as a piano player)
A good muck around	(boys' friendship group)

In class discussion some young people were quite open about charging individuals with responses such as *You only said that about her music because you're her friend.* The challenge for teachers is to make this part of the learning explicit to the pupils and offer young people alternative perspectives from which to draw language choices. For example, *If you weren't speaking as a friend of Louise's, would you say something different about her composition?* In this way, teachers may be able to encourage an alternative voice, which takes on different language choices, which in turn may liberate the individual to make new ways of constructing personal meaning. The examples at the end of the chapter illustrate another means of protecting personal meaning from peer pressure through collaborative work, especially where the music has been composed, performed and appraised in groups.

What we say depends on how we feel about ourselves making and sharing our music

Another consideration to take into account when we involve young people in making assessments of their own compositions as distinct from making assessments of others' work is that some pupils find it difficult to say anything about their own music, for example: *I did not say anything because I made it up*. For others, language choices are ruled by what is assumed to be socially acceptable public discourse. Some boys in the sample thought it was cool to promote their own work as *brilliant* whilst making negative statements about girls' work. Some girls believe it is cool to denigrate their own work. From my study, statistical evidence of pupils' ratings of their own compositions showed that, whilst boys only marginally rated their work better than girls at Key Stage 2, by Key Stage 3 boys' self-rating had increased and girls' self-rating significantly decreased. Denise's composition received positive comments from the rest of the class but her own comments are negative: *too many mistakes*. Without knowing the pupil better, it is difficult to know whether she is buying into the peer pressure to do her work down or genuinely is lacking in self-esteem or making a realistic assessment of her own work.

For some, the consequences of entering wholeheartedly into musical ownership in the public arena has personal cost, for example: *I liked mine when I made it up, but when I played it people laughed and I was very upset.* Indeed, for many young people, participating in the language of self-assessment is a risky business, where barriers of self-defence must be put in place. One means to do this, as we have seen, is through language. The implications for self-appraisal and social learning are inextricably linked. Teachers promoting self-evaluative techniques in the classroom are not only working towards a common understanding of value as learners within the art form, but are also entering the discourse of values education in the social, psychological and philosophical arena. It is a highly illusory area, where one verbal response is only ever a snapshot of a young person's continually evolving world.

Assessing learning

As I suggested at the beginning of this chapter, there are some tensions between learning and assessment methods in music. The SCAA documentation for music states that young people should be empowered as music users and reflective appraisers, *yet* prescribes a fragmented model of 'objective' assessment driven by standards. A curriculum led by this type of assessment can take away the joy and intrinsic worth of music making from its place in the world of personal meaning. Unless, that is, we redefine our relationship with 'assessment'. By considering pupil involvement in the language of self-assessment we can in one sense reclaim some ownership and independence in learning for the young people we teach. We can respect and enjoy the richness of the language which they demonstrate in their speaking and writing about their music, but more importantly, respect the place language has in bringing musical understanding home in its deepest sense.

The implications of the role of reflective language as part of the learning process can be summarised for music educators in three ways. First, the teacher has to create a classroom climate where the learners take ownership of their music making. The second move is to invite young people to share their ideas in their authentic voice. Through dialogue they come to a shared understanding of what constitutes the quality of value in their work. In this way the criteria for the learning are self-determined and the ownership of the music making remains with the learner. By drafting criteria in this way, the relationship between the learner and the learning objectives has a better chance of remaining intact. Assessment becomes integrated and sits naturally in the learning process. Learning objectives take account of both the content and the process of learning, seeing language not only as proof of learning but as part of constructing learning. Third, encouraging young people to engage in reflective stance on the language voices they have used gives learners a genuine opportunity to contemplate and choose alternative voices. In doing so, pupils make new language choices, extend vocabularies and exercise increasingly discerning judgements in the course of appraising their own musical and personal development. Offering ownership in this way opens out the path for promoting independence in learning and offer the opportunity for young people to take their place in public dialogue, further practical engagement and a certain kind of self-referencing for life.

Conclusions

The final word must come from the young people. I would like to end with some extracts from the lyrics of pupils' song compositions at Key Stage 3, alongside some of their self-assessments.

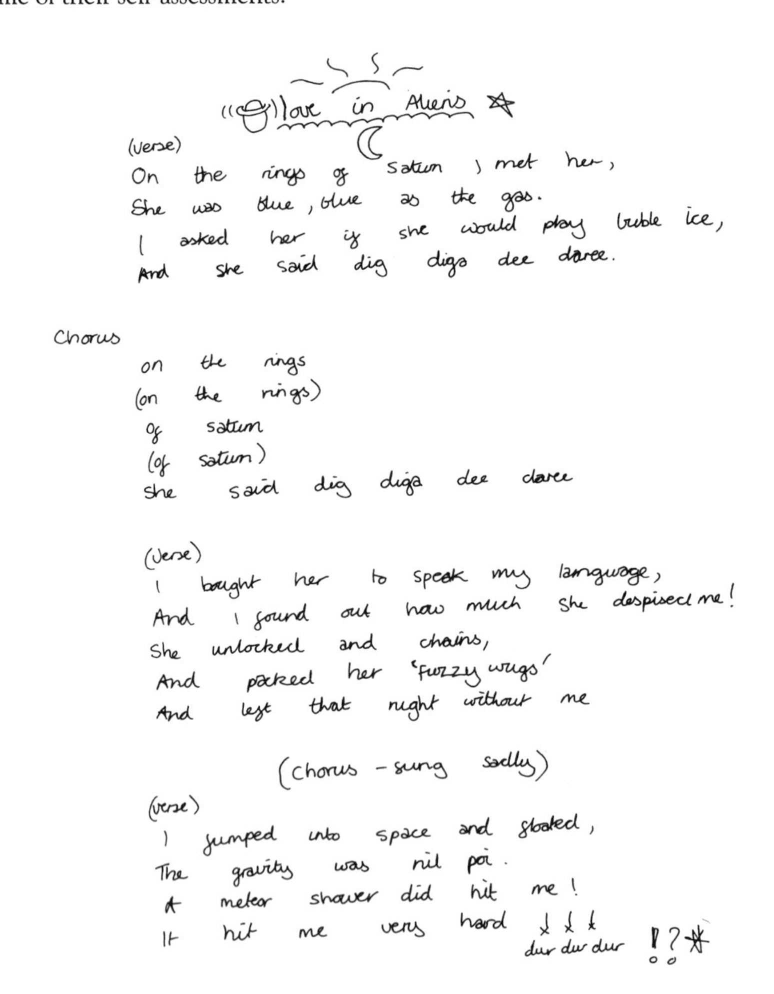

Figure 11.1 Love in Aliens

Lovin' you

Verse 1. I Saw her face Starring behind me
I, didn't know who She was, but then
I noticed who I was seeing the girl that
I dream of

Chorus. Loving you is such an Emotian
Seeing you Restores my Love.
asking you If you Love me is Something
that I'd never dream of.

Verse 2. I Saw her eyes Starring upon me
but then I thought I wouldn't be
but my body turned me around
To say I Love you.

Chorus

Verse 3 Your personnality is differenk to mine
I think I beter change my mind
I'm Sorry to Say this,
but this has to happen
but I dont Love you.

Chorus X3

Figure 11.2 Lovin' You

Love

love can stricke you anywhere
A kISS can take you ever where
Love is a dream— not what it may seem

Figure 11.3 Love

(Football rythem)

Football's great
I play it with my mate
we like to score
more and more

(Football rythem)

Football's cool
I play it with a ball
with my mate called Paul
who isn't very tall

(Football Rythem)

Football's brill
I play it with Phil
when I play I get a thrill
from all the fancy skill

(Football Rythem)

Figure 11.4 Football

In the lyrics themselves we see the relationship of music and language inherent in the art form. The language choices reflect their understanding of lyric form within the context of style, social, personal and public discourse. Further, their written statements capture the potential which this type of teaching promotes.

> *We decided as a class on the subject of love.*
>
> *We thought about all the different things about love and summer. We decided on a rhythm and got the music, i.e. the notes and the music.*
>
> *We were 'la-la-ing' different tunes until we found one we liked.*

I enjoyed doing it with my friends. Making the lyrics was great fun.

It all fitted together like a song should.

. . . the fact we wrote the song and got to sing it. I will always remember that!

. . . a sense of pride.

The chorus is always in my head and I can't get rid of it!

Acknowledgements

With thanks to the King Alfred School, London, and Netherhall School, Cambridge.

Note

1 I assigned the terms high/low status by observing how the pupils interacted and whom they held in esteem amongst their peers.

References

Balding, I. (1995) *Young People in 1994. The Health Related Behaviour Questionnaire Results for 48,297 Pupils between the Ages of 11–16*, Exeter: Schools Health Education Unit, University of Exeter.

Department for Education (1995) *Music in the National Curriculum*, London: HMSO.

Gilbert, E. J. [now Mellor] (1990) 'Aesthetic Development in Music: An Experiment in the Use of Personal Construct Theory', *British Journal of Music Education* 7 (3): 173–90.

Green, L. (1993) 'Music, Gender and Education: A Report on Some Exploratory Research', *British Journal of Music Education* 10: 219–53.

Hargreaves, D. J. (1982) 'The Development of Aesthetic Reactions to Music', *Psychology of Music*, Special Issue, 51–4.

McLaughlin, T. (1970) *Music and Communication*, London: Faber.

OFSTED (1996) *Subjects and Standards: Issues for School Development Arising from OFSTED Inspection Findings 1994–5. Key Stages 3 and 4 and Post 16*, London: HMSO.

O'Neill, S. A. (1997) 'Gender and Music' in D. J. Hargreaves and A. North (eds) *The Social Psychology of Music*, Buckingham: Open University Press.

Ross, M. and Kamba, M. (1997) *The State of the Arts*, Exeter University, sponsored by the Calouste Gulbenkian and the Paul Hamlyn Foundations.

School Curriculum Assessment Authority (1996) *Exemplification of Standards, Music: Key Stage 3*, London: SCAA.

School Curriculum Assessment Authority (1997) *Music and the Use of Language at Key Stage 3*, London: SCAA.

Shange, N. (1994) *i live in music*, Singapore: Stewart, Tabori and Chang.

Willis, P. (1990) *Moving Culture*, London: Calouste Gulbenkian Foundation.

12

USING REFLECTIVE PRACTICE TO MONITOR AND EVALUATE LANGUAGE AND LEARNING

Gill Venn and Ian Terrell

> Teaching, like nursing, engineering, journalism . . . is an activity which entails reflection on what one has done in order to become more accomplished. This kind of reflection on doing has been called 'practical reasoning'. It is a form of reasoning in which envisaged ends and practical means are considered jointly in order to improve practice. Whatever our criteria for judging effectiveness, such practical reasoning cannot be spelt out in operational terms, but only in terms of teachers' reflective understanding of their own practices with regard to specific areas of the curriculum, assessment and pedagogy.
>
> (Adelman 1989: 175)

There are many potential ways to monitor and evaluate the progress of language and learning in schools. Our aim in this chapter is to explore the possibility of teachers reflecting on the work and activities which take place in their classrooms in order to raise pupil achievement.

First, though, it would be useful to focus briefly on the distinction between monitoring and evaluation. Evaluation has been cited as 'the process of systematically collecting and analysing information in order to form value judgments based on firm evidence' (Bennett, Glatter and Levacic 1994: 16). Such a definition implies careful planning of how appropriate data will be collected, analysed and used in order to improve the situation – in this case, provision for language development. Monitoring is often viewed as a more informal activity, whereby individuals or groups 'keep an eye' on work in progress. We would wish to argue that for busy professionals this more informal approach is useful, but is more efficient when monitoring, too, is planned. In order to raise the achievement of all pupils, both informal and more formal approaches to reviewing provision need to be taken on board. These might be instigated by managers in schools, but in order for the review process to be effective, all staff need to be actively involved.

The importance of language in the learning process has a long history. Even if we take the Bullock Report of 1975 as the start of the modern era, we are talking about a twenty-year history. Yet, one could argue that outside explicitly language-based lessons, little attention is given to the importance of language and literacy in the learning process. OFSTED reports of underachieving schools often fail to make the connection between low levels of reading, writing, speaking and listening and low standards of achievement. While the key elements of effective schools, according to the OFSTED handbook, are the quality of leadership and the quality of teaching, very little mention is made as to how teachers use, develop and monitor language in the classroom.

It is interesting to question, therefore, why communication skills have, until recently and the introduction of the 'literacy hour', had relatively little attention from the teaching profession since the Bullock Report. One conclusion would be that teachers have a set of beliefs and values about the learning process which do not articulate a concern for speaking, listening, reading and writing in their subject areas. Such beliefs can impact not only on the quality of teaching and learning taking place in classrooms, but also on the quality and nature of monitoring and evaluation. Challenging such assumptions can be difficult.

We would suggest that a number of teachers have strong beliefs that low levels of achievement are caused by the ability of pupils or their social backgrounds rather than by classroom practices. Terrell and Venn (1996 and 1997) have outlined how fundamental beliefs and values about the nature of teaching and learning can be deep-rooted and difficult to change. Yet, articulating and discussing these beliefs and values must be the starting point for changes leading to raising achievement. Such articulation and discussion would form a vital, initial part of the review process. We would wish to concentrate upon the need for a developmental learning process for teachers investigating the use of language and literacy in the classroom. In this way, the approach to monitoring and evaluation becomes more holistic. Teachers reflect on their actions and contributions to learning whilst monitoring the progress of their pupils.

Our assumptions about school improvement and raising achievement are based on the following premisses:

- The key to improvement and raising achievement is staff development.
- The developmental process is a learning process for teachers.
- The learning process is about the construction of understanding.
- The learning process is facilitated by professional dialogue.

The learning process may take many forms including action research. Here we would like to outline a process of professional learning using reflective writing. Much has been written about reflection and professional practice (Schon, 1993; Kolb 1984; Eraut 1994).[1]

The purposes and benefits of using reflective writing

It might feel as though monitoring and evaluating language and literacy is time-consuming in itself. The suggestion of expanding the activity to incorporate reflection on professional practice might seem daunting. It is true that time is often a problem. However, if a more holistic approach enables more effective learning and professional practice, it would seem to warrant consideration. The range of potential purposes of reflective practice includes:

- clarifying thoughts;
- evaluating, reviewing, assessing and improving;
- being able to learn from experience;
- improving practice by thinking away from the classroom;
- applying what has been learned from previous experiences to future practice;
- developing and improving understanding;
- exploring feelings related to learning and teaching.

Planning

New terms are identified in the scheme of work.

Learning activities are planned to provide opportunities for extensive reading for understanding concepts.

Approach to learning

Students are encouraged to articulate what they already know and understand.

Classroom learning activities

Teachers use a range of closed and open questions.

There are many opportunities for students to talk at length and for extended periods.

Discussion in groups is about the subject and concepts rather than the task.

A wide range of texts is available for students to read from.

Video and audio tapes are used as sources of information.

ICT and CD-ROMS are used as sources of information.

Homework

Homework is set which encourages discussion with adults.

Independent learning

Students are encouraged to negotiate their learning targets and tasks with teachers.

Students discuss course plans and guides to gain understanding of what is required.

Figure 12.1 Good practice statements for developing language in classroom planning

Our conclusions are that considerable learning can take place through the process of reflective writing linked with discussion when the following elements are present:

- a clear focus;
- agreed time factors;
- a planned learning process;
- appropriate facilitation.

It is often helpful to decide upon a focus for reflective writing in advance. Some teachers find this difficult and a focus may emerge later. School inspection reports may give an indication for a specific focus. Alternatively, research reports or journal articles may suggest topics relevant to the group or department. Terrell, Rowe and Terrell (1996) have published some common statements of good practice derived from OFSTED reports. Some of these are illustrated in Figure 12.1. These items could form a 'checklist' to initiate discussion on deciding the focus. Alternatively, the aspects of learning and teaching which are to be evaluated could provide themes for the reflection.

It is important that a clear focus is established and maintained throughout. Whilst this is fine in theory, very often our thinking does not happen in neat chunks which are closely related to each other. Rather, when we start to evaluate and reflect upon a specific learning activity that we have undertaken with pupils, our thoughts can appear somewhat disorganised. The following quotation is taken from a teacher on an inservice module for which part of the required assessment was a reflective journal.

> I think what helped most was actually the reflective journal as much as I tended to complain sometimes it really made me sit down and discuss with myself what I really think in a not very organised way sometimes I think it is something I will continue with.

The process

The process of using reflective writing as a tool for evaluation is not always easy for practitioners and some take to it better than others. For those teachers who have never engaged with this type of activity, the process can seem daunting. One teacher on a mentoring programme confided, *I'd been teaching eleven years before I stopped and thought about what I was doing*. Our research with students on initial teacher education programmes points to the fact that some students believe that *good teachers are born, not made* and that because teaching is a *natural activity* you cannot learn how to do it better. Such attitudes can pose a significant barrier to reflective writing, particularly if they are never articulated. One way into the process of reflection might be to provide a 'safe space' for teachers to express their existing views and beliefs. This could enable a foundation for development to be laid and could be invaluable in aiding initial discussions.

We are focusing here chiefly on reflective writing. However, clearly, reflection can take many forms. Reluctant writers might be encouraged to take part in the activity if they are reassured that 'stream of consciousness' is not the only form of reflective writing. Simply making notes, recording feelings at times of critical incidents, devising different options or recording main points arising from discussions can all act as starting points for the reflective process.

Contracting

Before embarking on the use of reflective writing for purposes of staff development, clear agreement needs to be reached about the purpose and process. A fundamental question is whether participants feel that they need to develop language and literacy in their classrooms. If staff feel that there is no more that can be done, a full project is unlikely to be successful. In this case some agreement to initial data collection to see what actually goes on might be established. Decisions need to be made about a number of issues including:

- time to write;
- time to discuss;
- rules of confidentiality;
- participants' rights;
- purpose.

Teachers need to be given clear instructions, particularly about the scale of the exercise, for example, 20 minutes per week. It is vital that such activities are seen as providing a 'pay-off' for the teachers involved. Creating the time to discuss the writing is important. Many teachers welcome the opportunity to discuss their reflections, their beliefs and values about what is happening in their classrooms. Much teacher talk during meeting times is based firmly within the functional domain.

Time will always be a major issue and perceived lack of time can mean that the process never starts. Staff concerns about time need to be addressed at the start of the evaluation exercise and the intended outcomes shared. Reflective writing is usually best undertaken individually and this additional task may be resented by hard-pressed staff. This implies a need for an outcome which is shared and which is seen as being of real value. If time for writing is encouraged, time for discussion needs to be found following the writing process. The discussion as an outcome in itself can be highly fruitful. Creating the opportunity for staff to share their beliefs and values as part of a professional dialogue can impact positively on both teaching and learning.

Confidentiality is an important aspect to get clear within the contracting phase. Who will have access to these reflections? What will happen if it becomes clear that, as a department or a group of teachers, we have radically different and oppositional views as to the value of developing language and literacy within our subject area? What right do I have as an individual teacher to refuse to undertake the activity? These areas of potential conflict need to be clarified at the outset. Establishing a clear, shared purpose for the activity is critical. Agreeing the focus and process will help here.

Data collection – writing a journal

The importance of an established, agreed focus has already been discussed. If staff have agreed to undertake the process of reflective writing, they could now be asked to start a journal where they record their thoughts, observations, reflections on action, and questions. In terms of initiating evaluation, it would be possible to start with the following six questions:

- What are the pupils doing?
- What are they learning?
- Is it worthwhile?
- What am I doing?
- What am I learning?
- What do I intend to do next?

Brief written explorations of these questions can then be used as the basis for discussion.

Data analysis

Writing reflectively is but the first stage. It is essential that such writing should be analysed and reviewed. The task here is to interpret what the writing means on a number of fronts. You may ask what it means to the author. What might it mean about beliefs and values about their work and the pupils? Alternatively, what might it mean in terms of their approach to language and communication in the classroom? Leask and Terrell (1997) distinguish between reflection on self, reflection on others, the context you are working in, and the learning process. This distinction is useful when adopting an holistic approach to monitoring and evaluation, where insights about one's own practice are seen as being critically linked to the progress of the pupils.

In research terms there are a number of different processes of analysis that can be used. Content Analysis is a process where the themes within the content may be listed and categorised; as you read you may see contradictions or dilemmas. These may also be noted and discussed – Dilemma Analysis. It is helpful sometimes to distinguish between issues of continuing processes and action schedules and plans of action. Often the root of the problem practitioners face is not that they don't know what to do next but that there are all sorts of feelings, relationships and blockages related to developing practice. Examples of this may include negative feelings about joining in with a project or anger at certain leaders within schools. Here, the role of the facilitator is significant.

The role of facilitator

As facilitator of the group you may be a deputy headteacher, a senior manager, head of department or part of a team. There are many issues which arise when you are planning to lead a group of people who undertake reflective writing and discussion. First, what roles do you adopt? You might take on one or more of:

- friend
- encourager
- listener
- facilitator
- counsellor
- protector
- learner
- communicator
- adviser
- fellow practitioner
- 'parent'
- line manager.

Whatever role or roles you adopt, it is important that you feel comfortable with it and that your adopted role enables learning to take place. It is important to ask questions which develop reflection by being catalytic, affective and at times confrontational. Challenging your colleagues is sometimes difficult when the desired outcome is increased understanding and learning. Figure 12.2 shows some effective responses.

Expressed difficulty	*Response*
Excuses	I know that time is really short for you, but you said that this was a priority.
Omissions	We have talked a lot, but we have never discussed . . .
Discrepancies	You have said that raising the achievement of this group is important, but every time I suggest we discuss it, you haven't got the time.
Distortions	Do you feel that this is an accurate portrayal?
Oversimplifications	It is perhaps a little more complex than that. Shall we explore . . . ?

Figure 12.2 Challenging colleagues: effective responses

Time is clearly an issue. As an effective facilitator, you need to be aware of the potential time constraints and also be a good timekeeper. When the precious time has been made for these discussions, you need to ensure that you keep on task.

Improving learning through reflecting on practice

There are many ways in which to monitor and evaluate language and communication in classrooms and schools. In this chapter we have outlined the potential for involving colleagues in processes of reflection in order to achieve a holistic framework of evaluation. Undertaking such activities can improve the learning of both teachers and pupils and can challenge beliefs and values which might impede raising achievement. Carrying out structured activities in schools can mean that participants are required to observe and analyse everyday events which are often accepted as the norm, even though such accepted practices may be restricting progress and improvement. Evaluating through reflective writing should be purposeful and structured. As importantly, it should be an enjoyable, positive and rewarding experience. As one teacher explained:

> I must admit I was reluctant at first. I just wanted to get on with the job of reviewing the kids' progress. But having done the journal, well, I've learnt a lot – about myself as well as the kids' learning. It now seems like an important thing to keep doing.[2]

Notes

1 Our work in this area is derived from practical experience of working with teachers and school improvement and our work in Initial Teacher Education and Continuing Professional Development. In addition we have collected data from a number of research projects into the effectiveness and process of reflective writing as part of the evaluation cycle.

2 We have found that a great motivator for teachers is to use the development project as an opportunity to gain credit towards a graduate or postgraduate qualification. Many Higher Education institutions, including our own, are keen to tie in such project work.

References

Adelman, C. (1989) 'The Practical Ethic Takes Priority over Methodology' in W. Carr (ed.), *Quality in Teaching*, London: Falmer Press.

Bennett, N., Glatter, R. and Levacic, R. (1994) *Improving Educational Management*, London: Oxford University Press.

Eraut, M. (1994) *Developing Professional Knowledge and Competence*, London: Falmer Press.

Kolb, D. A. (1984) *Experiential Learning as the Sources of Learning and Development*, N.J.: Prentice Hall.

Leask, M. and Terrell, I. (1997) *Development and Planning and School Improvement for Middle Managers*, London: Kogan Page.

Schon, D. (1993) *The Reflective Practitioner: How Professionals Think in Action*, New York: Basic Books.

Terrell, I., Rowe, S. and Terrell, K. (1996) *Raising Achievement at* GCSE, Lancaster: Framework Press.

Terrell, I. and Venn, G. (1996) 'Educative Interventions in Reflective Practice', Paper presented at ECER 1996, Seville.

Terrell, I. and Venn, G. (1997) 'A Critical Evaluation of the Use of Portfolios and Journals as an Aid to Reflection in the Development of Competence', Paper presented at ECER Conference 1997, Frankfurt.

Part 5

DIFFICULTIES WITH LITERACY AND LEARNING

> I would like a future for my children in which they can lead productive lives, in a society which is positively engaged with the challenges of its time, and in which despair is, at the least, balanced by hope, difficulty by pleasure. I happen to believe that the possibilities of communication are the essential foundation for that.
>
> (Kress 1997: 164)

Surely all parents and teachers would agree. But for many children the difficulties of getting to grips with the ways society communicates are not balanced by pleasure. It does not take much imagination to appreciate the deeply damaging effects of not having access to literacy; lack of confident literacy affects not only learning opportunities but the fundamental human rights of any individual or group. This is why issues of entitlement have become more central to educational thinking recently. The state of literacy of the individual has its impact on the future of the nation. However, 'entitlement to a full and flexible curriculum' is so central to many current educational debates that the phrase – if not the principle of entitlement itself – is in danger of becoming a cliché. One of the threads in this book has been a retrospective on 'Language Across the Curriculum' and it is tempting to look back at earlier rallying phrases which expressed principles of entitlement – 'Education for All' and 'Equality of Opportunity' and view these with disappointment. In becoming slick educational and political shorthand, such phrases have lost their force and impetus.

One of the problems about articulating matters of principle is that if they are not translated into practice they stay at the level of resounding rhetoric and do nobody any good. Whilst debates about education should and must reflect issues of justice and human rights, it is in the everyday practice of education, in the school and classroom environments, that the principles of entitlement are kept alive and are seen to have effects. Teachers themselves can only get to grips with these important matters of equity if they have the chance to translate admirable ideals into what goes on daily in their own classroom communities. But putting principle into practice can be a complex process. This part of the book examines ways of doing this.

Literacy matters

Much of the curriculum is articulated through reading and writing and literacy holds a critically important place in life generally. In other words, literacy matters. Not having access to literacy matters too. Access to literacy is seen as an automatic right. Fair enough, but from there it is only a short step towards seeing the acquisition of literacy as a kind of duty and either pitying or blaming those individuals in society who are not as fully literate as is considered acceptable. At the moment there is great political attention directed towards levels of literacy accompanied by a sense that those pupils who leave secondary school with less than acceptable levels – however defined – are somehow less worthy human beings. In this way, of course, such young people receive a double blow; not only do they experience the de-powering effects of not being able to handle the literacy demands which others take for granted, but they also suffer from stigma because they lack that power. However, lack of power over the written word is not just a matter of technical skill; it is to do with the ways in which literacy opportunities are offered. Unquestioned assumptions about what counts as valid or valuable literacy can themselves create divisions and exclude some pupils from ever having the chance to exercise power over their own literacy and so over the social rights which literacy confers.

The matter of how young people get to grips with literacy, or, indeed, what constitutes literacy are two more strands in the complex interweaving of principle and practice. Being literate means more than simply being able to decode print, getting hold of the surface message. It means being able to bring experience and knowledge to bear on any text which is presented; being able to read the small print as well as read between the lines. Liz Plackett argues that literacy should mean more than basic literacy or functional *literacy*:

> Literacy should mean a great deal more than merely the ability to cope with tax or social security forms, letters from the council, or the front page of the *Sun*. The view which sees literacy for certain groups as merely the ability to cope with the 'demands of society' is one which sees these groups as passive, unlike others of whom a fuller kind of literacy is expected. We would like our pupils to use their literacy to become active members of that society which makes 'demands'; to be able to develop and extend their thinking in ways that only writing can provide; to see themselves as part of a community of readers and writers rather than as mere consumers of this community's products.
>
> (Plackett 1996: 197)

One of the demands which society is likely to make of its young people in the very near future is that they should be able to tackle new forms of communication; new 'literacies'. This makes demands on teachers themselves. As technology advances there is an urgent need to review assumptions about pupils' abilities in handling literacy demands. More varied and diverse texts are now available to young people – not just printed books but television, picture books, video, comic books, computer games, interest magazines, CD-ROMs and the Internet. The heavy influence of visual and media texts means that attitudes to literacy need to shift in order to help developing readers take a discriminating view. At the same time, new forms of representation are expanding pupils' knowledge. In different ways young learners bring a much more extensive range of 'literacy skills' than perhaps in earlier generations. This offers a challenge to teachers to hear the voices of young learners, who are often much more adept at reading the new forms of communication than adults are. There is a mass of out-of-school experience which cannot be energised in a classroom, where literacy is seen largely as skill building.

Differentiation and diversity

Differences between classroom and home experiences of literacy are well documented as important areas for scrutiny (Brice Heath 1983; Lankshear 1997). Avril Dawson examines these issues in her case study in Chapter 13. However, there are other significant conflicts in the ways in which teachers link learning with language. One of the most damaging of these is an assumption that literacy is an indicator of conceptual ability – or 'intelligence'. Much educational practice in the United Kingdom falls into the trap of assuming that a pupil who has difficulties with spelling, writing or reading is 'less able'. All such 'shorthand' definitions are likely to be inaccurate since not only does each person's 'ability' vary according to the task or curriculum area, it also varies according to what the teacher makes it possible for the pupil to achieve. Observing young learners during PE, art, design technology or working together on the computer yields evidence of cognitive ability which may not be matched by high levels of literacy. This is part of a perennial double bind for teachers. Whilst wanting to recognise and value the different strengths which pupils bring, they nevertheless have a duty to help each learner to reach the highest levels of attainment possible – and achievement is almost entirely judged through literacy. This means that there needs to be a thoughtful approach to the different qualities and experiences which are brought to the classroom – and in turn this implies a wider view of differentiation than labelling pupils 'more able' or 'less able'. There is potential for greater achievement when teachers can describe the learning strengths and needs of individuals or groups in ways which do not over-generalise or use unhelpful labels.

Helen Savva points to the dangers of such over-generalisations when working with bilingual pupils:

> One of the key lessons to be learned about bilingual children is that they are not a homogeneous group. There is a tendency to discuss them and their needs as if they were identical. Linguistically, socially, culturally, politically, the lives of bilingual children are complex and their experience diverse.
>
> (Savva 1991: 7)

It is all too easy for teachers to make assumptions about groups of pupils or about individuals whose English is insecure. The fact that they are not yet fluent in spoken or written English does not mean that they cannot learn. They may have a great deal of knowledge which they should be given the scope to use. Savva gives a poignant example of the kinds of assumptions made about bilingual learners' abilities:

> When working in a comprehensive school in the East End of London, I was told a story about a fourth-year pupil who had arrived recently from Bangladesh. Withdrawn from his mainstream mathematics lesson, he was taken to work with a small group on 'extra maths'. After completing a series of elementary calculations which the teacher provided, he pushed himself angrily from the table, chalked a complex algebraic equation on the blackboard and said: 'In Bangladesh, Me!'
>
> (Savva 1991: 8)

It is clear from this example that assumptions about ability and language can be misleading and that teachers need to look for the individual strengths, weaknesses and experiences which learners bring to the classroom. Even with pupils who are not bilingual, there are grounds for criticism of too inflexible an approach to 'ability' grouping. Grouping pupils is a perfectly acceptable classroom practice to promote learning. However, it is important to recognise that even if learners can be grouped according to common qualities, they are nevertheless not likely to form genuinely homogeneous groups. It is by no means a simple matter to group according to 'ability'. Such groupings beg the question *ability in what?* Every teacher is aware that pupils who show a high level of confidence and competence in one area of the curriculum may well experience difficulties in another area. A view of differentiation which focuses mainly on individual performance can lead to an exclusive approach to teaching and learning. Rather than open up opportunities, it can close them down and by focusing on the individual can evade taking a critical look at the arrangements for learning. In looking at differentiation in English, Peter Daw points out:

> If differentiation involves recognising differences between learners and pursuing these positively, it is clear that the areas of difference are many, with the ill-defined notion of 'ability' being only one and not the most

> important. Pupils differ in gender, in cultural background, experience of all kinds, in personality, in learning styles, in motivation and much more.
>
> (Daw 1996: 127)

This draws attention to diversity as a factor in classroom provision. In other words, differentiation needs to be perceived in terms of entitlement to as full and flexible a curriculum as possible and to be thought of in terms of how the curriculum might cater for and build on diversity. Not as easy as it sounds, but essential if future citizens are to be *positively engaged* with future challenges.

Another look at the curriculum

In her book *Differently Literate*, Elaine Millard researches the current concern of boys' achievements in literacy and so in education as a whole. She sees the issue as part of a much wider picture:

> While considering the reasons for boys' indifference to, and sometimes aversions for, the varieties of reading and writing most often set for them in school it seemed to me to be also symptomatic of a much larger concern. Most boys are less tolerant than most girls of activities which they consider to be irrelevant to their lives; girls, on the other hand, largely enjoy the 'literacy curriculum' whatever its function, often importing their interest in reading and writing to more practical subjects. . . . There is some ground, then, to consider boys' gradual alienation from current literacy activities in school as an important indicator of the need for a more appropriate and demanding curriculum for all pupils.
>
> (Millard 1997: 180)

Not only does the curriculum need scrutiny, but the newer forms of literacy need to be taken into account as well as the assumptions and practices which accompany more traditional forms of teaching.

The two case studies which form Part 5 address the complexities of issues surrounding literacy for pupils who experience difficulties. A theme which runs through both chapters is a sense that if teachers can help learners make connections between their existing out-of-school experience and the demands of the curriculum, they will be able to make more sense of learning. In Chapter 13 Avril Dawson gives a detailed case study of James, a perfectly capable boy, whose earlier experience of failure at school-type literacy has left him unsettled and unable to find his place in the demands of a curriculum which depends to a great extent on fluent reading and writing. She describes a mismatch between what is going on in James' mind and the intentions of the different teachers who try to teach him. Dawson argues that James is at the extremity of a kind of experience which faces all young learners – coping with the complexities of an *endless stream of undifferentiated experience* which is made worse by the fact that he has no stake in the learning activities which are presented to him. The discourse of school as an institution cuts no ice with James because he cannot locate a place for himself in it. He is an outsider to the curriculum, though, importantly, not an outsider to his peers. Neither his home nor his personal linguistic experience are able to feed his school-based learning. His oral fluency is diverted into misbehaviour and because the connections are not made, the gulf between what he knows and what he might come to know threatens to grow wider. This chapter ends with suggestions about how James – and pupils like him – can be given greater access to learning.

Peter Fifield's case study in Chapter 14 emphasises equally strongly the need to make connections between pupils' different experiences of literacy and learning. His work with children who have a range of physical, medical and learning difficulties means developing a finely tuned sense of how to cater for diversity. He feels strongly that special children should not be given a diminished curriculum; tasks should not 'be low level or trivial'. In teaching history with a small group of 12-year-old learners whose educational experience has been fragmented and difficult for them, he gives a reminder that if pupils' literacy is insecure this does not mean they cannot handle the demands of the rest of the curriculum: 'After all, the majority of the people who lived in the past were non-literate and much evidence about their past has been left to us in non-written forms.'

Using the pupils' experience of pictorial literacy, this case study account details the everyday classroom practices which can turn principles about entitlement into practice. By building on non-literate experience, these pupils are moving little by little into more fluent and assured literacy and this in turn opens up access to the wider curriculum. By making connections between what learners already know and can do and the demands of new learning, their grasp of new concepts is made more secure and enduring. For Avril Dawson and Peter Fifield, 'entitlement to a full and flexible curriculum' is no empty slogan, but a lived reality. They see a teacher's responsibility for language and learning involving:

- recognising the learner's existing experience and building on it;
- creating an environment where learners can take an active part in negotiating and organising their own learning;
- providing opportunities for collaboration, reflection and evaluation;
- having a clear view of (and discussing/explaining) aims, purposes and intended outcomes of activities;
- providing models and examples, including teachers' own use of language and experience;
- using what pupils say, in conjunction with what they do, as a resource for judging their levels of understanding and for planning activities that will help move them onwards;
- seeing the links between writing, talk, listening and reading, so that

language is recognised as the central means of making sense of experience and creating new knowledge;
- encouraging learners progressively to take charge of their own learning;
- having a theory of development as recursive, dynamic and cumulative, rather than a linear progress through clearly defined stages.

References

Brice Heath, S. (1983) *Ways with Words: Life and Work in Communities and Classrooms*, Cambridge: Cambridge University Press.

Daw, P. (1996) 'Differentiation and its Meanings' in M. Simons (ed.) *Where We've Been: Articles from The English and Media Magazine*, London: English and Media Centre.

Kress, G. (1997) *Before Writing – Rethinking the Paths to Literacy*, London: Routledge.

Lankshear, C. (1997) *Changing Literacies*, Buckingham: Open University Press.

Millard, E. (1997) *Differently Literate: Boys, Girls and the Schooling of Literacy*, London: Falmer Press.

Plackett, E. (1996) (revised) 'Helping Slow Readers: Principles and Practice' in M. Simons (ed.) *Where We've Been*, London: English and Media Centre.

Savva, H. (1991) 'Bilingual by Rights' in *Language and Learning* 5, pp. 6–10, Birmingham: The Questions Publishing Company.

13

MAKING CONNECTIONS I

James – a pupil with literacy difficulties

Avril Dawson

What the teacher teaches is not the same as what the pupil learns.
(Barnes, Britton and Torbe 1990: 45)

James has a statement of special needs.[1] At the age of 11 his reading age is assessed as being about three years behind his chronological age and he is unable to do very much in the way of independent writing – nor is he often inclined to make any effort in that direction. He has always been much more interested in what is going on around him, and this makes sitting still and quiet a very dull option.

This is James during a science lesson, on the subject of nutrition. The class have already done some work on the topic and are engaged in revising what they know, as well as learning more, through discussion and the use of a well-designed textbook. The book was chosen particularly with special needs learners in mind, and has attractive pictures, photographs and diagrams, with clearly headed print separated into manageable chunks and colour coded. The pupils are keen to answer questions and offer stories, sharing experiences of broken bones, favourite foods or the ones they find the most disgusting.

James is apparently not listening. His neighbour has a plaster cast on his arm, covered with writing in various colours of felt tip. James examines this with interest and, lacking his own plaster cast, covers his hand with felt scribbles. While he is engaged in this activity, his teacher asks a question about vitamins: James's hand shoots up and he is asked to answer (although his answer is incorrect). He rocks backwards and forwards on his stool as the discussion turns to the subject of scurvy, and becomes increasingly animated, delighted at the idea of sailors drinking their own urine. James relishes commenting *Skanky! Manky!* over and over. He turns round on his stool and tries to balance his pen, first under his nose, and then on his bottom lip. There is more discussion about the various food groups. The teacher involves the pupils, asking questions linked to their own experience, repeating key words in her statements and questions, using the textbook as a structure but ensuring the interest of the class through talk, before leading on to the drawing of a diagram of a food pyramid. She mentions dairy products; James immediately shouts out *Dairylea!* The teacher in the adjoining laboratory crossly calls the name of a student in her class and James repeats it, obviously taken with the idea that someone is in trouble, and revelling in the possibilities of what the offending student might have done. He perks up at the news that his own class will be looking at some packets: *Food!* (He is to be disappointed that the packets are empty.)

First, however, there is some writing to be copied from the board, to accompany the diagram the pupils have now copied into their books. James looks steadily at the blackboard, not once (until the teacher intervenes) at his exercise book, and talks constantly to his neighbour. He expresses his dislike of *boffs* (pupils who know things about science), invites my opinion on the subject, decides that his neighbour is acceptable as a *middle boff*. His characteristic writing pose is chin on arm, arm wrapped around the back of his neck. Unsurprisingly, his writing is totally illegible and wanders across the page at random.

With so much going on for James it is difficult to gauge how much he is involved with any focused process of learning, how much information he is taking in and what he is doing with it. How much does his learning match up with the teacher's teaching? Clearly there is a mismatch between the images in James's mind and those in the teacher's mind. My own mental picture when the teacher mentioned dairy products was based on cows on a hillside and childhood memories of butter being churned; James obviously saw little foil-wrapped triangles. Barnes, Britton and Torbe identify this kind of difference: 'This teacher teaches with his [*sic*] frame of reference; the pupils learn in theirs, taking in his words, which mean something different to them, and struggling to incorporate this meaning into their own frames of reference' (Barnes, Britton and Torbe 1990: 29–30).

There would seem to be more chance of James making learning fit his frame of reference and so reach an identifiable learning target in the relatively peaceful oases of one-to-one withdrawal lessons than in a whole class setting. In individual lessons he can concentrate on the learning of literacy skills without the exciting distraction of other pupils, as in the following example. The aim of this particular lesson, which I thought I had made clear to James at the beginning, was to familiarise himself with the computer keyboard in a quiet corner of the school, while becoming more aware of letter strings and learning to reproduce them accurately at speed. Implicit in my aims, though not expressed, was also the desire to give James some success in concentrating on a task, and to build up the length of time he could work without distraction:

James: What's that key for? What does that do? Did I tell you about me and my mate getting chased by the farmer? Yo! Ryan! Are those the photos of the Year 8 school trip?

Me: James, the computer's timing you on this game. I'll answer your questions in a minute.

A few seconds' concentration.

James: Oh, gone wrong again! Can we do something else now? Oh look! That kid's getting done! Why has that keyboard got dots on those keys? This one hasn't . . .

It's not that James can't concentrate. I've seen him totally engrossed, spending a 45-minute lesson colouring his own picture of a racing car while I've been reading to him, and he's been able to talk about the story in some detail afterwards. But there's usually just so much going on out there and he doesn't want to miss it.

Of course, James is identified as having special needs, but he's not the only one coping with the 'endless stream of undifferentiated experience' (Britton 1992: 37). In an attempt to probe what goes on in pupils' minds when they are in the classroom, I asked some more academically successful pupils to make impromptu notes recording what was going on for them in a lesson. They were certainly not blanking out all distractions. Their notes showed that they were thinking about playing tennis after school, contemplating the Test Match, wishing their neighbours would keep quiet, wondering whether they would make up with a friend, wishing the teacher would stop talking so that they could get on with the next bit of the lesson, listening for the bell, *this is boring, this is interesting, yuck! liver!* (the nutrition lesson again). My own 'quiet oases' of withdrawal lessons aren't any less full of distractions for me either. While I'm talking and responding to James, noting all the time what he is doing and saying, guiding him, explaining, suggesting, part of my mind is also reviewing plans for my after-school club, wondering whether one of my own children remembered to do something I had asked him to, sorting out the logistics of a trip at the weekend, noting a sore lip, overhearing the teacher in the next classroom, wishing I'd handled something differently in the previous lesson, wondering who will turn up for Parents' Evening, thinking it's about time I changed a wall display. . . . Each thought more or less fleeting, each more or less prominent.

Drawing the threads of one line of thinking together is easier for me, with years of experience, both in a private and professional sense. I also have the advantage that the direction of the lesson is necessarily under my control; although James is given a degree of choice, in that he is consulted about the order in which the activities I have planned are tackled and, to some extent, which activities out of a limited range of options he would like to do, the fact remains that I have chosen the activities according to my own plans, the result of my professional assessment of his needs.

Language and power

> [Words] acquire their meanings only in a context, and a crucial element of that context is the power relations operating within it.
>
> (Cameron 1995: 157)

My words to James – indeed anyone's words – are overlaid with a whole range of personal connotations, which are inevitably not the same as the connotations he attaches to those words, in the same way that my reading of certain books is intricately bound up with faint memories of the places I read them in, the mood I was in and so on; oral texts are part of a rich context of experiences, each experience infusing the others. James is in the position that, like me, he not only has to separate out the strands of experience – the aim and activities relating to the lesson, the sights around him, movements of other people, questions relating to equipment (the dots on the computer keyboard – a diversion as far as I am concerned – seem vital to him at the time, and certainly no less important than typing in letter strings), the practical difficulties of the activity (e.g. finding his way around the keyboard, sitting still), and so on – but has the added complication that none of this, as far as he is concerned, originated from any desire of his, but was imposed on him.

At school, James, like any pupil or, indeed, any member of staff, is bound by the conventions of the school as a social institution. Being told off for his behaviour is a familiar enough experience for him. The teacher determines James's stance, facial expression, gaze and body movements: James must look contrite, look at the teacher, stand upright and still, pay attention, not fiddle, not put his hands in his pockets. He is allowed only a limited range of responses, framed in polite language, speaking only when invited to, addressing the teacher in formal terms whereas the teacher addresses him by his christian name and may use the first person plural of themselves, reminding James of the weight of authority and the number of authority figures he has to deal with. His presence in the situation of being reprimanded, his clothing (uniform), even whether or not he is allowed to wear jewellery, are already determined by the social institution of which the teacher is a part. There is an assumption on the teacher's part of an agreement between teacher and pupil regarding goals. James is forced to voice agreement whether or not he agrees, pushed into promises he may have no intention of keeping. Of course he wants to behave better, not get told off, be seen as a responsible human being – at least, he knows he has to agree with this to get out of the immediate, uncomfortable situation. This may lead to a whole range of responses in James, including resentment regarding his impotence in school.

He must couch his responses in terms of the teacher's point of view, whereas he is, in fact, firmly located in his own. His immature, irresponsible behaviour (in the teacher's view) is, in James's view, a good laugh, which gives him a certain kind of status in the class (and is much easier to achieve than many other kinds of status). James is popular with his peers. Despite his sometimes bizarre behaviour and often ink-stained appearance, the girls in his year group (Year 7), particularly the more academically successful ones, rate him reasonably highly in the boyfriend stakes. The importance of peer relationships is not a trivial aspect of school, to be overlooked, but central to the lives of the pupils. For teachers, the central concern of school is education; when asked, pupils are very good at giving us the answers we want, assuring us that education is what school is about for them too, but, in reality, relationships have more immediate importance.

Meanings and intentions

This is James in a geography lesson. The pupils have been learning about the rainforest and the teacher has gathered them all around a table to explain a game that they are to make and play. James is sitting directly opposite the teacher, watching, repeatedly pushing his chin up with his fist to shut his mouth, pushing his hair back, tossing his head up and down. The teacher mentions colour coding and James immediately interjects: *Like Jumanji!* referring to the Robin Williams' film based around a game. The teacher recaps one of the things the pupils have to do in making the game, saying that they have to use a pen. An instant correction comes from James: *Pencil!* The class splits up into groups to start work. James joins in his group's discussion and insists (while practising golf swings behind his chair) *I'll be the cowboy!* The word *cowboy* has not been mentioned once during the lesson: the teacher referred only to *cattle barons*.

A few days later, I asked James what he remembered about the lesson, and the game in particular:

> You have this board game and it's called . . . I don't know. Can I call it Jumanji? . . . It's a strain, Miss [to remember]! You've got to fight for the area and whoever gets the most squares coloured in gets the area. That's about all. . . . I'm going to be the logger . . . chops down trees, burns jungle for money. . . . It's a job. It clears the area . . . you have to pick up cards and roll dice.

Although initially he said that he could remember nothing, brief prompting questions evinced the most salient features – and aim – of the game and showed that, contrary to his own expectations, he could actually remember what role everyone in his group was to play: 'Robert's going to be the cow person, a rancher. Ryan is going to be with Ben. Daniel's going to be the miner. He searches for gold with high powered jets.' Although James's image of what was happening in the rainforest was coloured by his delight in physical fighting, high speeds and the Wild West – presumably not the features the teacher, or designer of the game, had foremost in their minds – his interpretation was probably close enough to the shared meaning with which we can all agree. James has had long experience of making meaning in a variety of contexts. Each person's experience is unique, and this ensures that the meanings James makes are bound up with his own personal history and interests and are not necessarily defined in exactly the same way as the meanings his teachers intend.

This is not necessarily a big problem. It is inevitable that everything we say has a personal meaning for us and will be heard, personally translated, by the person listening to us. Generally, however, we make sense of each other.

Misunderstandings are the exception rather than the rule and the mismatches between our meanings do not usually present a practical inconvenience. Language is, after all, a social phenomenon, fundamentally dialogic in Vygotsky's terms.

However, genuine difficulties may arise where the participants in a speech event have very different personal histories and experiences, inevitable to some extent between adults and children, and certainly inevitable in the specialised environment of a school. Margaret Donaldson quotes Laurie Lee's experience on starting school: 'they never gave me the present . . . (they said) "Well, you just sit here for the present". . . . I ain't never going back there again' (Donaldson 1978: 17).

There is a danger that teachers may automatically assume that their words are unproblematic and difficulties will not be recognised. Misunderstandings such as Laurie Lee's expectation of a gift from his teacher may take a long time to become apparent; in that case, understanding may not have been crucial (though it certainly made its mark, to be remembered with such poignancy into adulthood) but other misunderstandings may lead to a real sense of alienation for the child and difficulty in making sense of learning opportunities.

Dislocations

> Have you ever hurt about school?
> I have, because I learned a lot of words from school
> And they are not my words.
>
> (Levine 1990: 15)

This extract comes from a poem written by a bilingual child. However, as Levine says, this is:

> no more than a sharpened version of what all children know about and often admit to: a sometimes anxious sense of being dislocated and fragmented by the need to behave quite differently at school from the way they behave at home.
>
> (Levine 1990: 20)

A group of Year 8 pupils, in a bottom English set, are discussing the problems they encounter at school. One of them explains :

> Teachers put you down sometimes, don't they? . . . Like if, like, I don't answer a question and I don't know it, [the teacher] goes, 'What's the answer?' and if you don't know, then she'll just embarrass you. . . . If you don't put your hand up, then you don't know it but she picks on you because she thinks you're not listening but you are, you just don't know it.

The pupils had easily grasped the problems a teacher faces in making sure that everyone understands the lesson, not always choosing the same pupils to answer questions, ensuring that everyone is paying attention . . . but they could go through the whole of their school life without the opportunity to make these issues explicit. At home, they would be more likely to be able to state that they do not know the answer to a question without fear of ridicule, but the competitive ethos of the educational context is different. This is not to say that competition does not exist outside the classroom; peer pressure is an obvious example with powerful consequences. However, the necessary power structures in school, maintaining the balance of status between staff and pupils, can dictate against the optimum conditions for individual learning, which are, after all, what we, as teachers, are trying to achieve.

Children have a long exposure to the kind of discourse that takes place in schools, but it is not necessarily a discourse in which they feel comfortable. Cazden and Michaels point to the dangers of dislocations between the discourses of home and school:

> Where teacher and child do not share a set of discourse strategies, the teacher – despite the best educational intentions – may be unable to build on what the child already knows, or may misassess the child's skills and needs altogether.
>
> (Cazden and Michaels 1986: 138)

Such research shows the advantage some children have over others when they start formal education already versed in the kinds of discourse favoured in school.

Shirley Brice Heath's study, for example, of the communities in Roadville, Trackton and the neighbouring township (Brice Heath 1983), demonstrates the deeply complex varieties of literacy and oracy existing in one relatively small area of the Piedmont Carolinas in America. Expectations and uses of literacy and oracy are shown to be quite different, not only from each other, but from the expectations and uses which are (covertly) valued by school. Children from both Trackton and Roadville came into school already very familiar with the written word, but unprepared for the school's ways with words. The township, in contrast, was strongly oriented towards school; school success was seen as integral to success as an adult in general. The children of the townspeople entered school prepared by their community's literacy and language environment, familiar with the distinctions between contextualised first-hand experiences and decontextualised representations of experience, already acting as literates before they could read. This had significant effects on their chances of success in schooled literacy. As practising teachers, we cannot be familiar with the patterns of discourse of all the pupils we teach, even in a restricted, stable environment. There are inevitably subtle differences between communities, between families in those communities and between individuals in those families. What we need, however, is an awareness of those differences so that we can be flexible, as the teachers described in *Ways with Words* learned to be flexible, finding ways to make reading and writing make sense, and so that we can learn to believe that pupils like James can learn.

Different ways of knowing

Teachers may have had very different backgrounds and a variety of experience of discourse patterns, but we do have in common at least a certain amount of academic success. While this is a necessary qualification, there is a danger that we see school discourse as the only true discourse of thinking and learning. It is worth reminding ourselves that there are different kinds, not only of discourse, but of intelligence: Howard Gardner (in Meek and Mills 1988: 101) speaks of mountaineers and dancers displaying *spatial intelligence* and *bodily kinaesthetic intelligence*, for example. James, for all his apparent inability to sit still and follow instructions, is a keen sportsman. He swims with a club, wins judo belts and is accomplished at karting, all skills which require discipline, a sense of timing and good co-ordination.

Knowing that James has these abilities in other areas but does not use them to improve his literacy skills can make it even more frustrating for those of us who teach him. While I do not believe that James is unable to learn literacy skills – far from it – it is worth noting the research by Scribner and Cole among the Vai in Liberia (in Gee 1994: 189), which points out that different literacies allow different skills to be practised. Gunther Kress reminds us that the Australian Aborigines have been referred to as 'illiterate', yet they have at their disposal a complexity of forms of representation (Kress 1997: 102).

The 'essay-text literacy' valued so highly by western society is only one literacy among many. It is, of course, valued by those who have power and its importance gains significance with increasing globalisation:

> Where life opportunity exposes children to the patterns of language actually rewarded in an education, they come to school very much advantaged over those not so exposed. For so long as we continue to leave the linguistic choices necessary for school success a matter of the 'invisible' agenda of schooling, so too we perpetuate disadvantage.
>
> (Frances Christie, in Green 1993: 90)

Children who do not feel comfortable with school patterns of discourse very soon find that they may be doubly disadvantaged. Some quickly learn the approved ways of operating, even if they are not their natural ways. Other young learners find that they are unable to make the shift. This has implications for their learning in the classroom. They are less likely to have their oral contributions incorporated into the process of the lesson, or to be given the opportunity to clarify and expand what they have to say. This in turn makes it more difficult to internalise the required discourses of literacy. Without easy access to literacy, the students spend more time confused, having to work harder towards a more difficult goal than their peers, and, often, giving up.

There is plenty of scope for confusion in school. Learners experience an increasing amount of technical vocabulary as they progress in their schooling. For some pupils this adds to their sense of confusion and alienation. They encounter words in maths such as *kite* and must learn that this is the name of a very particular kind of shape which may resemble some of the kites they have experienced in the world outside school, but is totally different from many others, whose shapes must not be called kites. Neither is it just a matter of jargon: it may also be a matter of appropriateness, using different ground rules. Areas for exploration in school, for instance in science, are usually defined by the teacher, whereas outside school children's exploration generally occurs as a natural part of their experience and interest, informing and reforming their concepts, as it did pre-school. Pupils who can produce perfectly punctuated work in exercises may seem incapable of transferring these skills to writing in general. We teach the importance of punctuation without making explicit what they already know from their own experience – that punctuation is not always important or appropriate – in notes to each other, or on the blackboard, or in some advertising. Poetry and literature often work precisely *because* the conventions of punctuation are flouted; for example, publishers do not refuse to publish Gabriel García Márquez on the grounds that he writes single sentences five pages long.

Establishing shared understandings

When they come to school, children are required, in a sense, to leave the ordinary world behind, to 'disembed' their thinking. James finds this very difficult; his mind is constantly caught up in his world outside school, or at least in the world outside the teacher's planning of the lesson, making connections which do not always lead to better understanding. While he accepts this world which is so familiar to him – he has by now had several years of schooling – it is doubtful whether he really feels part of it. He is a passive recipient, rather than an active participant in his learning at school.

There are ways of making it easier for children to take ownership of their learning. Genuinely validating their own talk can allow them to work towards a better understanding. A colleague who is particularly sensitive to the need to build up a common knowledge frequently calls on pupils to explain their ideas. After the first explanation, a series of pupils are invited to explain the same idea: *Samantha, can you tell us what Richard has just said? . . . Michael, can you put what Samantha has said into your own words?* And so on. I stumbled across a similar technique one day in exasperation. Several of the pupils complained that they could not understand what they had to do, though it seemed obvious to me. I explained again, two or three times. A few more understood. At a loss as to how to explain any more clearly, I asked them to explain to each other. I am not sure what they said that was different, but there was complete success and all started working productively. Perhaps it is a case of *not what you say but the way that you say it*. Another colleague weaves a multitude of anecdotes into her science lessons, riveting the students (and any colleagues fortunate enough to be present!) so that they are eager to make the connections between the science they are learning and their own experience.

Classroom talk like this gives the children with literacy difficulties equal opportunities with their peers, and a real stake in their learning. They do not always have this benefit. In many classrooms it is the teachers who do most of the talking. Research shows that the teacher asks, on average, two questions a minute; the students average two an hour per class (Norman 1992: 204). This is not necessarily a bad thing – teacher talk is essential for a number of reasons, not least the teacher's greater knowledge and expertise in guiding the students – but it does not encourage pupils to be active learners. If the pupils' task is only to guess what the teacher has in mind, to respond rather than to initiate; if initiations are only seen as an unwelcome distraction and therefore ignored, then the pupil may be justified in feeling alienated from the whole experience. For some learners, speaking up in class to offer a contribution or answer a question, even if they are confident they know the answer, may be intolerable because they hate being in the spotlight. Class discussion is vital, but we should also be aware of its disadvantages.

Talking in a small group may give the pupil with literacy difficulties – as well as the shy one – more chance of active participation. Group talk offers a chance to try out ideas, to work together towards a common understanding, to admit when they don't understand, to use their own language, to ask questions, be given immediate responses, absorb their ideas into their own cultural references. They are also given the opportunity to be exploratory in what they say, rather than present a 'final draft'.

For the teacher, however, sometimes pupil talk may feel threatening. They may not explore what we intend them to, or come to the conclusions we want. They may wander off the point and start discussing something else. There is the question of behaviour management. It is interesting that taped discussions often show pupils taking 'time out', but this also has the effect of giving them time to think, to return to the discussion with fresh, or clearer, ideas. From another angle, informal social talk also often shows evidence of reflection on what pupils have been learning. For the curriculum to work we must ensure that pupils come to a *common knowledge*, in Edwards and Mercer's phrase (Edwards and Mercer 1987). This means that group talk must be planned carefully. It must be given validity and seen by the students as valued both as a means of learning and as a method of assessment.

Talking with other people undoubtedly helps to generate and clarify thoughts, but talking to ourselves can be equally useful in sharpening ideas. James's contributions on tape, made on his own, are in marked contrast to his talk in the classroom, where he has developed ways of behaving which mask his fear of failure with reading and writing. On tape, when he knows he is being taken seriously, he talks with interest and enthusiasm, showing a level of commitment to his own learning which is otherwise lacking. It is true that the conditions have been quite different as he is in a one-to-one situation where he does not have to impress his peers, but this does not seem an adequate explanation for his increased confidence. Talking on tape allows him to show his kind of knowledge; in his experience, the demands of classroom literacy have for many years prevented this. Instead of trying to draw James back in from the edges of his learning experiences, by insisting on the routine and sometimes incomprehensible classroom practices, it seems wise to make better and more frequent use of his stronger oracy skills to support his weaker literacy skills – to make it clear that his knowledge is worth listening to. Recognising his kind of knowing places him more firmly where he should belong – at the centre of his own learning.

Note

1 Names have been changed throughout the text to protect identity.

References

Barnes, D., Britton, J. and Torbe, M. (1990) *Language, the Learner and the School*, London: Heinemann.

Brice Heath, S. (1983) *Ways with Words*, Cambridge: Cambridge University Press.

Britton, J. (revised 1992) *Language and Learning*, Harmondsworth: Penguin.

Cameron, (1995) *Verbal Hygiene*, London: Routledge.

Cazden, C. and Michaels, S. (1986) 'Teacher/Child Collaboration as Oral Preparation for Literacy' in *The Acquisition of Literacy: Ethnographic Perspectives* vol. 21, Norwood, N.J.: Ablex.

Donaldson, M. (1978) *Children's Minds*, London: Fontana.

Edwards, D. and Mercer, N. (1987) *Common Knowledge*, London: Methuen.

Fairclough, N. (1989) *Language and Power*, London: Longman.

Gee, J. P. (1994) 'Orality and Literacy: From "The Savage Mind" to "Ways with Words"', in J. Maybin (ed.) *Language and Literacy in Social Practice*, Milton Keynes: Multilingual Matters Ltd in association with The Open University.

Green, B. (1993) *The Insistence of the Letter: Literacy Studies and the Curriculum*, London: Falmer Press.

Kress, G. (1997) *Before Writing – Rethinking the Paths to Literacy*, London: Routledge.

Levine, J. (ed.) (1990) *Bilingual Learners and the Mainstream Curriculum*, London: Falmer Press.

Meek, M. and Mills, C. (eds) (1988) *Language and Literacy in the Primary School*, London: Falmer Press.

Norman, K. (ed.) (1992) *Thinking Voices – the Work of the National Oracy Project*, London: Hodder and Stoughton.

14

MAKING CONNECTIONS II

Access to learning for pupils with special educational needs

Peter Fifield

If children's literacy is insecure, it is often supposed that they cannot handle the demands of the rest of the curriculum. This case study describes some of the learning activities in a history class over two terms. All the pupils attend a special school and have a variety of learning difficulties. None of them is particularly confident with writing and most are only happy with reading fairly simple written texts. Presenting the curriculum for pupils with special educational needs involves careful thought and planning. Enabling pupils to demonstrate understanding without relying on extended writing tasks or independent reading of complex texts, can be difficult. For those who have little confidence in literacy, there is a danger that the tasks they are asked to tackle may be low level or trivial.

This small class of 11- and 12-year-olds were embarking on the Key Stage 3 programmes of study. These pupils attend special school for a variety of diverse and complex medical, physical and emotional reasons, for example:

Michelle has significant learning difficulties but is also very emotionally vulnerable.

Peter has Asperger's syndrome and his behaviour can be obsessive and bizarre. He finds writing difficult but is more confident orally.

Shaun has also been diagnosed as having Asperger's syndrome. He is emotionally very unstable. He enjoys collecting facts but is not keen to engage in written tasks. Shaun has a lively mind but is happier in reality rather than in imaginative tasks.

Lee has had a serious medical condition that has meant long stays in hospital. He lacks self-confidence.

Ellie also has had long spells in hospital and has therefore missed important parts of her schooling. She is not as emotionally developed as other pupils of her age and finds it hard to concentrate, mainly due to her particular illness.

Other pupils in the class have experienced interruptions to their learning because of their medical or physical conditions, but I have chosen these five to concentrate on since their work over this unit of work showed some interesting – and surprising – capabilities.

A good level of literacy is often seen as a prerequisite for developing historical skills. However, this need not be so. History offers the opportunity to develop language in different ways – much of it is generated by powerful story lines that are very appealing and accessible to children. There is enormous potential for storytelling and discussion in this subject. Historical information is gained not just through written texts but also through pictures, diagrams, artefacts, site visits, models, films, CD-ROMs, videos, older people's memories. These are all resources that can be drawn on to make history accessible to pupils from the whole spectrum of capabilities. After all, the majority of people who lived in the past were non-literate and much evidence about their past has been left to us in non-written forms. Although I am keen to use history to develop more confidence in written work, I also want to develop the pupils' historical skills through other means – storytelling, role play and, particularly, the extensive use of pictorial texts.

I began planning by referring to aspects of the five Key Elements of the National Curriculum for history. I also wanted the pupils to have experience of using a range of learning materials relevant to historical enquiry. In covering these learning objectives in history, I was also hoping to strengthen their confidence, fluency and accuracy in reading and writing. The National Curriculum study Unit 1 at Key Stage 3 is Medieval Realms. Because I wanted particularly to focus on those areas which lend themselves to storytelling, I decided to spend most time on the Norman invasion of England in 1066; the death of Thomas Becket; and aspects of life in medieval times (and later), especially disease and medicine. I chose these because they offered scope to develop the key areas through a variety of non-writing or small writing tasks which I wanted to build towards more extended narrative. The last topic (disease and medicine) also offered a bridge from medieval times to later periods of history. Figure 14.1 shows my planning outline.

Reading the pictures

The 1066 story was ideal for my objectives since one of the main historical sources is in narrative pictorial form – the Bayeux tapestry. All the pupils were familiar with and enjoy comic books and picture story books. The cartoon-style format of the tapestry was recognisable to them, the pictures themselves are very accessible and are simple and even appear childlike themselves to modern pictorial readers. I planned for the work to take about half a term. Using the Bayeux tapestry I wanted to develop all the strands identified in the National Curriculum:

Medieval realms	*Main activities*	*NC key elements*	*Learning outcomes*
1066: setting the scene	drama and role play	Communication	**Knowledge** of the Norman invasion: dates; names; places; way of life; warfare; sequence of events
The Bayeux tapestry	class discussion role play information gathering using primary evidence	Communication Chronology Historical enquiry and understanding	**Concepts**: invasion; causes of warfare; consequences of Harold's actions
Northern invasion	storyboarding sequencing	Organisation and communication and Historical understanding	**Skills and techniques**: gathering and interpreting evidence from primary sources – pictorial, oral, buildings, artefacts; skimming and scanning for pictorial and verbal information; ordering pictorial narrative
Battle of Hastings	model making diagrams	Historical understanding	
Waltham Abbey	fieldwork – using primary evidence	Historical enquiry	
Becket	retelling narrative using models – pictorial and captions sequencing and role play	Chronology, Historical understanding and Communication	**Knowledge** of the assassination: names; dates; places **Concepts**: duty and loyalty; relationship between church and state **Skills and techniques**: as above plus constructing sequenced pictorial narratives with brief written text
Disease and medicine	Slides – Eyam story class discussion picture/word note-making tapes	Communication, Chronology and Historical understanding	**Knowledge** of medical practices; health and hygiene in medieval and post-medieval times **Concepts**: causes of epidemics before modern medicine; consequences – spread of disease; self-sacrifice **Skills and techniques**: as above; summarising; explaining; giving reasons; constructing oral, pictorial and written narratives; evaluating oral texts

Figure 14.1 Planning outline for history

- chronology: looking to sequence certain key events;
- historical understanding of these events;
- interpretations: looking very carefully at specific pictures in order to gain meaning;
- historical enquiry: beginning to form questions about the tapestry itself;
- communication and organisation: being able to retell part of the 1066 story using the Bayeux tapestry format.

I began the topic by telling the class the story of Edward the Confessor's problem: he was getting old and did not have an heir. I explained how Harold Godwinson was sent to Normandy to tell Duke William that he should be the next king. We turned the classroom into England on one side and Normandy on the other. Some pupils acted out these first scenes in the story in a very simple way, with me providing 'voiceover'.

Then began our main work using the Bayeux tapestry. I described what the tapestry was and at first we focused on three particular pictures. The first was a picture showing Norman soldiers crossing a river in Normandy during a flood. This is an action picture with plenty going on. The picture shows a significant event in the story – Harold carrying a soldier on his back to safety, as well as many historical details – for example, weapons, armour and horses. There are also top and bottom border illustrations of birds, fish and snakes and some Latin text. As a class we looked carefully at the picture and tried to work out what was going on and spot as many details as possible. All provided opportunities for discussion.

The second frame of the tapestry that we looked at was of Harold swearing an oath to Duke William. The picture again enabled discussion of how we make promises and the consequences of broken promises. The pupils used the picture to act out the scene in pairs. This very simple role play helped to reinforce the main events in the story; it also began to introduce concepts of cause and consequence.

The third picture was of the star that was seen as an omen in 1066. There is one picture of the people looking up at the sky at what was clearly a strange sight. We talked about comets and also about luck, fortune telling and superstitions. The pupils' knowledge of current events, including, by good fortune, the appearance of the Hale Bopp comet, their interest in horoscopes in newspapers and the frequent appearance of Mystic Meg on the television, all helped to link the present with the past and establish a sense of chronology.

I gave the pupils photocopies of these particular pictures in the tapestry so that they could refer back to them later. I wanted them to use them in the same way as they might have used written notes to remind them of key events in any historical narrative.

We continued with the story of the year 1066 as we would if we were reading a book or watching a TV soap opera together, looking at an episode at a time. The next major event was the invasion of northern England by King Harald of Norway. This part of the 1066 story is not included in the original Bayeux tapestry and so it was a good opportunity for the class to create their own frieze showing these events in the style of the original. I told them the story of how the king of Norway landed in Yorkshire and of King Harold marching his army north to York. As a class we story-boarded the significant events, sketching out what the main frames of the cartoon should be. Then in pairs the pupils were given the task of producing their own part of the frieze to draw. I wanted them to concentrate on the pictures telling the story and giving information as the original tapestry had done. The results were pasted together to form a display in the classroom. The activity proved a valuable and enjoyable one. The pupils used the conventions that had been used on the original tapestry – a decorated border top and bottom, little written text, with the detailed pictures showing all the action.

Lee demonstrated his good imagination and drew a detailed picture of Scarborough being burned down. There are soldiers with flaming torches and fire issuing from all the buildings. The detail is remarkable (see Figure 14.2). He showed that he knows about the kinds of buildings of the period and their vulnerability to attack, the weapons, methods of fighting, as well as an understanding of the conventions of pictorial depictions of different kinds – the border on his part of the frieze, for example. Whilst the factual details which he shows could be expressed in writing, his grasp of the concept of symbolic and narrative representation through pictures would be very difficult to express in words.

Shaun, who finds imaginative work much more difficult than fact gathering, decided to draw the route of Harold's army from London to York as a map.

Figure 14.2 Scarborough is burned to the ground

He chose to draw England lying sideways across the map so that it would better fit the tapestry format. He has included written text to indicate the direction of the journey Harold's army took and to show where Harald Hardraada's men landed. In this way he has captured a great deal of information – the landing at Scarborough, the extent of the journey north and then south again, the type of ship used – in a highly abstracted form, indicating sound conceptual grasp of the main events (see Figure 14.3). Michelle and Peter both produced pictures of the invasion by finding pictures of Viking boats in books. This meant much scanning and searching for information and they used the pictorial texts they had consulted as models for appropriate drawings. They both include details of the armour and ships: Peter has a painstaking picture of a soldier in armour where every link in the chain mail is clear; Michelle's drawing captures the idea of a dangerous journey with small ships being tossed in a rough sea. Ellie used pictures of battle in the Bayeux tapestry to give her the information to draw the defeat of King Harald's army at Stamford Bridge. For her, the people and their reactions to events were central; she has used facial expression to differentiate between the conquerors and the vanquished.

When all the pictures were completed we laid them out and put them in order. This again reinforced the pupils' learning about the story and helped them to sort out the chronology. The end product was not simply a very attractive piece for

Figure 14.3 King Harold's army

display, but a collaborative piece of work which also demonstrated a good understanding of this part of the history of the invasion. They were not only giving evidence that they had knowledge of the topic but were also interpreting picture evidence well and communicating their understanding in a clear way. None of them could have demonstrated their understanding of the northern invasion of England so successfully through extended writing, which for them is laborious and slow.

Building on this success, we again turned to the original Bayeux tapestry and looked at a fourth frame in detail. This time I wanted them to write down some of their observations. This picture showed Duke William's army crossing the English Channel. I asked the pupils to write down what they could see in the picture. Some of them simply described the picture and others showed signs that they were using the information to piece together something more about the story:

Lee: I think they are putting up the sails and one man looks like he is looking at the sea . . . also there is a funny looking head at the front of the boat.

Peter: . . . The man at the front of the boat is looking for danger.

Michelle: One of the men is rowing and the other man is hanging on the sail and the other man is telling the one man to Row the boot and the other man is looking out for a man to kill.

I was interested in Michelle's version because it concentrates solely on the men on board. It describes what two of them are doing and infers from the picture and previous knowledge what the other may be doing. For Michelle, who has significant learning problems, this demonstrates that she had a pleasing grasp of the material and was making confident predictions – she knows they are soldiers looking out for the enemy and she has drawn out a narrative from the picture.

So far, we had looked at the events in the tapestry piecemeal. In order to gain an overview of the events of 1066, we laid out a copy of the entire tapestry on the dining hall floor and spent a lesson looking at the whole piece in different ways. First we located the four pictures that they were already familiar with. We then looked at the Battle of Hastings. Then I gave pairs of pupils specific tasks. They were all asked to look for certain details and to make a note of them in drawings or in words. One pair looked for weapons being used, one looked for armour, one found all the animals they could see, another concentrated on clothing styles, another on forms of transport and so on. Laying out the whole tapestry enabled the pupils to see the length of the story and also allowed them to move around the story physically to research their given details. They saw the tapestry as a giant cartoon strip telling the story and also as a piece of evidence to interrogate as historians to obtain information in addition to the narrative.

Our work on the 1066 story continued by concentrating on the Battle of Hastings – drawing diagrams and making models of Norman and Saxon soldiers.

We also visited nearby Waltham Abbey in Essex, where King Harold was reputedly buried after the battle. We consolidated our 1066 work by putting all the key events into order. Sequencing is a skill that many pupils with special educational needs find difficult, but using pictures and some simple texts from School Council materials (Shephard and Moore 1994: 57), each child was able to arrange the main events in order. As a means of finding out what they had come to know about historical evidence, I asked them to write down how we know about these events. Some of the responses were:

Peter: We know these things from our history books.
Lee: . . . because there was a tapestry showing the scene.
Shaun: We know this by the tapestry nuns made. This information is very old.

Teaching the 1066 story with the Bayeux tapestry as the main resource gave access to historical understanding for all the class – those who find reading written texts difficult and those who are not confident writers. They had used pictures to make interpretations of historical events as well as to develop their sequencing skills; they had successfully communicated facts and concepts and had shown historical understanding of cause and consequence. I now wanted to take these achievements even further.

Building stories from pictures

The comic strip format was a successful way of getting the pupils to sequence a story and thus gain a better understanding of events. I wanted to build on the success of the 1066 work by choosing another powerful narrative – King Henry II's quarrel with Thomas Becket. Over the next few weeks I wanted the class to consolidate their earlier learning of using pictorial text as a technique for ordering key events through story-boarding. The quarrel between church and state involves difficult concepts. I decided that I should give them a model for the beginning of the story which they could build on. I drew some simple cartoons on the board showing King Henry and Becket as friends, the Archbishop of Canterbury refusing the king's wishes, Becket being made the new archbishop and also refusing to obey his old friend the king, and finally Becket having to leave England because of this argument. I then gave out copies of these scenes with simple captions which had to be placed in the correct order. Having story-boarded in pictures the events previously, I was pleased to see that the pupils had little problem in correctly sequencing them. This activity also demonstrated their developing historical understanding. They were beginning to analyse reasons for and results of historical events.

The next part of the work involved role playing the scenes when the exasperated king asked *Who will rid me of this troublesome priest?* and Becket's resulting murder. Having acted out the scenes with some dialogue improvised and some given, the pupils were asked to draw them as a cartoon strip, adding a suitable written text, as in the Bayeux tapestry. Again, the results showed that they had absorbed and understood certain details:

Figure 14.4 shows Peter's picture of the king complaining about Becket and the four knights in the background watching the king's fury. He has captured a complex series of events and emotions in one frame.

Figure 14.4 Who shall rid me of this troublesome priest?

Shaun's cartoon of events is much more like a narrative. Figure 14.5 shows the meeting with the four knights; the knights riding towards Canterbury; the knights finding Becket with a cross symbolising the cathedral; and the final frame showing Becket lying dead, the assassin holding his sword over him. This was a

Figure 14.5 Who shall rid me of this troublesome priest? *and* Where is Thomas Becket?

particularly encouraging breakthrough for Shaun because at the start of the topic he had been reluctant to engage imaginatively with any story, yet this piece of work shows that he has used the basic facts creatively to describe the main events in pictures. He has embellished the bare narrative to capture the atmosphere of the events. His use of the quotation and *you shall die this instant* shows his grasp of the kind of formal language needed to express the gravity of the events. Michelle (Figure 14.6) has helped the reader by adding a caption explaining the action. The horror of the event is shown by somewhat stylised dripping blood and Becket calling for help.

Figure 14.6 Thomas Becket has been killed by King Henry's soldiers

Again the use of pictorial texts enabled these pupils to learn something of the internal conflicts in the medieval state as well as being able to understand the events leading up to the death of Thomas Becket. They were also able to organise their ideas and express them both pictorially and in words. Their confidence in expressing historical ideas and concepts was growing.

Telling their own stories

The third area that I concentrated on was looking at medicines and disease. Again, I wanted to use the skill of retelling a story with pictures. This is always a popular topic with children as it contains many gruesome and unpleasant facts. In order for this group to practise the skills they had developed with the Bayeux tapestry and Becket work I linked work on the Black Death of the fourteenth century with the Eyam plague story from a slightly later period. One of the problems inherent in a curriculum which separates historical periods over different key stages is that pupils lose a sense of historical continuity if, for example, they learn about the Tudors in Key Stage 2 then later learn about the medieval period preceding the Tudors. In order to help them gain a sense of continuity it is useful to make links between historical periods through themes such as medicine.

Again I used pictures as a starting point. I had visited the plague village of Eyam in Derbyshire and had taken a set of slide transparencies of the buildings, churchyard and signs. I used these to explain the story of how the plague broke out and how the vicar encouraged everyone to stay in the village and not travel outside. In this way the plague was contained and although many of the people of Eyam died, the disease did not become an epidemic in the neighbouring villages and towns. I wanted to build the skill of note-making into this part of the work. Children who find sequencing difficult also often find selection of information tricky. As a progression from the earlier experience of sequencing, I wanted the pupils to make picture notes of the story that they could remember, add written notes to remind them of other details and then use their notes to retell the story on tape. Again I helped the process by giving the pupils a model on the board as a guide to start them off. I drew pictures of the beginning of the story and together we added suitable captions. The pupils were then encouraged to continue the picture sequence – the quiet village – a weaver coming to the village and delivering wool – Sarah Sydal's family falling sick – The Reverend Mompesson calling the village together to explain the sacrifice that they were going to make – the death toll rising – the end of the epidemic. I reminded them of their work on the northern invasion frieze and on Becket and we discussed how some written text might help to describe events. They set off on their task with the evocative slide pictures of Eyam fresh in their minds.

Some, like Peter, decided to use no written text. Shaun, who is not a confident writer, used a minimum of written text (see Figure 14.7); however, the captions to his pictorial notes were short and helpful: *Eyam the village – merchant delivering – Sarah Sydal – Sarah and her family died – the plague attacked the whole village – the local vicar said that people can't go in or out – this idea worked a little bit – at the great fire the plague ended.* He sequenced the work well and in his last two captions he relates previously learned information about the Great Fire of London (covered at Key Stage 2) to events in Eyam.

Other pupils, including Michelle, wanted to have more written text to supplement what they could draw. Michelle asked for help to write: *People in the village went to church to pray, more and more of them fell sick, most of them died.*

The next challenge for the pupils was to retell the story on tape. I had explained that after they had made their taped stories we would listen to them

Figure 14.7 Sarah Sydal

together. They went to a separate room accompanied by a classroom assistant to make their recordings, taking with them their pictorial and verbal notes. I hoped this would show how well the story could be retold just by referring to their notes. I was impressed at how eager the pupils were to volunteer to go to a quiet spot to record their version of events. All of them spoke confidently and used their notes effectively.

Peter, whose notes included no writing, told the story like this:

> One day there was a village and Sarah went out to get some wool . . . then she got the plague. The fleas off of the rats come off the wool and bit Sarah. No one could come in or out of the village. . . . Sarah's got the plague and she died. Her husband died as well.

Shaun's story was brief, but complete:

> This is the story about the great plague of 1665. Okay, in Eyam the village there was this merchant delivering sheepskins and fleeces. Sarah Sydal was making these sheep fleeces into wool. But suddenly Sarah and her family died. The plague that caused this attacked the whole village. The local vicar said that people can't go in or out of Eyam. This idea worked a little bit. At the Great Fire of 1666 the Great Plague ended.

Ellie's account began:

> A merchant delivered wool to be made into cloth. The merchant put the wool in a shed and went off. But some rats got in and they had fleas and the rats went to sleep on the wool and the fleas went on to the wool . . .

The mechanics of how the plague spread were of great interest to Ellie and she was able to embroider her version with a lot of imaginative detail that was certainly in keeping with the story. This activity demonstrated that the cartoon version of the Eyam plague could be used to recall and recount information. All of the pupils had a good understanding of the story and were keen to find out more about medicine and diseases in history.

Individual progress

These pupils had certainly been able 'to communicate their knowledge and understanding of history using a range of techniques, including extended narratives and descriptions and substantiated explanations'. They were showing evidence of being able to 'describe, analyse and explain reasons for and the results of historical events and they had used a range of sources of information'

(DfE 1995: 11). All of them grasped something of abstract ideas such as invasion, loyalty, betrayal, self-sacrifice. Individually they have all moved on:

> Michelle managed to stay focused in all areas of the topic. Her confidence increased and her graphic portrayal of the Becket assassination reveals a positive move towards communicating her understanding.
>
> Peter had his own history of difficulty in sustaining concentration. However, throughout this topic he was absorbed by the pictures which he was able to interrogate – asking clear questions and demonstrating understanding. His taped narrative showed that he had understood the main ideas of the Eyam story and he was able to express himself confidently in the unfamiliar medium of taping.
>
> Shaun had demonstrated success in following and describing a number of complicated narratives. His caption in the Becket story shows that he is now able to move on to construct more lengthy written texts. His previous keenness to collect facts has been augmented by increasing empathetic understanding of historical events.
>
> Lee also followed the storylines, despite absences during this topic. He enjoyed the work and found success in demonstrating his knowledge through detailed pictorial text as well as writing. The most striking improvement in Lee's work was in his attitude and concentration, gained through the experience of successful communication of his knowledge.
>
> Ellie was again absorbed by all the different activities. The pictorial texts enabled her to focus on particular events in a way that she couldn't achieve through writing. She still has a long way to go but her enthusiasm for historical detail is well represented in her taped story.

The methods and activities used to teach this class are not ground-breaking or new. The work was simply an attempt to give a small group of pupils who find learning very difficult the opportunity to develop their historical skills and enjoy the subject. By using pictorial narrative – both as a source of information and as a means of the pupils communicating their knowledge – I found that they became more involved and enthusiastic as the work went on. Their own drawings provided me with information about their learning, showing not just that they had taken in facts about the medieval period but that they could select and abstract from the texts and sources of information which they had seen and heard to interpret and explain historical events. The move from pictures to oral and written narratives may be taken for granted with pupils in mainstream classes. For this class, it was a significant step towards tackling some of the more formal demands of the history curriculum.

References

Department for Education (1995) *History in the National Curriculum*, London: HMSO.
Shephard, C. and Moore, A. (1994) *Medieval Realms: Teachers' Resource Book*, London: John Murray.

15

CONCLUSION

Language in use – from policy to practice

> We have been opposed from the outset to the idea that reading and the use of English can be improved in any simple way. The solution does not lie in a few neat administrative strokes, nor in the adoption of one set of teaching methods to the exclusion of another. Improvement will come about only from a thorough understanding of the many complexities, and from action on a broad front.
>
> (DES 1975: 513)

> For pupils' knowledge, understanding and skills relating to the use of language to be developed most effectively, there needs to be a coherent approach, clear goals and common expectations across the school. Agreed priorities and procedures across the school are important to realise this.
>
> (SCAA 1997: 2)

This chapter of the book is designed to tackle some of the complexities of the use of language in all curriculum areas. The frameworks and review formats are intended to contribute to the development of 'a coherent approach, clear goals and common expectations' on the 'broad front' of the whole school. Whilst recognising the need for negotiated agreements about practices and teaching approaches, however, there is no suggestion that teachers should adopt such a common approach that the richness of diversity in teaching styles is lost. The balancing act – amongst so many in teaching – is to maintain individuality whilst having shared understandings of what the classroom and school enterprise is all about. What follows is a range of suggestions for ways in which colleagues might reach shared understandings through developing policy and reviewing practice. The chapter traces a process of:

Change and development
Establishing priorities
School structures for change
Looking at pupil performance
Looking at classroom practice

Looking at departmental provision
The role of the Language, Literacy and Learning Group
Looking at whole school provision:

- processes of getting and conveying information
- the library
- group work
- the use of information and communications technology
- equal opportunities
- responding to and assessing writing
- assessment, reporting and recording
- partnerships with parents over literacy

Putting ideas into action
Timetabling events

Year 1 – investigation
Year 2 – implementation
Year 3 – consolidation

Monitoring and evaluation

The frameworks offered here are founded on the view that one of the most effective starting points in any process of development is to identify current good practice and work from there. Another foundation stone is a definition of policy as what happens in practice. There are schools throughout the UK where policy documents gather dust on the shelves, only to be brought out and dusted off when OFSTED come to call. This is emphatically not the kind of policy development suggested here. A recent report by HMI lists some good examples of documentation which were noted during the survey of secondary schools:

- departmental audits of literacy needs or expectations;
- guidance on drafting in all subjects;
- guidance for parents;
- literacy action plans for pupils of all abilities;
- guidelines on classroom support for literacy;
- departmental key word lists; and
- sections of departmental, library and school development plans.

(HMI 1997: para 15)

This chapter includes all of these and much more; it is about policy-in-practice evident from what teachers do in the classroom and accessible through documentation which informs parents, governors and others about *what we do in this school*. The paper version of the policy should act as a source of reference for teachers and a means of informing others about practice. Just as important, however, is the enacted version of the policy which takes place every day. There is no place here, however, for bland hopes or brute sanity. The previous difficulties encountered in trying to use the wisdom of *A Language for Life* provide a few pointers for tackling some of the complexities.

The diagram in Figure 15.1 represents a process for developing the curriculum. At the extremes, the need for change becomes apparent either when something is going awry or when everything is going smoothly. In the first case it is necessary to take some action to get the school back on course; in the second, having reached some equilibrium, it is essential not to fall into stagnation. This is not to recommend change for the sake of change, or hasty sandbagging; there will also, of course, be schools whose situation falls between those two extreme positions or where some areas are falling apart and others are going very nicely indeed. The most healthy situation is where development is seen as an abiding element in the school plan. There is a neat, but important, distinction between *change* and *development*. The first suggests a shift of gear or direction; the second a steady, planned process. Schools experience both, and both are necessary in

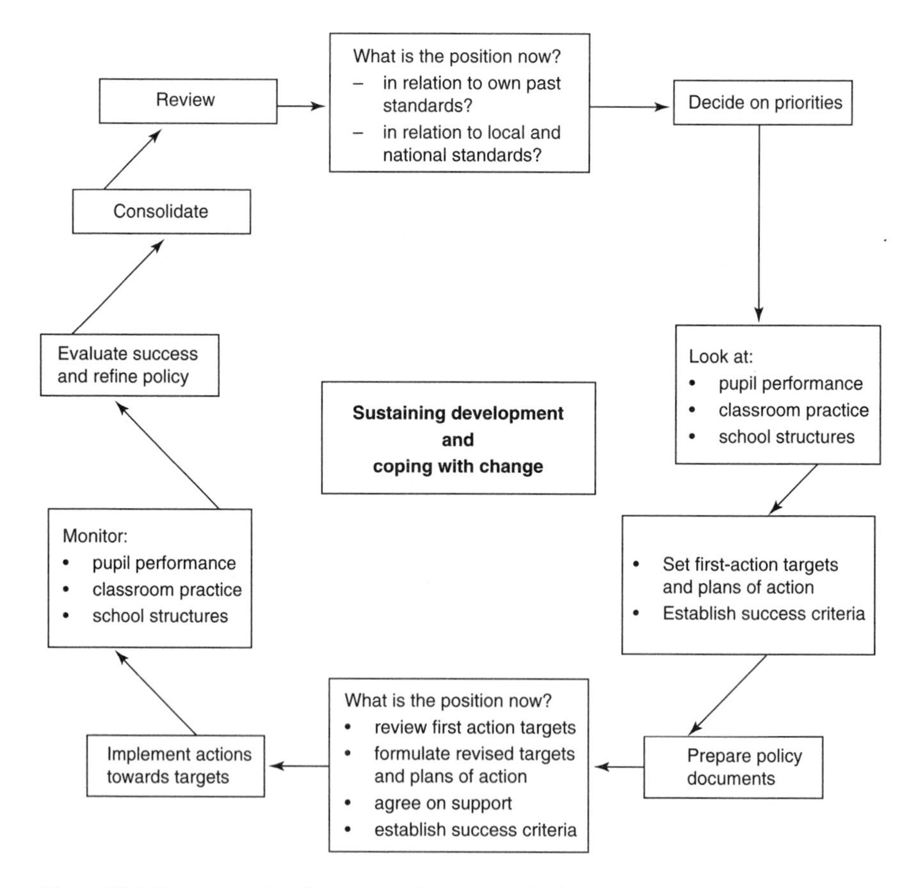

Figure 15.1 Sustaining development and coping with change

any institution; whilst every well-managed school will continually plan for development, external demands often require change. In terms of developing or clarifying a school's approach to the use of language and the promotion of successful literacy, there is great pressure from national concern and government demands. Whilst these may well coincide with teachers' own desires to extend pupils' language and literacy capabilities, yet another set of requirements can seem just one burden too many. The diagram in Figure 15.1 describes a process which might serve to quiet some fears by taking a steady, systematic and realistic view of change and development.

The SCAA core document *Use of Language: A Common Approach* summarises the principles which should guide a whole school approach:

- developing a shared understanding between all staff of the role of language in pupils' learning and how work in different subjects can contribute to and benefit from the development of pupils' ability to communicate effectively;
- helping teachers be clear about the ways in which their work with pupils contributes to the development of pupils' communication skills;
- knowledge and understanding of pupils' standards of achievement in speaking and listening, writing and reading, and the identification of any areas of strength and weakness;
- taking account of the needs of all pupils, including the more able, those with special educational needs and pupils for whom English is an additional language;
- structuring lessons appropriately in ways that support and stimulate language development and showing how learning objectives for pupils are to be achieved;
- recognising how resources will be organised and used to support this teaching;
- monitoring and evaluating the impact of common goals and clear, shared expectations of pupils' developing ability to talk, read and write effectively, and, specifically, establishing whether targets have been achieved.

(SCAA 1997: 3)

Change and development

Establishing common aims is more likely to be a consequence of curriculum development than a goal in itself. The process of looking at how to raise standards of achievement in literacy, for example, will raise issues about just what literacy implies and what kinds of teaching will best promote it. As Part II outlines, it is necessary to establish a culture of change and this depends on solid school structures set up to manage change and development. Throughout the process of development there are requirements for structural support if teachers are to get to a position of shared understandings. A view of balance between pressure and support is relevant here: too much pressure can result in discord, disaffection and delay; too much support can lead to stasis and complacency. This is very like what happens in the classroom. Learners tend to be recalcitrant if there is undue pressure and self-satisfied if there is too much support. For teachers genuinely to feel that they are committed to development, they need to be treated as learners who deserve the kinds of support necessary to tackle the demands of the pressures put on them.

All the ingredients for effective learning in the classroom hold good for teachers developing their own practice. There needs to be some purpose or motivation, some relevance in the task, opportunities for sharing ideas, exchanging opinions and choosing areas of investigation, frameworks which will extend and challenge, advice from more practised people, status given to individual experience, the chance to explain and justify beliefs and scope to experiment, revise and change. All of these depend upon an environment which will support and stimulate ideas. What is needed is an opportunity to keep revisiting learning so as to place new experiences beside more established ideas. Meetings between teachers offer such opportunities. They need, of course, to be structured. Just talking with colleagues, stimulating and comforting as it may be, is not enough; there needs to be some kind of framework which will require a more consciously explicit examination of the issues raised in conversations.

Establishing priorities

The responsibility for ensuring balance falls to school senior management. At the beginning of any initiative the senior management team will also need to take into account other factors which can stand in the way of development. The earlier attempts to make Language Across the Curriculum work and experience gained from large-scale curriculum development projects like the National Writing Project, the National Oracy Project and the Language in the National Curriculum Project have clarified some pointers to success in curriculum development. Any new initiative, in this case the development of a Language in Use policy should:

- not be seen as an extra burden;
- be central to the school's work for the period of development and allied with the school's other development concerns;
- build on existing sound practice and areas of development – e.g. language policy or collaborative work between departments;
- involve teachers from a range of subjects, not just see the English department as responsible for language development;
- give the initiative a high profile and status by senior management involvement and accountability and governor involvement;

- allow for adequate resourcing and support in time and personnel;
- build in opportunities for consultation, consensus and agreement;
- have considered how development will be monitored and evaluated;
- make explicit who is ultimately responsible for issues of language, literacy and learning.

Consideration of these factors should help the senior management team to establish priorities.

School structures for change

Once the senior management team has taken account of the issues detailed above, the starting point for any development has to be an audit of the current position. You can't plan a route if you don't know where you are in the first place and taking the scenic route may not be an option. One of the first decisions is to identify the responsible senior management team member and the brief of the group. The senior management team will look at statistics and compare them with the school's own previous standards and with levels of achievement locally and nationally. Discussion will help to clarify the main thrust of the initiative. Key issues may arise from targets set by OFSTED inspections. Whether the impetus comes from external or internal demands, the senior management team will need to have some view of priorities.

Decisions will also need to be made about whether work will involve:

- all year groups;
- all staff – including support staff;
- feeder schools;
- governors;
- all the language modes at once – reading, writing, speaking and listening.

Reaching these decisions will be a key to future progress, so it is advisable to have a representative group of teachers who will steer the initiative. Putting structures into place to make it possible for the group to meet regularly and to be supported will be essential to success. This group should have at least one senior manager as a permanent member – perhaps convenor and scribe – who is accountable both to the staff as a whole and to the senior management team. Past practice suggests strongly that it is not the best idea to expect the head of English or a member of the department to chair and lead the initiative. Of course, English teachers are the colleagues who can give advice and guidance on the structures and practices of language and literacy. However, if they are seen as the ones who do it all, then other colleagues may feel that their contributions are less relevant or valid or that they are not 'expert' enough to get involved. Over-dependence or control by English departments contributed significantly to the 'failure' of the Bullock initiative. Members of the group are most likely to participate fully if they are volunteers and departments might equally decide to be represented by their newest colleague who is keen to get involved or by the head of department who perhaps has lengthy experience. It is often a good idea to have two nominated members in a department. Discussions between them will generate more ideas than one person can come up with and, if one cannot attend a meeting, continuity is assured because the other can.

Once the composition of the Language, Literacy and Learning Group is settled, their working brief should be made explicit. This might be to:

- gather and analyse information;
- lead inservice sessions;
- prepare draft policy;
- decide on a timetable for long-term development;
- identify key areas for more focused investigation;
- establish targets and success criteria;
- liaise with governors and/or feeder schools.

There are many ways of investigating the current position. Decisions about which to use will depend on whether pupil performance, classroom practice or school structure is the focus. In practice, of course, all three will need to be examined, but any initiative needs to be systematically carried out if it is to succeed and both quantitative and qualitative information are important. A full investigation will involve:

- looking at examination or SAT results;
- surveys and questionnaires;
- focused observation;
- pupil shadowing;
- departments identifying their own concerns;
- departments and individuals carrying out audits of their own provision and practice.

After the initial investigation, departments will decide on first-action plans. These should be focused and designed to try out modest and reasonably short-term targets. The idea is to use these first-action plans to firm up ideas for longer term targets. For example, a department may decide to look at the subject-specific vocabulary used in particular units of work and make sure that pupils understand it. A test of this as an effective first-action target would be when pupils begin to use the terminology accurately themselves. Figures 4.2 and 4.3 (pp. 64 and 65) give examples of first-action plans.

Looking at pupil performance

Departments may already have analyses of examination results. There will also be information from routine assessment, reporting and recording procedures. It is important to have a balance between numerical and descriptive information if a full picture of pupil performance is to inform future planning. Tests are often seen by teachers as necessary, but partial, informants. Often, broad-spectrum test results prompt questions which can then be followed up by more precisely focused or longer term methods of investigation. One common difficulty is that SAT results on transfer from primary school may not reach the secondary school in time to be useful in informing sharper observations. Those schools which have opportunities for meetings with feeder school colleagues, or even better, chances to visit each other's classrooms, are at an advantage. There are some schools, however, like the one in Chapter 4, whose large number of feeder schools prevents such close liaison. In such cases, exchanges of writing between pupils in Years 6 and 7 can be a helpful way of teachers finding out about the literacy practices and expectations of colleagues in the other sector. In the future, of course, such exchanges could easily be happening through web-sites. Whilst exchanges like this may take effort to set up, the Language, Literacy and Learning Group might see this as a valid part of their work in establishing some knowledge of what pupils can do with language when they come to secondary school.

Numerical data can yield information about comparative levels of literacy in different year groups, disparities between chronological ages and reading ages, differences between boys' and girls' levels of achievement. Part II gives examples of a range of different ways of getting information and the ways in which schools acted on these initial analyses. Once such information has been collated, the Language, Literacy and Learning Group will be in a better position to decide how to get hold of more detailed information.

Questionnaires and surveys can yield useful information, as the teachers in Chapter 6 found. Figure 6.1 on p. 94 gives an example of a reading questionnaire designed to discover the reading tastes of the whole pupil cohort. One of the surprises Nigel Spratt and Ruth Sturdy had when they carried out their research was that school reading is only part of a very wide range of young people's reading. It is well worth discovering the kinds of reading pupils do at home and at school. Reading diaries are a useful way of researching the reading demands made on young learners over a week in school and their reading preferences at home. This could be done by specific groups or individuals and introduced during PSE or form time. Figure 15.2 suggests a possible format.

Writing diaries can be equally informative, particularly in terms of the purposes for writing (Figure 15.3). Often, pupils can find that the reasons for school writing are not clear to them apart from 'for the teacher to mark'. Teachers' purposes may not be clear to the learners. Whilst writing diaries can inform both teachers and pupils about the types of writing and the extent of writing carried out in classrooms and homes, writing samples are more helpful in looking at pupils' writing capabilities. Departments might decide to look at a 'top', 'middle' and 'bottom' in each class throughout a year group, or a sample of boys' and girls' writing. A close look at a few examples can provide a model for looking at all writing. One departmental or whole staff meeting dedicated to

Day	*Subject*	*Reading in school* **Type of text** (e.g. information, numerical, fiction, poetry) and **format** (e.g. history textbook, poetry anthology, encyclopaedia, CD-ROM)	*Time spent*	*Reading at home* **Type of text** (e.g. report of football match, novel, problem page) and **format** (e.g. newspaper, book, magazine, computer)	*Time spent*
Monday					
Tuesday					
Wednesday					
Thursday					
Friday					
Saturday					
Sunday					

Figure 15.2 Investigating reading at home and at school

Day	*Subject*	*Writing in school* **Type of text** (e.g. notes, fiction) and **purpose** (e.g. for reference; for assessment)	*Time spent*	*Writing at home* **Type of text** (e.g. letter, diary) and **purpose** (communication, to record events/feelings)	*Time spent*
Monday					
Tuesday					
Wednesday					
Thursday					
Friday					
Saturday					
Sunday					

Figure 15.3 Investigating writing at home and at school

Name: **Age:** **Languages spoken:**

Subject area:

Context: (teacher-directed/collaborative work/self-chosen/part of research)

Stage of completion: (draft/notes/proofread by writer/proofread by teacher/finished piece)

Purpose of writing:

Teacher's purpose – what was the writing supposed to do?

Pupil's purpose – what does this piece show about the writer's success in making her/his own meaning and intentions in writing clear?

Audience/readership:

Who was the intended readership?

How does this piece show the writer's understanding of the needs of a reader?

Structure/form:

What was the expected format? How does the form fit with the intended task?

What does this piece indicate about the writer's ability to present ideas clearly and coherently?

Technical features:

What features show the writer's competence in handling the transcription elements of syntax, punctuation, vocabulary, spelling?

How effectively has the writer varied technical features in relation to purpose and readership?

Figure 15.4 Guide questions for discussing samples of pupils' writing

looking at a sample of writing can pay great dividends. In looking at samples, however, it is important to look beyond the surface features of technical accuracy towards matters of purpose, audience and organisational aspects. It is important to have some information about the origins of individual pieces of writing which might be looked at as part of a writing sample, as well as covering the different aspects of writing. Figure 15.4 offers a set of guide questions which might be used in discussing pupils' writing.

Looking at classroom practice

This is the other area of investigation which can inform plans for language and literacy development. Teachers may wish to look at their own methods, or work with colleagues in examining a specific aspect of classroom practice. Focused observation can be helpful for reviewing both oneself and others but it is best to have a clearly defined purpose or question. This might be aimed at looking at teacher and pupil talk, for example, or at the management of group work or at the use of resources. Some areas for focused observation or self-audit might be:

Speaking and listening

Is classroom talk purposeful and productive? For example,

- Are teacher instructions clear? Do the pupils generally know what they're supposed to be doing?
- Are teacher explanations clear most of the time?
- What kinds of questions does the teacher ask? (open/closed; hypothesising/challenging)
- What kinds of questions do the pupils ask? (for clarification of task/for further information/for interest or hypothesis)
- Are all pupils involved in question/answer sessions?
- Are all pupils involved in talk activities? For example, do boys/girls dominate? Are 'quiet pupils' getting their share of discussion in group settings?
- Do pupils listen attentively and courteously to each other – and the teacher?
- Do pupils seem to value talk for learning?
- What variation is there for talk? (paired discussion/small group discussion/whole class discussion/giving presentations and feedback)
- Are spoken contributions sustained or extended? How does the teacher prompt pupils to contribute more extensively?
- How does the teacher act as a model of variety and effectiveness in speaking and listening?

Reading

- What reading resources are provided in the classroom? (books/magazines/ displays/computer texts, etc.)
- How do these match the reading fluency of the pupils?
- What is the range of types of text used within a series of lessons/unit of work? (pictorial, graphic, numeric, instructional, etc.)
- Does the reading material in the classroom cater for all pupils' tastes and needs? (boys/girls; more/less fluent and experienced; graphic/verbal text readers, etc.)
- What reading activities are expected? (getting information/analysing ideas/reading for inference/for pleasure, etc.)
- What reading strategies do pupils use? (skimming and scanning, reading in detail and depth, re-reading, etc.)
- How does the teacher check for understanding at literal and inferential levels?
- What opportunities are there for pupils to give considered responses to what they are asked to read?

Writing

- Are writing tasks clearly explained in terms of purpose, audience/readership, expected extent of proofread and revised text?
- What range of forms and formats are pupils asked to write in?
- What opportunities do pupils have for writing at length, in their own words, exploring information, issues and concepts in depth?
- Do writing tasks offer an appropriate level of challenge to the pupils?
- Do pupils have opportunities to redraft writing and present it for others (beside the teacher) to read?
- How confident/experienced are pupils in taking/making notes? What strategies or formats are used to help them?
- How is pupils' writing responded to? – as spoken comment/in writing?
- What is the response intended to do?

Audits or focused observations based on some of these questions can throw a useful light on good practice – and gaps in practice – in any teacher's classroom. However, a pupil's experience spans several classrooms and it can be helpful to take a 'horizontal' audit, either by groups of colleagues within a year group getting together to examine their practice, or by pupil shadowing throughout the curriculum. Some of the questions above might be considered if the staff decide on pupil shadowing, but it is important to be sure that colleagues are aware of just what the area(s) for observation will be. Figure 15.5 offers a format for 'horizontal observations' across subject areas.

Year: **Observer:**

Area of focus	*Subject*	*Time of day*	*Length of time observed*	*Observations and key points*

Figure 15.5 Format for horizontal observations by colleagues or for pupil shadowing

Looking at departmental provision

Departments might decide to act on observations gathered from questions like those above or the framework in Figure 15.5 might also be used within a department to review practice across a particular year. A similar approach could be taken to sampling work throughout Years 7–9 or 10–11. Once observations of pupil performance and regular classroom practice are collated, they can form the basis for further discussion and setting priorities. The surprises and confirmations generated by reviews or surveys will already have begun a process of thinking about principles and practice. This process needs to be given shape in both those areas – in the preparation of draft policy statements (principles) and draft first-action plans (practice).

Information on pupil achievement and classroom practice lay the foundations for more ruminative discussions about principles – about what matters in raising standards of achievement in language and literacy. Department meetings are often good places for such discussions. On-the-spot observations can be informative about regular practice, but cannot answer questions about the balance of language experience or literacy teaching in any subject area nor about staff confidence in their own knowledge about the structures and techniques of literacy. Fed by information collected through observation or review, groups of colleagues within a department might consider such questions as:

- What issues about language and/or literacy have been raised by our preliminary investigations?
- What are the language/literacy demands of our subject? How effectively do we make use of language to support learning, including speaking and listening, reading and writing?

Considering the 'readability' of textbooks and worksheets

What does the text look like?

- size of print
- the font / typeface used
- the layout and use of 'white space'
- organisation of headings and sub-headings
- differentiation of text which serves different purposes
- colour and contrast
- use of upper **and** lower case
- quality and appropriateness of diagrams and illustrations

What kind of vocabulary?

- the proportion of new or difficult words
- the extent of technical and subject terminology
- clarity and ease of interpretation

How difficult is the content?

- the number of new concepts and ideas that are introduced
- the clarity and relative detail of explanations
- the style employed
- coherence: the way in which content is put together

How clear is the organisation?

- clarity of any written instructions
- logical sequencing of ideas
- use of 'summary' statements
- clear definitions at appropriate points

How straightforward is the syntax?

- active rather than passive verbs
- use of active verb rather than abstract noun formed from the verb
- sentences which can be easily followed, with subordinate clauses kept to a minimum and subject and verb close together

Figure 15.6 Considering the 'readability' of textbooks and worksheets

Checking readability using cloze procedure

The 'formal' method . . .

Extract a passage of 250 words; delete every fifth word and replace it by a line (of uniform length).

Leave punctuation (other than apostrophes within words) intact.

Ask pupil(s) to complete passage, using the correct words.

Only count responses which match the original text as 'correct'.

The proportion of correct responses indicates the readability of the passage for the pupil in question and shows whether he/she is reading the text at:

- **an independent level**
  - score of 60% or more
  - where the pupil can read the passage with understanding without requiring extra help
- **an instructional level**
  - score of between 40% and 60%
  - where the pupil would not be able to understand the language sufficiently well without a substantial source of support
- **a frustration level**
  - score of less than 40%
  - where the language would be too difficult to understand, even with additional help

An 'informal' method . . .

Select a passage of shorter length and delete words in one of the following ways:

- at random
- every *n*th word
- nouns or verbs
- 'key' words.

The 'level' criteria described above can't be used with this method and results will need careful interpretation. However, the information obtained can provide a useful quick guide.

Figure 15.7 Checking readability using cloze procedure

- What are our priorities in making our practices more effective in teaching language and literacy?
- What challenges do we face in tackling those priorities?
- What support do we need?

Staff might find sets of guide questions like those in Figures 15.6 and 15.7 useful in department meetings aiming to establish first-action plans.[1]

The role of the Language, Literacy and Learning Group

The issues which a department might tackle can equally well be taken on by a working group. Policy takes a time to develop, since it needs to be a record of consensus rather than a neat and tidy document. In fact, the most enduring and genuine policy development often comes about through the discussions between colleagues as they hammer out ideas. Even draft policy statements need to be discussed and agreed over a period of time. A preliminary step might be to consider why a language policy is important in the first place. Figure 15.8 shows the notes from the working group from the school in Chapter 4 after they considered the question *Why have a language policy?* They were able to identify key points about entitlement and equal access to learning for all pupils and their discussions formed the basis of a shared view of the principles which guide practice. The statements were then used as a basis for the draft policy document.

In agreeing policy which will lead towards 'a coherent approach, clear goals and common expectations across the school' (SCAA 1997: 2), some of the areas which might be considered are:

- the role of language in learning;
- the balance and relationship between reading, writing, speaking and listening;
- the range of talk activities which can support learning in all subjects;
- the management of oral work;
- the range and balance of different kinds of reading required of the pupils;
- the appropriateness of reading resources;
- the use of school, departmental and class libraries;
- the range and balance of different kinds of writing required of the pupils;
- the teaching of different writing strategies;
- the purposes for writing in lessons;
- approaches to marking and responding to pupils' work;
- classroom management to cater for the range of pupils' learning needs – language, gender, cultural diversity, special educational needs.

Group A

Central to learning – means of learning

Use language to communicate – demonstrates learning

Entitlement – all students should be critical users of language by the end of compulsory education

Equal opportunity – access to the curriculum

Need to know the language demands that we make on students within the different learning areas – written / spoken / reading, including subject-specific language

National Curriculum requirement – use of language

Employers' requirements – key skills (communication, application of number, IT)
– effective communicators – spoken and written

Need to be clearer about the relationship between language and thought

Need to empower students through language development

Needs of students where English is an additional language

Appreciate the contribution of all languages to language development

Self-confidence, self-esteem in terms of the student's use of language – being able to express oneself

Group B

Should this be practice?

To share information, strategies, resources

To clarify roles and responsibilities – all staff share responsibility
– monitoring

To develop procedures and a consistent approach

- developing expertise in dealing with the issues
- early stage learners of English
- SEN e.g. dyslexia
- concentration, listening skills
- inability to express ideas clearly on paper
- encouraging talk

To raise achievement across the curriculum

To develop awareness of speaking
listening
reading
writing
as skills which need to be explicitly and systematically taught

Figure 15.8 Why have a language policy?

Looking at whole school provision

The agenda for whole staff meetings will vary according to already established priorities, but might draw on questions such as those outlined for departmental discussions or for the Language, Literacy and Learning Group. They might also use inservice provision from outside the school to support areas identified through reviews of present practice or through discussions in department or working group meetings. Chapter 12 makes some suggestions for staff development work through reflection on practice. This section lists some of the significant areas of discussion about language, literacy and learning which can form the focus for whole staff discussion. Each area has a set of questions or statements which can be used as starting points for group or whole staff consideration.

The processes of getting and conveying information

Starting points for whole staff meetings might be documents like those in Chapter 4. Figure 4.1 (p. 62) lists terms which are used in examination papers. The question might be asked: *When do we teach pupils these terms?* Figure 4.5 (p. 70) outlines the stages which a pupil has to go through to complete a coursework assignment. Discussion might deal with the question *When do we teach pupils the skills needed to go through the processes involved?* First-action plans might involve the use of formats like the one in Figure 4.2 (p. 64) which gives a framework for individual departments to identify areas of focus; actions/tasks; the person responsible for heading up the work; the deadline and the success criteria.

The library

Other productive uses of whole school meetings might be to discuss the uses of the library and other resources. The school library can be one of the most effective supporting mechanisms for raising standards of achievement, yet in many schools its use is undeveloped or undervalued. Figures 15.9 and 15.10 offer frameworks which could form the basis for discussion of the library as a resource centre and the roles and tasks of the school library team.[2]

Group work

Discussion across a whole school might equally well focus on teaching approaches such as the use of talk or group work in the classroom. An outside speaker might be invited in to work on groupwork techniques such as those shown in Figure 15.11 and consider such questions as: *What is effective group work?* in other words, *What will really get the learning done?* The whole subject of group work is complex and diffuse, but certainly bears scrutiny if organising for learning is to be as effective as possible. Starting questions might be:

- What kinds of groupings do you use?
- How do you decide who will be in particular groups?
- What kinds of tasks lend themselves best to group work? How much do you vary them?
- What expectations do you have for group behaviour and co-operation? How do the pupils know about your expectations?
- What guidance will you give for the management of the tasks and group procedures?
- Are instructions for tasks or activities usually written or verbal?
- What use do you make of the time when groups are working? – for example, individual observation, assessment of curriculum coverage and grasp of concepts or of pupil performance.

Discussions of group work are often related to issues about provision for supporting boys' and girls' language and learning in the classroom. The OFSTED report *Boys and English* noted that girls were sometimes more reticent and took less part in class discussion and, in low-attaining groups in particular, boys dominated oral work (OFSTED 1993); more research is being done which shows boys' achievement as an area for concern (Millard 1997). An inservice provider could also help guide colleagues through the tricky waters of considering issues of gender and talk, for example.

Getting a balance can often be achieved through careful group management, as the examples in Figure 15.11 suggest.

Use of Information and Communications Technology

Another fruitful area for whole staff discussion might be the role played by ICT in promoting language, literacy and learning. The use of Information and Communications Technology can promote and develop explanatory, predictive and hypothesising talk as well as encouraging negotiation and collaborative practices. Computers provide very good opportunities for individuals or groups to work independently of the teacher: word processing can give a chance for pupils to draft, revise, edit and proofread writing together; databases involve a great deal of discussion about what should be entered and how it can best be entered. CD-ROMs offer opportunities for explanations, questions and the display of a pupil's knowledge which the teacher may not have known about. In terms of reading, the advent of the CD-ROM is probably the most significant development, enabling quick referencing and, importantly, the capacity for several pupils to research at once. This means that the added value of discussion can enhance their learning and shift information gathering very quickly towards genuine understanding. Desktop publishing packages mean that books, pamphlets and newspapers can be produced to a professional standard. Databases can

The library as a resource centre

Aim: To transform the library into a resource centre.

Issues to be addressed.

1 **Who does a library serve?**

Pupils
- with all levels of interests, ability, ages and experiences;
- a multi-ethnic population with a diversity of cultures, languages, religions.

Teachers
- with a wide range of qualifications, experience and subject disciplines;
- and levels of professional development.

2 **What should the library provide?**

Librarian/s and subject teachers
- work in partnership;
- are facilitators.

Each have a unique role.
Librarian should (supported by teachers):

- stimulate an interest in and respect for books for the enjoyment of:
  - literature;
  - knowledge/ideas;
  - research.
- help pupils to locate the most appropriate resources to:
  - enhance their learning;
  - complete coursework/homework;
  - undertake projects;
  - do research;
  - widen their experience.
- teach information handling and research skills.
  - information retrieval skills.
- help teachers find the most appropriate materials for effective curriculum delivery.
- examine aspects of the National Curriculum and direct teachers to relevant materials.
- work with, stimulate, enrich gifted pupils by facilitating/setting up:
  - projects;
  - research;
  - special programmes.
- provide opportunities/resources/information direction on professional development.

- act on/accept recommendations/suggestions from other professionals on resourcing and learning methods.
- support topical/national/school initiatives – eg Book week, Health awareness etc.
- raise awareness of world (current) issues.
- arrange talks, readings, exhibitions.
- provide opportunities for independent learning.

3 **How is library to be resourced?**

(Related to 1)
Multi-media resources
- Books
- Encyclopaedias
- Dictionaries
- Audio tapes/CDs, junction boxes
- Computers and software
- Catalogues
- Newspapers
- Magazines
- Posters
- Journals
- Cuttings/clippings
- Videos
- Brochures
- Internet.

4 **What changes? The way forward.**

Librarian – from book stamper and chaser to facilitator of 2. (Roles)

Library
- User friendly accommodation/attractive.
- Easy access to books.
- Spacious/roomy/uncluttered.
- Designed for classes and for independent use.
- Flexibility essential to accommodate change.

Figure 15.9 The library as resource centre
Source: Guidelines developed by Mary Bryning and Marie Stacey. This document owes a great debt to *School Librarianship in the United Kingdom* by Helen Palin (British Library 1987)

List of roles and tasks of the successful school library team

Governor

- Develop understanding of library's unique value to school and communicate this to others.

Senior Management Team

- Development and implementation of a library policy.
- Set up a cross-curricular library management team to include HoDs, Teacher/Librarian, member of SMT (consider including your governor and pupil and parent representatives).
- Agree job description of teacher/librarian, librarian and/or clerical assistant.
- Monitor use of library resources across curriculum. Look at value-added; programme study skills.
- Ensure that progressive library skills are included in curriculum planning.
- Target setting.
- Accountability in relation to results.

Library Management Team

- Development and implementation of library policy (with SMT).
- Overall budget planning and allocation.
- Promotion – using all means to make the whole staff aware of the contribution that library resources can make to subject teaching and to education in the wider sense; being responsive to needs expressed by staff; encouraging all staff to use resources both in their teaching area and by bringing their classes into the library resource area.
- Evaluate use of library (e.g. age, sex, evidence of achievement, purposes).

Teacher/librarian

- Promotion – using all means to make the whole staff aware of the contribution that library resources can make to subject teaching and to education in the wider sense; being responsive to needs expressed by staff; encouraging all staff to use resources both in their teaching area and by bringing their classes into the library resource area.

- Organising and participating in programmes of teaching progressive library/study skills including work related to specific subjects.

- Encouraging positive attitudes to, and facility with, books and other media including IT; promoting literacy and learning through effective use of the library by all students.

- Regularly helping individuals and groups to locate and use resources; promoting self-reliance and self-confidence.

- Promoting involvement of pupils and parents in the work of the library, as a social and educational benefit, and encouraging parents to be aware of the value of reading.

- Ensuring that accounts are kept as necessary.

- Supervising ancillary staff and instructing them in their duties.

Clerical Assistance

- Monitoring use of library – keeping statistics

- Making available books and materials for classroom use; providing lists of topic materials as needed.

- Arranging displays in the library and elsewhere, including publicity for the library; liaison with subject departments for this purpose.

- Regularly helping individuals and groups to locate and use resources; promoting self-reliance and self-confidence.

- Ensuring that accounts are kept as necessary.

- Day to day running of the library, cleaning, repairing and shelving books and other resources, filing.

- Maintaining records of loans, sending overdue notices.

Figure 15.10 List of roles and tasks of the successful school library team

Single sex grouping: This can be useful, particularly in areas where boys might traditionally be seen to dominate, such as technology or science. However, it is worth deliberately mixing groups at times for these activities; this might be done at a second stage of the work when the boys and girls have had a chance to develop some expertise or knowledge which can be shared. This strategy is also useful for a group of pupils who share the same community language; they can work together first to establish their knowledge then change groups to share that knowledge with others.

Organising roles within groups: Identifying a group chairperson, a scribe, a listener/reporter can be a very effective way of sharing roles. Equally, giving specially assigned roles ensures that all have a chance to contribute. This might also be a chance to subvert traditional stereotyping by deliberately assigning specific roles to particular individuals.

Listening triangles: In groups of three, pupils take on the roles of speaker, questioner and note-maker. This can be done with almost any activity but may need to be demonstrated first. The speaker explains to the others about the topic decided on; the questioner finds two areas which might need clarification or prompting for further detail; the note-maker reports back briefly at the end. (It is sometimes useful to give time limits, and to practise keeping to them.) The next time round, the roles change and so on.

Group observers: One member of the group, using prompt questions devised beforehand, acts as the observer to reflect back to the group the way it has been working. The observer watches, listens and notes as the group works. This information is then fed back to the group to be discussed.

Pair building: One of the most automatic groupings in the classroom is the idea of working with a partner. It is always useful to build on pupils' established ways of collaborative working, but pairs can also be the basis for more extended mixing and varying groups. They might join up in fours or sixes according to the kinds of science experiments they have been doing – to compare or contrast findings; they might have been working on the same maths investigation or have read similar books or poems. The content of the mixed paired discussions can be managed by the teacher, of course, deliberately to get pupils working together for particular reasons.

Jigsawing: This will need careful explanation, tight timing and management of resources. *Home groups* of about six pupils research a topic over a specified period of time. The teacher decides on six (or other appropriate number) areas within the topic which can be researched with supporting materials. Each pupil is assigned a particular area within the topic with the aim that he or she is to become the *expert* in that area. During the work of the Home groups, time is allocated for each of the experts to share their findings with the whole group. Pupils then re-form into Expert groups made up of all those from the Home group who had the same topic. After the Expert groups have met, they return to their Home groups to recount the additional information they have picked up and to plan any final display or presentation for the whole class.[3]

Envoying: This can ease the teacher's load of always having to be the expert and consultant. One member of the group may be sent to the library, to another group, teacher or individual to find out or check a particular fact, detail or procedure. It is wise to limit the number of envoys to be sent on research jobs at any one time! An envoy can also be sent to explain a group's findings to another group.

Figure 15.11 Different groups to promote productive learning

be used to store and retrieve information about texts. In all curriculum areas, the requirements to input data in abbreviated form also means attention to language and more genuine comprehension of information texts.

Discussion amongst colleagues could discover the extent to which ICT is being fully exploited to develop language. Questions to consider would be:

- How many of the following types of texts are available to the pupils in an electronic form?

Fiction	Non-fiction
Drama texts	Newspapers
Magazines	Reference books
Encyclopaedias	Dictionaries

- How many of the following ICT resources are available to the pupils?

Word processors	Desktop publishing
Simulations/adventures	Language development software
Talking books	Databases
CD-ROM	Internet and e-mail
Overlay (concept) keyboards	

- Approximately how often do the pupils have opportunities to use ICT to develop their reading, writing, speaking and listening – daily/weekly/termly/yearly?
- What aspects of ICT are used in developing language, literacy and learning?
- Do all the pupils have equal access to using the computers?
- How might ICT be used more effectively to support language, literacy and learning?

Equal opportunities

Some issues related to equal opportunities have been dealt with in earlier sections, but it may be worth having a special slot in a whole staff meeting to consider the language, learning and literacy needs of boys and girls, pupils for whom English is an additional language and pupils with special educational needs.[4] It is all too easy to descend into a slough of despond about the difficulties of staffing which mean that conscientious teachers feel they may not always be doing their best for certain groups. It is important, therefore, to be able to identify good practice as well as using discussion to set some manageable targets for support. Questions might be:

- How do we cater for diversity in our classrooms?
- Are our expectations high enough?
- How do we make links with homes to foster learning relationships?
- What are the issues we want to pursue about entitlement and equal

opportunities? – are they related to gender? SEN provision? provision for bilingual learners?

English as an additional language

Very often teachers find that good diverse classroom practice is the most effective way to support bilingual learners who are gaining fluency in English. However, they cannot be left 'just to get on with it'; conscious planning is necessary. Colleagues might want to review practice by asking the following questions:

- How do we select and use materials to reflect cultural diversity?
- How do we help learner bilingual pupils ask questions?
- How do we use visual texts of different kinds to support activities requiring careful reading and comprehension?
- What other reading activities do we use to help support developing English users?
- How do we organise for pupils working in their preferred language as a support to their developing English?
- How do we push bilingual learners on to the leading edge of their conceptual competence?
- How do we use the family (including the extended family) as a resource for supporting the development of English?[5]

Responding to and assessing writing

This is one area where consistency is critically important to the pupils. However, colleagues do not always have common views on what marking (or responding) is supposed to do in promoting learning – and language. Discussions often range around the technicalities of spelling rather than seeing the importance of responding to the meaning of a whole piece of writing.[6] A single staff meeting is not going to deal with all these issues, but might start the ball rolling. Some general questions to be tackled in cross-curricular small groups might be:

- What are the different ways we respond to pupils' writing?
- Why do we use these different practices?
- How effective are our current approaches?

It is worth carrying out some preparatory work within a department to be done before such discussions. For example, colleagues might be asked to look at the comments they have made on a sample of pupils' writing in one year group or colleagues could take a sample across subject areas – perhaps the same five pupils – and look at the pupils' different experiences of response across subjects. Figure 15.12 offers some more detailed questions which could be used in departmental or follow-up work accompanied by looking at examples.

WHY?

Is the response intended to:

- encourage/promote confidence?
- give further ideas for writing or thinking?
- point out general or recurring faults?
- provide feedback about content?
- suggest additions/amendments which will help the reader make sense of the piece?
- give an indication of the level of success of the piece in achieving what it set out to do?

WHAT?

- What is the writing intended to do?
- What/who is the intended readership?
- What kind of response will best help the writer?
- What is important in responding to this piece – ideas? audience awareness? structure/organisation? technical features?
- What aspects of the work can be left for the moment?

WHEN?

Is the response being made:

- at the beginning – to help sort out ideas?
- in the middle – to monitor progress, organisation of material, reader appeal?
- at the end – to give feedback on interest, success in getting the job done, or suggestions for next time?

HOW?

Is the response going to be:

- spoken?
- written – in ink? pencil? on the work?
- in some other form – publication, sent for other people to read?

WHO?

Is the response being made by:

- the writer herself/himself?
- other pupils in the classroom?
- a wider audience?
- the teacher?

Figure 15.12 Key questions about response to writing

Another approach might be to develop a school statement to be given to parents about marking and assessment, beginning something like:

School Marking Policy

Marking is only useful if the writer reads the comments and acts on them. Ideally, marking should be like a conversation between teacher and pupil, where the teacher's comments are taken into account and acted on as the pupils work to improve their techniques. Marking can have different purposes:

Showing appreciation
Improving
Replying to ideas
Assessing, etc.[7]

Each of these areas could then be explained in more detail.

Assessment, reporting and recording progress

Two important questions to be asked when reviewing or establishing policy for assessment, reporting and recording are:

- What do we want our ideal recording and assessment system to do for us?
- How does our present system match up?

These questions raise others:

- What records of progress are kept in each department for reading, writing, speaking and listening?
- What evidence is collected?
- Are the records the same for all departments in the school?
- What records are passed on from year to year or at transition across Key Stages?
- How does the school ensure progression?
- Who else is involved in keeping records? (parents/helpers/the pupils themselves?)
- How do pupils evaluate and comment on their own progress?
- What arrangements are there for screening for language and literacy difficulties?
- How is information given to parents?
- What formal assessments are made?
- How are the results recorded and passed on?

Partnerships with parents over literacy

It is important to be able to establish dialogues with parents and carers where they can both give and receive information and ideas. Often, however, the place of parents in the partnership is to hear about school practice in language, literacy and learning and to do what the teachers ask them to do. Discussions might involve the parent–teacher group or parent governors. In reviewing or beginning to establish policy for working in partnership with parents or carers, the following questions might be helpful starting points:

- What do parents think literacy is? Is it the same as teachers think? How and when do we share views on language and literacy with parents/carers and establish common ground?
- How might we include parents/carers' views about development?
- How do we find out what pupils know about language and literacy when they first come to school?
- How do we gain the confidence of parents, carers and families, especially those who don't (or can't) usually get involved? How can we show them we value their opinions and experience?
- Are parents involved in formulating policy documents, creating information booklets, choosing reading material . . . ?

Putting ideas into action

After preliminary investigations and meetings, it is time to develop first-action plans. These should be seen as exploratory – *we think this might be a way to improve things* – and focused (as in those shown in Chapter 4). They should also have a date for review and agreed criteria for success. It is important to decide on dates for review of first-action plans at the beginning. The time should be relatively short and the pay-off should be apparent (see the introduction to Part 2 p. 53). Members of the Language, Literacy and Learning Group could offer guidance on manageable first-action plans.[8]

Timetabling events

This is essential. Of course, timings will vary according to school contexts but an approximate time plan might be:

Preliminary

June/July	Senior Management Team (possibly including a governor with a specific brief for literacy/raising standards of achievement) identify priorities, member(s) of SMT responsible for the Language, Literacy and Learning Initiative and build dates into school calendar.

Outline plans to whole staff and ask for two representatives from each department (where possible) to join the Language, Literacy and Learning Group.
SMT member prepares relevant statistics.

Year 1 – investigation

September	First meeting of Language, Literacy and Learning Group. Presenting ideas for discussion/investigation to departments via members of group. Plan for whole staff meeting this half of term. Department meetings to decide on areas for investigation.
October	Whole staff meeting for information and discussion of key issues. This could be the time to discuss why a policy is important and might be led by an inservice provider from outside the school.
November/ December	Language, Literacy and Learning Group meeting to feed back on departmental progress, discuss drafting of policy statements from staff meeting and plan for first meeting next term. Senior management team briefed by Language, Literacy and Learning Group member. Begin review of library and other school resource provision.
January	Departments meet to discuss findings of investigations or observations and to identify key issues/areas for first-action targeting emerging from these. Language, Literacy and Learning Group feed back on departmental priorities emerging from investigations or focused observations. Also consider draft policy document and make preparations for whole staff meeting to formulate first-action plans. Senior Management Team review library and school resources provision. Plan briefing paper for staff to be issued later in the term.
February	Whole staff meeting. Groups to discuss key issues collated by Language, Literacy and Learning Group from departmental feedback. Whole staff agree to formulate first-action plans and to report back in three months' time. Departments meet to firm up first-action plans and agree on success criteria.
March	Language, Literacy and Learning Group continue drafting policy statement. Report on first-action plans and progress.

Senior management team briefed by Language, Literacy and Learning Group member and discuss resourcing implications for following year. Report back on library and school learning resources review.

April — Language, Literacy and Learning Group meet to prepare for whole staff meeting. Feed back on first-action plans and emerging priorities/issues.

May — Whole staff meeting. Cross-curricular groups feed back on first-action plans. Identify common concerns across departments. Begin to identify further inservice needs.

June — Joint Language, Literacy and Learning Group and Senior Management Team to review work so far and discuss plans for target-setting for next year. Targets must be accompanied by plans of action.

Whole staff meeting. Inservice provided to cater for identified needs. Briefing about target-setting for next year. Clear guidelines about supported, manageable targets given by senior management. Draft policy circulated.

Departments meet to set targets and plans of action to reach the targets. Respond to draft policy.

July — Language, Literacy and Learning Group finalise first stage policy in response to departmental comments.
Decide on meetings for implementation year (Year 2).

Senior Management Team meet to receive policy, approve targets, confirm support and inform departments.
Make own targets and plans of action for library and school learning resources and inform departments.

Assessment co-ordinator and Senior Management Team collate statistics from examination/test results and incoming SATs to circulate to departments.

Year 2 – implementation

Term 1 — Language, Literacy and Learning Group feed back on plans of action towards targets. Discuss any problems of support which need to be referred to senior management.

Whole staff meeting. Inset provided as identified and/or across subject groups discussing progress of plans of actions towards targets. Senior Management Team brief staff about library and school learning resource targets.

Departments look at comparative statistics for last two years and identify trends/focus on areas for special attention. Update on action towards targets. Identify any problems and report back to Language, Literacy and Learning Group.

Term 2 Language, Literacy and Learning Group make plans for monitoring policy-in-practice.

Whole staff meeting. Inset provided as identified. Agree procedures for monitoring policy-in-practice.

Departments look at samples of pupils' work in each year group to assess effects of action towards targets so far.

Senior Management Team make provision for monitoring and feedback.

Term 3 Language, Literacy and Learning Group carry out monitoring (see p. 267 and Figure 15.13). Prepare feedback for whole staff meeting. Update on action towards targets.

Departments review action towards targets and look at success criteria. Identify success and areas for future action/targets.

After test/exams analyse results in relation to actions/targets.

Whole staff meeting. Receive and discuss monitoring report. Identify key issues of policy for following year and what should be done to address them. Discuss successes of actions towards targets and problems. Agree to set revised targets for next year (consolidation).

Senior Management Team outline plans for revised actions/targets in respect of library/school learning resources.

Assessment co-ordinator and Senior Management Team analyse exam/test results to feed back to departments

Year 3 – consolidation and evaluation

Departments will be working on revised targets. The Language, Literacy and Learning Group will make plans for collaborative monitoring of actions/targets throughout departments and of the library and school learning resource provision. The Senior Management Team will receive updates on targets and relate these to financial expenditure.

There will be a whole school evaluation exercise in the summer term to prepare for the school's next cycle of development involving language, literacy and learning.

Monitoring and evaluation

This will involve the three areas: pupil performance, classroom practice and school structures as for the initial investigations. The recent HMI report on raising standards of literacy in secondary schools commend those schools which have set targets for improvement linked to the school's short-, medium- and long-term planning and where there is 'longitudinal, coherent and consistent monitoring and evaluation of pupils' progress (1997: para 13.iii). This firmly links overall school management and organisation with the success of individuals. Pupil performance can be monitored through school assessment records. Monitoring classroom practice and school structures is best done with the full agreement of the staff. Time has to be set aside for monitoring and procedures negotiated. The Senior Management Team play a key role in this and their lead in monitoring their own procedures will set the tone for the whole school. Monitoring can be a tricky aspect of school work if it becomes associated with assessing staff performance. Some teachers fear that anyone who comes in to observe teaching is necessarily making negative judgements. It is important to establish through whole staff and department meetings a view that everyone is monitoring and evaluating the process of development. It is a joint and collaborative venture, intended to be supportive in identifying success as well as noting areas for future attention. Before deciding on a programme of monitoring it is worth being explicit about what monitoring means and asking colleagues to answer a few questions, as in Figure 15.13.

Once the monitoring and evaluation process is completed, it is important to have a year (at least) of consolidation. The Senior Management Team member of the Language, Literacy and Learning Group will have a watching brief, but this

Monitoring and evaluation

Over the next two terms we have been allocated time for monitoring the Language, Literacy and Learning Initiative. This is to observe how the actions towards targets are progressing. The aim is to identify good practice and to help individual staff and departments focus on areas for future development. It would be helpful if all colleagues could respond to the following:

What aspects of your classroom work are you satisfied with?

What areas of your work are you trying to develop?

What kinds of support have you been given?

What support might still be necessary?

When would you like a colleague to observe an area which you are pleased with?

When would you like a colleague to observe an area you want to develop?

Figure 15.13 Guide questions to help collaborative mentoring

should not involve any major changes. Problems involving school structures and continuing concerns should be documented and put on the agenda for the next three-year (or whatever period seems suitable) review. The consolidation period is essential for the cementing of new relationships and practices to promote standards of literacy. Only in this way will there be 'a coherent approach, clear goals and common expectations across the school' (SCAA 1997: 1) in order to raise and maintain higher standards of the way language is used to promote learning.

Acknowledgements

I am grateful to Richard Landy, chief executive of the Education Support and Inspection Service, Mid Glamorgan, for significant contributions to this chapter and to teachers in different places who have worked with parts of this material.

Notes

1 These sets of questions were developed by the Education Support and Inspection Service in Mid Glamorgan.
2 Ellen Lebethe developed Figure 15.9 and Marie Stacey provided Figure 15.10. My thanks to both of them.
3 This idea and envoying were first explained widely by the National Oracy Project. The Project book *Teaching Talking and Learning at Key Stage 3* is a mine of useful and practical information.
4 Relevant resources and background materials are:

    School Curriculum and Assessment Authority Boys and English Working Group (1995) *Boys and English*, London: SCAA. This has some other references and useful activities.

    The final sections of each of the following include sets of questions to guide practice:

    National Writing Project (1990) *What are Writers Made of? Issues of Gender and Writing*, Walton-on Thames: Nelson/National Writing Project.

    National Writing Project (1990) *A Rich Resource: Writing and Language Diversity*, Walton-on Thames: Nelson/National Writing Project.

5 Two helpful books are *A Rich Resource* (see n. 4) and Hilary Hester (ed.) *Patterns of Language*, Centre For Language in Primary Education/London Borough of Southwark, 1991.
6 One of the most comprehensive manuals for looking at spelling is Margaret L. Peters and Brigid Smith, *Spelling in Context: Strategies for Teachers and Learners*, NFER-Nelson, Windsor, 1993.
7 A great deal of useful material can be found in National Writing Project (1990) *Responding to and Assessing Writing*, Walton-on-Thames: Nelson/National Writing Project.
8 The NATE document *Use of Language in the National Curriculum* has some helpful

guidance and questions. It is available from National Association for the Teaching of English, 55 Broadfield Road, Broadfield Business Centre, Sheffield S8 0XJ.

References

Department of Education and Science (1975) *A Language for Life* (known as The Bullock Report), London: Her Majesty's Stationery Office.

Her Majesty's Inspectorate (1997) *Second Literacy: A Survey by HMI Autumn Term 1997.*

Millard, E. (1997) *Differently Literate: Boys, Girls and the Schooling of Literacy*, London: Falmer Press.

Office for Standards in Education (1993) *Boys and English*, London: Department for Education.

School Curriculum and Assessment Authority (1997) *Use of language: A Common Approach*, London: SCAA.

INDEX